Free Trade and the US–China Trade War

This book provides an analysis of the global trading system and its implications. The author uses network theory to examine the sustainability of the free trade system and its future. The book attempts to find out what the future of free trade could be and how the global trading system would unfold.

The book assesses four main waves of challenges to free trade and open society: the COVID-19 pandemic, the US–China trade war, economic nationalism, and the Fourth Industrial Revolution. While some of these challenges have been casting their shadows on the global economic system for some time, others are relatively novel, and their full effects are yet to be seen. This book also looks at the challenges they would present to multilateralism and global trade development.

This book will interest those who wish to have a better understanding of the US–China trade war and the challenges to the global trading system.

Yoon Heo is a Professor at Sogang Graduate School of International Studies and Director of Sogang World Trade Institute. He served as a member of the National Economic Advisory Council for the President of Korea. He has been a policy advisor to the World Bank and various Korean government agencies.

Routledge Studies in the Modern World Economy

For more information about this series, please visit: www.routledge.com/
Routledge-Studies-in-the-Modern-World-Economy/book-series/SE0432

Free Trade and the US–China Trade War

A Network Perspective

Yoon Heo

Routledge
Taylor & Francis Group

LONDON AND NEW YORK

First published 2023
by Routledge
4 Park Square, Milton Park, Abingdon, Oxon OX14 4RN

and by Routledge
605 Third Avenue, New York, NY 10158

Routledge is an imprint of the Taylor & Francis Group, an informa business

© 2023 Yoon Heo

The right of Yoon Heo to be identified as author of this work has been
asserted in accordance with sections 77 and 78 of the Copyright, Designs
and Patents Act 1988.

All rights reserved. No part of this book may be reprinted or reproduced
or utilised in any form or by any electronic, mechanical, or other means,
now known or hereafter invented, including photocopying and recording,
or in any information storage or retrieval system, without permission in
writing from the publishers.

Trademark notice: Product or corporate names may be trademarks
or registered trademarks, and are used only for identification and
explanation without intent to infringe.

British Library Cataloguing-in-Publication Data
A catalogue record for this book is available from the British Library

Library of Congress Cataloging-in-Publication Data
A catalog record has been requested for this book

ISBN: 978-1-032-30562-2 (hbk)
ISBN: 978-1-032-30563-9 (pbk)
ISBN: 978-1-003-30570-5 (ebk)

DOI: 10.4324/9781003305705

Typeset in Galliard
by codeMantra

To Don and Jay

Contents

Preface

The world we live in has never been this interconnected, making it look like a labyrinthine *network of networks*. This resulted in what the experts label as *hyper-globalization*. However, the trend in which interdependency among different countries around the globe continues to increase is coming to an end. After the global financial crisis in 2008, globalization began to slow down. With a series of events involving the trade and technology war between the US and China and the subsequent offset of the COVID-19 pandemic, globalization is now on the ebb. Throughout this book I aim to provide an analysis of the global trading system relating its implications to the globalization process. Applying *network theory* to the analysis, I place the focus of the study on the sustainability of the free trade system and its future. I organized the contents of the book starting with the analysis of the evolution of the global trading system.

During the Cold War era from 1945 to 1989, the world was dominated by two contrasting superpowers: the US and the Soviet Union. The US pushed for liberalism, establishing multilateral institutions, while the Soviet Union utilized communism and created its own sphere of influence. After the collapse of the Soviet Union in the early 1990s, the USA's influence increased, and under the liberal international order that the US created, the proliferation of regional trade agreements (RTAs) and free trade agreements (FTAs) had started. Fast forward to the present, the liberal international order is now being greatly shaken by various forces. This research assesses the four main waves of challenges: the COVID-19 pandemic, the US–China trade war, economic nationalism, and the Fourth Industrial Revolution. I will offer some straightforward explanations, in addition to analyses that are simple to follow, and examples regarding how these challenges would impact free trade and multilateralism. While some of these challenges have been casting their shadows on the global economic system for quite some time, others are relatively novel and their full effects are yet to be seen.

From Chapter 2, the study introduces the *network theory*, which will be the main lens through which we are going to analyze the different RTAs and FTAs. The network theory highlights the importance of a network's elements: nodes (vertices) and links (edges). Through the observation of these elements, we can identify important aspects of a network such as the collision of inner and outer networks, network power, network structure, and communication patterns within the network. In the following chapter, an analysis of various FTAs and mega-FTAs of global superpowers will be provided.

Thereafter, I will move toward the four waves of challenges and conduct a more detailed analysis of their impacts on the world's three biggest economic blocs: the US, China, and the European Union. I look at how these global superpowers are currently being affected and how they will respond to these challenges. Throughout this study, I try to give an answer to the ultimate question: is free trade doomed? If so, how will the future of the global trading system unfold? It is important to be aware of these topics as our lives are being affected, whether directly or indirectly, by the changes that the global trading system faces and will be facing.

In preparing this book, I have benefited from comments and discussions by many scholars whose names I cannot enumerate here. I also owe a great intellectual debt to the many authors who have contributed to the body of knowledge presented and synthesized in this book. Finally, I thank my team of research assistants, Giuseppe Peressotti from Italy, Sherwin Mariano from the Philippines, and Pham Thuy Hong and Pham Thi Hong Ngoc from Vietnam, all students at Sogang Graduate School of International Studies (GSIS), for the stimulating and excellent contribution they provided in the preparation of the manuscript.

1 Rising Threats to Free Trade

The origins of the free trade system, in their basic form, can be traced all the way back to the 16th century. Free trade is a form of trade policy that does not restrict or discriminate against imports and/or exports; it is *laissez-faire* applied to international trade. Levels of trade openness in the past few decades were the highest since free trade was conceived.[1] However, free trade as we knew it is now approaching the end. The world today is facing four strong waves of challenges that will considerably reshape the flows of goods and services and the global trading system itself: the COVID-19 pandemic, the US–China trade war, economic nationalism, and the Fourth Industrial Revolution (4IR). These challenges are having significant impacts on most countries in the world, and although similar on the surface, their effects differ in terms of degree and also timespan, which ranges from a few years to several decades into the future. But regardless of the timespan, it is certain that the impacts of the four waves can trigger a paradigm shift that will forever change the way trade is conducted. In the later chapter of this book, we will be looking at how the three biggest economies in the world, namely the US, China, and the European Union (EU), are and will be reacting to these waves, in addition to analyzing their foreign policies and administrative decisions on trade. In particular, the focus will be on examining the following questions: How does each wave reshape the global trading system? And what are the signs that explicitly show the threat that these waves carry with them? Now, let us begin by exploring how the current global trading system was created.

1.1 Evolution of the Global Trading System

A global order has many sub-orders, including a trading order. According to Mearsheimer (2019),[2] "[A]n order is an organized group of international institutions that help govern the interactions among the member states." He also stated that during the Cold War era, from 1945 to 1989, "there were two bounded orders, one largely confined to the West and dominated by the US and the other consisting mainly of the world's communist countries and dominated by the Soviet Union."[3] The US led the bounded liberal order as its leading node, and the Soviet Union created and controlled its own illiberal order of communist allies.

DOI: 10.4324/9781003305705-1

The US-led Western order established a host of international economic institutions, such as the International Monetary Fund (IMF, 1945), the World Bank (1945), and the General Agreement on Trade and Tariffs (GATT, 1947). The rise of liberalism shaped the multilateral world trading network through the GATT. After the Soviet Union collapsed and the Cold War ended at the beginning of the 1990s, the US became the undisputed global hegemon. The earlier bipolar period faded, and the newly established unipolar moment arrived. As Comecon and the Warsaw Pact dissolved in the summer of 1991, the liberal international order, based on liberal principles, began a new epoch. In trade and investment, the US pursued a multilateral free-trade network. The 1992 Maastricht Treaty was a substantial step in accelerating European integration, and in 1999, the euro, the European single currency, made its debut. The EU also expanded into Eastern Europe. As a result of the Uruguay Round, the World Trade Organization (WTO) was established in 1995. China and Russia joined the WTO in 2001 and 2012, respectively. Under American leadership, both industrialized and industrializing economies took a number of initiatives to lower their trade barriers. The relatively stable political environment, the common interest of free trade, and the improvements in transportation and communication technology enabled global trade to expand rapidly.

Meanwhile, RTAs (regional trade agreements) and bilateral FTAs (free trade agreements) also proliferated rapidly, beginning in the early 1990s. They spread without geographical limitations and tended to overlap with one another in scope and location. This liberal international order was based on the principles of the free market system and comparative advantage. Policymakers worldwide, including in China, believed that the free flow of goods, services, labor, and capital would bring greater economic prosperity. The rapid economic globalization was also supported by technological development, especially the decreased transportation costs and the rise of the internet. As Gilpin (2001)[4] mentions, "[N]ovel technologies in transportation have caused the costs of transportation, especially transoceanic travel, to fall greatly, thus opening the possibility of a global trading system." Additionally, the growing public awareness of the internet, beginning in the early 1990s, and additional advances in telecommunication technologies have accelerated global financial flow; these developments have been invaluable for enabling multinational firms to pursue global economic strategies and operations. The compression of time and space resulting from these technological changes has significantly reduced the cost of international commerce.

However, globalization and the global trading network have begun to face serious challenges from the system's member states. Mearsheimer (2019)[5] states that

> *hyper-globalization*, which began gaining traction in the 1980s and accelerated after the Cold War, effectively overturned the Bretton Woods consensus. The new order, created largely by Western policymakers, was designed to greatly reduce regulation of global markets by removing controls on capital flows and replacing GATT with the WTO.

According to him, the Bretton Woods Consensus, understood to extend from 1945 to the late 1980s, calls for moderate and limited globalization, only to the point where governments retain considerable scope for protectionist policies when it is in their interest to do so.

Colantone and Stanig (2019)[6] discuss the economic roots of the recent political backlash against globalization. Providing a data analysis of evidence from 15 Western European countries over the past three decades, they explain how and why the legitimacy of the liberal global order has been undermined. The first relevant factor is the China shock, which is defined as the growing exposure to Chinese competition that has resulted from the Chinese economy surging as a leading global exporter over the previous three decades. They find that the China shock led to lower employment rates and lower wages in local labor markets in the US and Europe. This shock has stronger implications for low-wage and low-skilled workers, who face higher rates of job turnover and worse losses of earnings. Second, technology shock resulted from the information revolution, especially from the early 1990s onward. It led to an increase in the polarization of the labor market of both the US and the EU, thus compounding the economic and political effects of globalization created by the China shock. The third factor is immigration. Colantone and Stanig (2019) provide empirical evidence that the overall direct effects of immigration, in terms of natives' employment and wages, tend to be small, but generalized fears of potential economic or social harm caused by immigration are nevertheless widespread and drive anti-immigration sentiment. In Western Europe, the Great Recession of 2008 to 2009 began as a financial crisis and then became a second recession that lasted from 2011 to 2013, driven by a sovereign debt crisis. Each of the factors listed here has played a role in the backlash against the liberal trading order and globalization.

As Hays (2009)[7] and Fukuyama (2018)[8] notice, many individual losers in globalization consider themselves to have been disregarded by the elites. Furthermore, these losers' demands for compensation and redistribution for the losses caused by trade liberalization have not been met due to the ineffectiveness of the relevant governments and the inability to perform collective decision making. People have been wearied of the global trade system, which seemed to have been captured by the interests of multinational corporations, big domestic exporters, and the political establishment, including the mainstream political parties. Moreover, between 1994 and 2007, a globalization-induced rise was seen in the income tax burden of the middle class in 65 sample countries (Egger et al., 2019).[9] As a result, Colantone and Stanig (2019) find (1) an increase in support for nationalist and isolationist parties, (2) an increase in support for radical-right parties, and (3) a generalized shift to the right throughout the electorate.

Fukuyama (2018) finds the reasons for the rightward drift of voters in the US and Europe in the failure of contemporary left-leaning parties. In the US, working-class voters overwhelmingly supported the Democratic Party from the New Deal period of the 1930s to Ronald Reagan's Republican presidency in the 1980s. European social democracy was built on a foundation of trade unionism and working-class solidarity. However, the working class in most industrialized democracies began to merge with the middle class in the 1990s. The left, in response, shifted its agenda from its earlier emphasis on the working class to the demands of the widening circles of marginalized minorities leaving the old working class behind. Although members of the white working class are members of a dominant ethnic group, many see themselves as victimized and marginalized. Their tax burden has risen, and their requests for compensation for their economic losses from globalization and free trade have been ignored by the establishment and elites, including the mainstream parties of both the right and the left. This created opportunities for right-wing identity politics to emerge in its most extreme form – economic nationalism. So far, I have discussed the evolution of the global trading system from its structural point of view. Now, let us look at its current status and see how rapidly the situation is changing.

1.2 Four Waves of Challenges to Free Trade

1.2.1 The Corona (COVID-19 and Its Variants) Pandemic

Ever since the coronavirus has taken the world by surprise in early 2020, many countries have imposed lockdowns and travel restrictions to control the spread of the virus, first in Asia and then in Europe, North America, and the rest of the world. These measures have been impacting the global trading system as the world shifted away from normalcy, thus disrupting the flow of goods, capital, and human resources. In the midst of this seeming turmoil, we must remind ourselves that it is essential for global leaders to maintain a smooth flow of trade so as to sustain the supply of products needed in these trying times, as well as to demonstrate confidence toward the global economy (OECD, 2020).[10]

The COVID-19 pandemic continues to upset both the demand and the supply sides of the global economy, and this alone is a major source of difficulties for keeping global trade and investment stable. Many governments have also temporarily closed manufacturing establishments for non-essential items especially during the early days of the pandemic. Some corporations experienced a decrease in production due to reduced labor resources and also due to the change in their supply chains (Gruszczynski, 2020).[11] These lower production and trade volume clearly affected the global economy, and one of the main indicators is the year-on-year change in the volume of global trade in goods. According to the COVID-19 Special Report by UN ECLAC (2020),[12] the volume of global trade in goods fell drastically by 17.7% in May 2020 compared to the same time previous year. The drop in exports was particularly severe in the US, Japan, and the EU.

In addition, countries have started to implement export controls and import restrictions due to the pandemic. At the start of the COVID-19 epidemic, many countries restricted exports of medical products to allocate domestic supplies to their own citizens. In mid-April 2020, around 75 governments had implemented export curbs on medical supplies and medicines, with the same goal of securing supplies for the domestic market. However, many observers have emphasized that export controls or restrictions are inefficient and ineffective, as both can cause harm to trade partners, leading to retaliation by affected parties (Hoekman et al., 2020).[13]

There are considerable changes that the global trading system is going through. First, there is an accelerating trend toward regional value chains (RVCs) from the previous global value chains (GVCs). This means that the production of goods and the sourcing of certain materials that were previously being conducted through the wider GVCs are starting to be localized either regionally (RVCs) or by establishing self-sufficiency. This new pattern is being further pushed by supply chain and travel disruptions caused by COVID-19, and most analysts concur that the pandemic will reinforce relocation and reshoring trends (Fortunato, 2020).[14] Relocation also comes in the form of nearshoring, which is a practice of transferring a business operation to a nearby country, especially in preference to a more distant one. The trend is expected to be more prevalent in countries close to major consumer markets as manufacturing supply chains diversify and become more regional. Some countries also started onshoring, or simply transferring a previously offshored business operation back to the country from which it was originally relocated. According to Savills World Research (2020),[15] greater diversification of supply chains is expected in the future, together with a rising level of nearshoring. But full-scale onshoring is "likely to be limited to critical or less cost-sensitive goods, though longer-term increased automation in the manufacturing process may play a role." Looking at the general data gathered by the WTO in its 2021 Statistical Review (WTO, 2021),[16] GVCs were hit the hardest during the first half of 2020, and the export of intermediate goods dropped 10% on a year-to-year basis. As James (2021)[17] put it,

> *COVID-19 looks like it is completing the work of the 2008 financial crisis: the Great Recession produced more trade protectionism, forced governments to question globalization, increased hostility to migration, and, for the first time in over four decades, ushered in a sustained period in which global trade grew more slowly than global production.*

Nevertheless, after the initial chaos started to settle and the vaccine rollout managed to bring great hope among the general public, economies around the world began to move toward their own recovery paths. Indeed, following the World Economic Outlook from the IMF (2021),[18] we can see how the challenges that the international community should be aware of are tied to a stable, worldwide coverage of the vaccination plan. Most *rich economies* are projected to witness exceptional growth in the next couple of years (of course, counterweighing more than one year of social-economic disruption), while low-income countries appear to be struggling with their vaccination programs and, hence, slowed in their recovery. This dichotomy, paired with the economic shockwaves caused by the disturbance in international trade (late shipping, lack of materials, high commodity prices, and shortages of resources), will further spread uncertainty among international players and make these changes in GVCs and RVCs even more prevalent.

1.2.2 The US–China Trade War

To put into perspective what happened between the US and China, we might want to recall that on the first day of the US–China trade war, July 6, 2018, was marked by the imposition of a 25% tariff on 'List 1,' which includes 818 imported Chinese products valued at US$34 billion. Since then, the situation worsened, and China retaliated by mirroring the move. Soon after the US raised the stakes by announcing additional duties on $200 billion worth of products, China followed by increasing its duties on products for $60 billion worth of US products (Herrero, 2019).[19]

The immediate results for both the US and China were a sharp decline in bilateral trade, price increases for many of the related goods, and increased imports from other countries (Nicita, 2019).[20] According to Herrero (2019)[21] and the data gathered by the World Bank in its Global Economic Prospects report (2019),[22] the impact on Chinese and American economies has been relatively mild compared to the effects on their financial markets. This could be explained by the fact that economic forecasts, contrary to the stock market, do not take into consideration of the effects on investments through a worsening market sentiment toward the future. It is true that investors inside and outside of China started to worry that their investment opportunities could be completely blocked by the US or negatively affected by the worsening relationship between China and the US. The multilateral economic order maintained by the US is likely to be massively transformed.

This whole scenario, mostly escalated by Donald Trump, can be linked to his *America First* Policy at the expense of values tied to multilateralism and institutions like the WTO (Fehl and Thimm, 2019).[23] Trump's motives revolved around the idea that China should be kept in check through several policies that he implemented. During his presidency, the Committee on Foreign Investment in the US (CFIUS) opened almost 600 investigations, with an average of 150 per year, doubling the average of Obama's administration.[24] Some examples of these investigations included the case of acquisition of MoneyGram International Inc. by Ant Financial, the Chinese financial-services giant controlled by billionaire Jack Ma, and the proposed sale of Lattice Semiconductor Corp. to Canyon Bridge Capital Partners LLC, a private-equity firm backed by a Chinese state-owned asset manager. Moreover, the Foreign Investment Risk Review Modernization Act (FIRRMA) passed by the US Congress in 2018 further restricted unwanted investment in the US, particularly Chinese technology investments (Capital Watch, 2018).[25] Suspicion against China had been continually growing, and Trump utilized all available avenues to scrutinize China.

However, the US has also viewed China with suspicion under the Obama administration, even before Trump pulled the trigger in the form of the trade war. China adopted a development model during Former President Hu Jintao's administration. In 2005, Hu launched his *harmonious society initiative*, and according to Chan and Zhong (2019),[26] this initiative "attempted to maintain economic reforms and further open China's economy while also using government intervention to solve a variety of social problems such as unemployment, poverty, and regional disparities."

Up to this day, under the Biden administration, America continues to demand major structural reforms in China but without a satisfactory response from the latter. It is no secret that the trade war is also an indication of the ongoing hegemonic rivalry between the US and China. Indeed, China already overtook the US as the world's largest trade partner. This only serves to add salt to the wound, considering China's technological rise. The US has never been this anxious over the possibility that China will not only dominate the world as the major trade partner of all countries but also take the lead in the future as the main innovation powerhouse in the world. Chinese leader Xi Jinping was keen on expressing his great ambitions for the country through China's strident *Made in China 2025* (MIC 2025), an industrial upgrade strategy introduced in 2015. Although it is unlikely that China will take over the US lead in technology in the next decade, it is clear that MIC 2025 has caused more fear than appreciation among advanced economies such as the US and the EU.

It does not look like this sentiment is going to change much under the current administration. Indeed, Joe Biden has reinforced the anti-China stance of the Trump administration, albeit with some differences. He strongly expressed his opposition toward China's human rights record, which encompasses several issues such as the current situation in Hong Kong, the repressive policies of the Chinese Communist Party (CCP), and the issue of forced labor of Muslims in Xinjiang. Biden also emphasizes that with traditional allies who share the *American values*, the US will seek to build coalitions to strengthen their position in this hegemonic war. In his article in *Foreign Affairs* magazine, Biden states that "if China has its way, it will keep robbing the United States and American companies of their technology and intellectual property" (Biden, 2020).[27] Biden also expresses that he is an advocate of *fair trade* and pledged not to enter into any new FTA without the strong protection of the environment and labor rights. "Until we have invested in Americans and equipped them to succeed in the global economy," he promised to put his policy priority on the domestic economy (Becker et al., 2020).[28] Putting these things together, it is certain that the competition between the US and China is far from over.

The US-China trade war definitely poses a threat to free trade and multilateralism. As we will shortly see, the influence of China is growing rapidly, and the number of countries with China as the major trading partner continues to rise; the great game is being exacerbated as both giants start shifting among their trading partners more strategically to mitigate the negative impacts of the trade war. The change in the US administration will outline a mandate in which China will still be considered a fearsome opponent, to be fought through alliances rather than with *sheer brute trading power*.

We can clearly see how the trade war affects free trade and multilateralism. The trade war, as mentioned earlier, can be traced back to Trump's *America First* Policy. And this policy is a part of economic nationalism, which will be discussed next.

1.2.3 Economic Nationalism

Gilpin (1987)[29] describes *economic nationalism* as "the idea that the economic activities are and should be subordinate to the goal of state-building and the interests of the state." Furthermore, the analytical core of economic nationalism argued by Gilpin (2001)[30] bears similarities to that of *state-centric realism* since it "recognizes the anarchic nature of international affairs, the primacy of the state and its interests in international affairs, and the importance of power in interstate relations."[31] According to Colantone and Stanig (2019),[32] three key elements of economic nationalism are (1) isolationism in the form of protectionist stances on international trade and investment, (2) economic conservatism in the form of lower income taxes and a skeptical attitude regarding the welfare state, and (3) a nationalist narrative in the form of appeals to national sovereignty and national identity. Economic nationalism oftentimes glorifies protectionism, shaping economic policies typically in realist terms. Nationalism and national identities exert power over economic policymaking, ultimately shaping the geopolitical situation, be it local or global (Helleiner and Pickel, 2005).[33] Protectionism, after all, seems to be shaping most of the big players of the global trading world. On a global scale, the phenomenon seems to be widespread as more nationalist leaders have either gained power or are on the rise. The Japanese Prime Minister and his Indian equivalent Narendra Modi, and the Turkish government guided by President Recep Tayyip Erdoğan are all examples of this (Bieber, 2018).[34] In the EU, the trend manifested in the form of the Brexit phenomenon and by the success of far-right parties in Italy, Germany, and Austria.

An analysis of the largest political parties' policy platforms in the G20 (Group of Twenty) countries made by the Peterson Institute for International Economics (De Bolle, 2019)[35] shows that more parties lean toward policies that reflect national interests while rejecting multilateralism. The same paper mentioned that policies prioritizing domestic industries and workers, and against migrants and foreign goods, are more appealing to voters. These results suggest that economic nationalism definitely hampers policy coordination among countries at a time of a global slowdown, which is what we are experiencing now due to the COVID-19 pandemic and the US–China trade war.

There are several reasons why a country implements protectionist measures. But in general, countries impose such measures to protect domestic jobs, industries, and national security. That is why we can directly tie protectionist measures to economic nationalism, which follows the emotional invective of ensuring the domestic economy's stability and protecting it from too much foreign competition. These measures are implemented through government intervention as it holds the power over a country's border and in regulating the flow of goods, products, and commodities going in and out of the border. Although trade protectionism has been controversial, an upward trend can be easily confirmed. Indeed, protectionist measures have increased steadily since 2008, especially with trade defense measures, such as anti-dumping, subsidies, and safeguards at the top (Guarino, 2018).[36]

In China, economic nationalism has different aspects. The Chinese trade system operates under tight government controls. It is known to have high tariff rates, complex and non-transparent non-tariff barriers, and a wide range of discretionary practices. Even during the second stage of China's economic reform in 1994, the country still had a system of high tariffs, with an average of 36% – much higher than most developing countries.[37] China's import administration also suffers from overlapping authority and multiple objectives. It is also possible that it is a means of keeping tariff rates high, as set by both the central and the local governments, reflective of China's economic nationalism. Aside from these high tariff rates, countries such as China rely on other protectionist policies as well to safeguard their economic interests. But not to single out China, other countries implement such measures as well, such as the US, the UK, and Germany. However, economic nationalism in China not only stands out for its structural nature, visible in such areas as SOEs (state-owned enterprises), but also shows up in the form of subsidization, disregard for intellectual property rights, and theft of technology, long the target of opprobrium from the Western world.

In the US, the revival of economic nationalism was initiated by the Trump administration. The motivation and issues of concern to the Trump administration in this regard included bilateral trade deficits, currency manipulation, and disastrous trade agreements.[38] The ideology is best depicted in the *America First* Policy, in which "every decision on trade, on taxes, on immigration, on foreign affairs, will be made to benefit American workers and American families" and to "protect the borders from the ravages of other countries making our products, stealing our companies, and destroying our jobs."[39] Furthermore, Trump attacked the WTO through several measures: an offensive against the WTO's Appellate Body (AB), a return to unilateral adjudication and remediation of trade disputes, and an interpretation of the WTO's national security exception that would permit economic concerns to qualify (Brewster, 2018).[40]

The remarkable transformation from globalism to protectionism under Trump's regime, of course, has had enormous impacts on multilateral cooperation in the world. Brewster (2018),[41] Bown and Irwin (2019),[42] and Wyne (2020)[43] concurred that the economic nationalism ignited by the US pushes the international trade law back to the GATT-era system, in which WTO members resolve their disputes by an economic-power-based dispute settlement process. Economic size and power, not the principle of law, determine the outcome of trade disputes. Moreover, as the US invoked the national security rationale to challenge WTO rules, other great powers will likely imitate the tactics and push the multilateralism to the verge of collapse. And the world trading system run by discriminatory trade blocs (US-led and China-led) will hurt small countries and push them to align with more powerful ones for self-preservation, creating a historical fragmentation in the global trading system. It is true that multilateralism has reached a point where "even if Trump loses reelection in 2020, global trade will never be the same" (Bown et al., 2019).

Although the US managed to stall the WTO's two-step dispute settlement process, its influence was not powerful enough to destroy the institution completely.

Without waiting for the US to remove the blockage, the EU and many WTO members established the Multi-party Interim Appeal Arbitration Arrangement (MPIA), which has the same function as the WTO Appellate Body, to provide parties with "an independent and impartial second and highest instance of appeal."[44] With the Republican term coming to an end in 2020, the major events that ended up derailing the multilateral trade system could be somewhat reversed but not back to the pre-Trump era. What about economic nationalism in general, then? Given the uncertainty lingering over this topic, it's hard to imagine that things will change for the better in the short term. In the next section, let's talk about the current industrial revolution and how this can help countries further advance their interests.

1.2.4 The Fourth Industrial Revolution (4IR)

The 4IR concept, which is considered a new chapter in human development, was brought to the world by the World Economic Forum in 2015. It is depicted as a new round of technological revolution and industrial change in artificial intelligence, big data, quantum information, and biotechnology. In this 4IR framework, China and the US appear to be the front-runners and are competing against each other for the position of the world's technological leader.

At first glance, it seems like the 4IR would guarantee positive changes and developments as it can make industries more efficient regarding production capacity through smart factories, artificial intelligence, and big data. Even during the Third Industrial Revolution, the advancement of these industries not only improved factors of production and hourly wages but also created jobs in new industries. The 4IR can also affect improvements in quality of health and life span through advancements in biomedical science. Then, how can these improvements pose a threat to free trade and multilateralism?

First, the 4IR brings changes in the employment structures. With artificial intelligence being pushed to its limits, it will not be surprising to see jobs being automated, which will eventually eliminate the need for real human workers. This will directly impact trade in services through the automation of jobs as demand for workers will decrease.

Second, the 4IR creates issues in privacy and trust. There are specific cases such as the espionage on the part of China, and other cybersecurity concerns involving Huawei, TikTok, and WeChat that will be discussed in the latter part of this book, but it is undeniable that the development in technology also enables different countries and companies to facilitate and advance their agenda of collecting confidential information, from other governments and private individuals. These issues prompted some countries to refrain from using those suspected services to avoid compromising private data. This directly affects trade as import and export issued through specific software and hardware could eventually change and shift markets.

Third, the 4IR has accelerated the proliferation of disruptive technologies. Although innovation is good for digital development, technological advancements also raise legal and regulatory concerns around the world. There are issues concerning artificial intelligence and how humans can control *deep-learning* algorithms fed by data and how it can also turn into an issue of human liability and accountability for machine activities. Drones also pose a security threat as these devices can be utilized to conduct surveillance and intelligence gathering. Blockchain, on the other hand, raises legal concerns as it would affect e-commerce, online agreements, and online dispute resolution (Singh, 2019).[45]

Lastly, the 4IR brings changes in production processes, location, and trade. The development of a country's manufacturing technology changes not only the final product but also the sourcing and its supply chains. For example, if country A currently sources certain parts of an electronic product from country B, then trade is being facilitated. But with the 4IR developments, the locational advantage that country B possessed disappears and country A is now able to produce the parts to complete the electronic product. Then, trade between country A and country B for that specific part will stop.

The technological advancements brought by the 4IR might also result in more onshoring, nearshoring, and reshoring, which will then change the existing industrial models and GVCs, and make them more regional oriented, thus strengthening RVCs, or worse, the country might stop trading altogether if it becomes fully self-sufficient. This is one of the negative aspects of the 4IR, which might prove disadvantageous to emerging markets. Reshoring is one of the prominent risks from automation, as there is a lesser need for low-cost, unskilled labor. One visible example of this is the clothing brand Adidas, which now has a new and highly automated production facility in Germany, its home country, for manufacturing trainers. Trainers were originally produced in Asian countries with low wages but are now being produced back in Germany, making this case an Industry 4.0 (4IR)-enabled reshoring.

The 4IR is more than just 'advancements' in tech: it brings essential changes in the production process, value chains, and trade. Whether the positive effects will prevail is yet to be discovered as the world moves forward. But certainly, we should be aware of the possible negative impacts of the 4IR and focus on reaping its benefits rather than on its drawbacks.

In this chapter, I have discussed the evolution of the global trading system and the four waves of challenges that are currently reshaping the way countries interact and deal with each other. These challenges, as mentioned, have different timespans and scope of effects. The global trading system and free trade are being challenged by the said waves, and I will be looking at specific cases in the latter part of this book. In the next chapter, I will start incorporating *network theory* and use it as a lens to look at these changing patterns for us to better understand the global trading system.

Notes

1 Federico, G. and Tena, J. (2018), The World Trade Historical Database, Vox, CEPR.
2 Mearsheimer, J. (2019), Bound to Fail, *International Security*, 43(4), p. 9.

3 Mearsheimer, J. (2019), Ibid., p. 18.
4 Gilpin, R. (2001), *Global Political Economy: Understanding the International Economic Order*, NJ: Princeton University Press.
5 Mearsheimer, J. (2019), Ibid., p. 39.
6 Colantone, I. and Stanig, P. (2019), The Surge of Economic Nationalism in Western Europe, *Journal of Economic Perspectives*, 33(4), pp. 128–151.
7 Hays, J. (2009), *Globalization and the New Politics of Embedded Liberalism*, NY: Oxford University Press.
8 Fukuyama, F. (2018), Against Identity Politics, *Foreign Affairs*, 97(5), pp. 90–114.
9 Egger, P., Nigai, S. and Strecker, N. (2019), The Taxing Deed of Globalization, *American Economic Review*, 109(2), pp. 353–390.
10 OECD (2020), Covid-19 and International Trade: Issues and Actions, OECD. https://www.oecd.org/trade/documents/covid-19-international-trade-issues-actions.pdf
11 Gruszczynski, L. (2020), The Covid-19 Pandemic and International Trade: Temporary Turbulence or Paradigm Shift? *European Journal of Risk Regulation*, 11(2), p. 338.
12 UN ECLAC (2020), The Effects of the Coronavirus Disease (COVID-19) Pandemic on International Trade and Logistics, Special Report COVID-19 No. 6, Sandiago: UNECLAC. https://www.un-ilibrary.org/content/books/9789210054706
13 Hoekman, B., Fiorini, M. and Yildirim, A. (2020), Covid-19: Export Controls and International Cooperation, pp. 79; Baldwin, R. and Evenett, S. (eds), *Covid-19 and Trade Policy: Why Turning Inward Won't Work*, London: CEPR Press, pp. 77–87.
14 Fortunato, P. (2020), How Covid-19 Is Changing Global Value Chains, United Nations Conference on Trade and Development (UNCTAD), Geneva: UNCTAD. Retrieved from https://unctad.org/news/how-covid-19-changing-global-value-chains.
15 Savills World Research (2020), Covid-19 and Global Manufacturing Supply Chains, *World Research–July 2020*, p. 5.
16 WTO (2021), WTO World Trade Statistical Review, p. 7, p. 14, https://www.wto.org/english/res_e/statis_e/wts2021_e/wts2021_e.pdf.
17 James, H. (2021), Globalization's Coming Golden Age, *Foreign Affairs*, May/June, 100(3), pp. 1–16.
18 IMF (2021), Fault Lines Widen in the Global Recovery, IMF World Economic Outlook Update (July 01, 2021). https://www.imf.org/en/Publications/WEO/Issues/2021/07/27/world-economic-outlook-update-july-2021.
19 Herrero, G. (2019), Europe in the Midst of China–US Strategic Economic Competition: What Are the European Union's Options? *Journal of Chinese Economic and Business Studies*, 17(4), pp. 403–423.
20 Nicita, A. (2019), Trade and Trade Diversion Effects of United States Tariffs on China. *UNCTAD Research Paper*, No. 37.
21 Herrero, G. (2019), Ibid.
22 World Bank (2019), *Global Economic Prospects: Darkening Skies*, Washington, DC: World Bank.
23 Fehl, C. and Thimm, J. (2019), Dispensing with the Indispensable Nation? Multilateralism Minus One in the Trump Era. Global Governance. *Review of Multilateralism and International Organizations*, 25(1), pp. 23–46.
24 McLaughlin, D., Mohsin, S. and Rund, J. (2020), All about CFIUS, Trump's Watchdog on China Dealmaking, *The Washington Post* (September 15, 2020).
25 Capital Watch (2018), PERSPECTIVE: FIRRMA to Decrease Chinese Investment in U.S. Amidst Trade War (August 08, 2018).
26 Chan, J. and Zhong, W. (2019), Will China Fold on Structural Issues? An Algorithm says Not Any Time Soon, *China Business Review* (March 11, 2019).

27 Etzioni, A. (2020), Biden Joins the Anti-China Chorus, *The Diplomat* (August 24, 2020).

28 Becker, S., Fischer, N., Moeller, E., Oresman, M. and Rosenberg, S. (2020), Trump vs. Biden: An International Trade Briefing, *Pillsburylaw* (October 29, 2020).

29 Gilpin, R. (1987), *The Political Economy of International Relations*, Princeton: Princeton University Press.

30 Gilpin, R. (2001), *Global Political Economy: Understanding the International Economic Order*, Princeton: Princeton University Press.

31 Helleiner, E. (2002), Economic Nationalism as a Challenge to Economic Liberalism? Lessons from the 19th Century. *International Studies Quarterly*, 46, pp. 307–329.

32 Colantone, I. and Stanig, P. (2019), Ibid.

33 Helleiner, E. and Pickel, A. (Eds.) (2005), *Economic Nationalism in a Globalizing World*, NY: Cornell University Press.

34 Bieber, F. (2018), Is Nationalism on the Rise? Assessing Global Trends, *Ethnopolitics*, 17(5), pp. 519–540.

35 De Bolle, M. (2019), *The Rise of Economic Nationalism Threatens Global Cooperation*. Washington, DC: Peterson Institute for International Economics (PIIE).

36 Guarino, A. (2018), The Economic Effects of Trade Protectionism, *FocusEconomics* (March 1, 2018).

37 Shuguang, Z. (1998), An Assessment of China's Trade System; *Measuring The Cost of Protection in China*, Peterson Institute for International Economics (PIIE), pp. 31–32.

38 Noland, M. (2018), US Trade Policy in the Trump Administration, *Asian Economic Policy Review*, 13, pp. 262–278.

39 Trump, D. (2017), Remarks of President Donald J. Trump – as Prepared for Delivery, Inaugural Address. White House, https://www.whitehouse.gov/briefings-statements/the-inaugural-address/.

40 Brewster, R. (2018), The Trump Administration and the Future of the WTO, *The Yale Journal of International Law Online*.

41 Brewster, R. (2018), Ibid.

42 Bown, C. and Irwin, D. (2019). Trump's Assault on the Global Trading System and Why Decoupling from China Will Change Everything? *Foreign Affairs*, 98(5), pp. 125–137.

43 Wyne, A. (2020). How to Think about Potentially Decoupling from China, *The Washington Quarterly*, 43(1), pp. 41–64.

44 European Parliament. (2020), Trade Policy Review, Including WTO Reform Initiative: Legislative Train for a Stronger Europe in the World. Retrieved from https://www.europarl.europa.eu/legislative-train/api/stages/report/current/theme/a-stronger-europe-in-the-world/file/wto-reform

45 Singh, N. (2019), How Can We Regulate Disruptive Technologies? World Economic Forum. Retrieved from https://www.weforum.org/agenda/2019/02/how-can-we-regulate-disruptive-technologies/

2 The Global Trading System from a Network Perspective

Global trade has faced many setbacks in recent years. Mounting trade tensions, growth in trade restrictions, and continued economic uncertainty caused by the four waves of challenges have posed substantial threats to world trade. In this regard, virtualizing the situation in the image of a network provides us a clearer view of the interaction among countries and the impact created by one country on the whole system. Network theory also helps to answer the questions of whether non-state factors can call the signals in the world, what the determinants of power in the world trade system are, how the structure of the system is shaped, and how member countries connect with each other. Since traditional economic and political theories no longer seem capable of clearly presenting the issues involved, we examine the major tenets of network theory and apply them to the analysis of the global trading system. This analysis incorporates the collision of inner and outer networks, network power, network structure, and communication patterns within the system.

2.1 Why Network Theory?

A *network* can be defined as a complex system with two core elements: *nodes* (vertices) and *links* (edges). This concept appears in academic discussions and commentaries on an enormous range of topics. It often appears in assessments of information networks, where the nodes represent information resources, such as Web pages or documents, and the edges represent logical connections, including hyperlinks, citations, and cross-references. In social networks, the nodes are people or groups of people, and the edges represent diverse types of social interaction, possibly mutual exchanges of goods and ideas. In transportation networks, the nodes are cities or destinations, and the edges show direct connections among the vertices.

Two main theories are used to analyze networks: graph theory, which studies network structure, and game theory, which provides models of individual behavior in settings in which outcomes depend on others' behavior (Easley and Kleinberg, 2010).[1] Euler's celebrated 1735 solution of the Königsberg bridge problem is often cited as the first true proof using network theory, and during

DOI: 10.4324/9781003305705-2

the 20th century, graph theory developed into a substantial body of knowledge (Newman, 2003).[2]

Although network theory is relatively young, its use is growing as more people recognize that it helps us understand the world both practically and in a schematized sense. Traditional analysis would call for a separate assessment of each independent component in a system, gradually building up a picture of the operations of the entire system. However, an important feature of the contemporary world is that its elements are mutually correlated, and things are not isolated from each other. Relationships among the elements are not merely unilateral or bilateral but have multiple correlations and layers. Properly representing these features in a network requires a holistic approach, in which vertically and horizontally entangled connections among nodes define the system overall.

The concept of networks has attracted attention in the social sciences for several reasons. First, the concept is generally flexible, as part of an open analytic platform that enables researchers to examine phenomena of interest in a pragmatic manner. Additionally, the concept of a network identifies structural patterns from a relational perspective and enables understanding of the idea of a micro-macro link. For example, social networks mediate among individual actors in larger macro-social processes (Diani, 2003).[3]

Network theory is applied to a variety of areas, including social relations, biological connections, and logistics. Network studies analyze nodes and their relations within a network, as well as the structure and property of the network. Thanks to the availability of advanced communications technology and high-powered computers, networks allow us to gather and analyze data on a scale that is far larger than was previously possible. Nevertheless, drawing a picture of a network using actual points and lines and eyeballing images of networks are still excellent ways of understanding the structure of the network. However, a picture cannot replace the statistical methods recently developed for quantifying large networks. Castells (2012)[4] explores social movements in a network society and reports that such networking depends on communication; further, he argues that autonomous communication is the essence of social movements. These social movements are spread through the internet and move toward the occupation of urban spaces, motivated by a common interest. Finally, members build their projects by sharing their experiences. Indeed, networked social movements have different characteristics in different forms, such as the hybridization of cyberspace and urban spaces (this unity constitutes the third place, referred to as the space of autonomy) and the creation of togetherness. Movements are simultaneously local and global and usually leaderless, and they are political in a fundamental sense.

Network theory has been used in many studies of trade. For example, Hamashita (2001)[5] uses network theory to present East Asia's entry into the era of negotiation from the 1830s to the 1890s, which marked a shift from a tribute order to a Western trading-type order. He reports an increased dynamism in relationships within East Asia, as treaty ports were interwoven with commercial networks and novel and redirected trade routes throughout Asia and between Asia, Europe, and the Americas. Degain et al. (2017)[6] use network analysis to present the evolution of global value chains (GVCs) and to show how, between 2000 and 2015, the GVC network changed dramatically. In particular, GVCs of the North American Free Trade Area, East Asia + Association of Southeast Asian Nations (ASEAN), and the European Union (EU), respectively, became relatively isolated. Scholars are developing an increasing interest in economic regionalism, such as the formation of networks of free trade agreements (FTAs) and the developed understanding of FTA-network formation as a game (Goyal and Joshi, 2006;[7] Furusawa and Konishi, 2007;[8] Daisaka and Furusawa, 2014[9]).

Studies that adopt a network perspective share some common ground. First, each individual's actions are understood to have implicit and explicit consequences for others connected to that individual. Second, the role of leadership is not broadly recognized. The function of a leader is, mostly, to facilitate communication among members. Finally, networks are not static but dynamic. A network expands or contracts, its links are strengthened or sometimes severed, and its nodes can get stronger or weaker or even exit the network altogether.

Grewal (2008)[10] links the concept of network power to globalization and economies of scale, writing that "the greater is the number of people who use a particular standard, the more valuable it becomes for others to adopt the same one." The network's power imposes standards on members of the network and those who are not members. Because common standards enable cooperation among a range of participants, the constitution of standards can be seen as a form of power. Therefore, when a standard becomes compulsory for members, it is said to gain network power. In other words, a standard that has network power is generated by the connectivity of actors on the grid. The standard might be a language, a law, or a convention that members of the network follow.

For example, English can be described as a standard that possesses great network power, derived from the reasonable and forced choices of non-native speakers to speak English. It is reasonable to speak English because English is the best option for communicating with others; it is also a forced decision because English's global dominance causes other languages to lose their attractiveness. This, in turn, increases English's prominence and erodes the viability of other languages as a possible second global language. People may have intrinsic or extrinsic reasons for adopting a new standard. An intrinsic reason is one by which a new standard simply functions better for a given individual's purposes, and an extrinsic reason is one that causes the individual to simply find a network desirable for other reasons, such as size or compatibility with other standards. As the network power of a standard grows, the intrinsic reasons for its adoption become less important relative to the extrinsic coordination benefits that the standard provides. The external value of a standard comes to outweigh any intrinsic merits or demerits.[11]

Therefore, network theories have an advantage for the analysis of large-scale connection patterns, and they focus on the relationship among components. Previous literature on network theory offers us a rich resource for analyzing the global trading system from a network perspective.

2.2 Network Theory and the Global Trading System

2.2.1 *The Collision of Networks: Inner vs. Outer*

Network analysis in the context of diplomacy has certain limitations, in that the network inside the state (the inner network) has largely remained unexplored. When we speak of a state network in the context of diplomacy, we are usually focusing on its external effects or its relations with other nodes; as such, we overlook its interactive influences among domestic players. States in a global trading network are connected with other states, but a single state is linked with and constrained by many domestic actors.

It is true that, in a global trading system, powerful nodes (great powers) create and manage networks. If we visualize the world as one network, it is easy to see the US and China as the leading nodes due to their sheer power and the size of their individual networks. Under their respective circles, there are complex networks of smaller nodes that are heavily dependent on the two leading nodes. Some of the links among these nodes overlap, and it makes the whole network more complicated. As we have mostly discussed in the other chapters of this book, the US and China's own networks, be it their multilateral trade agreements or FTA networks, are undeniably influential. Therefore, any collisions between the two leading nodes could hurt the smaller nodes. Obviously, when the impacts of the US-China trade war, COVID-19 pandemic, economic nationalism, and the Fourth Industrial Revolution are combined, it forces small countries in the middle to ultimately pick a side and determine which side has what it takes to be the leading node.

However, the above argument is based on the realist assumption that inside the state, domestic nodes are either non-existent or their views are consistent with those of the state.

The rise of non-state actors in the international trading system emphasizes the trade-offs faced by states. The state becomes trapped in various value dilemmas. This can include the trade-off between economic growth and social development in relation to the environment, culture, and labor abuses, to name only a few. The state can make a broad choice between industrialization and the environment, while consumers can only decide whether to buy a cheap product made by child laborers or an expensive one that meets labor standards. Each side of the trade-off represents a benefit to a pressure group. Civic groups actively push the government to either stop trade or open markets and harmonize the interests of all parties, both within and outside of states. Free trade leads to a trade-off between wealth and inequality as well. The US is $127 billion richer each year, thanks to the additional trade growth due to NAFTA (North American Free Trade Agreement) (PIIE, 2014).[12] However, unskilled US workers face the threat of job loss and wage reduction as imports from Mexico and China increase and production facilities move to these countries. The trade-off between current and future generations also shifts from one period to another. The decision to adopt protectionism to support a young industry to allow it to ultimately become a powerful industry requires domestic consumers to shoulder the burden of higher costs and higher taxes. Domestic nodes influence the poli-cymaking process of the states and make it more complex and difficult. Globali-zation became unsustainable as the gains from free trade were not evenly shared within a society.

We are currently observing the growing participation of a range of social groups, labor unions, minority groups, multinational corporations (MNCs), and local organizations in the policymaking process. Many non-state players may affect, promote, or constrain a state's behavior, with a range of groups and collective actors seeking to maximize their interests by influencing the state.

In the financial sector, for instance, non-state actors actively participate in the global trading system, leading to investment flows among sovereign states. The World Association of Investment Promotion Agencies (WAIPA) has 170 members, but over one-third of them are agencies for cities or regions and not countries. On a global scale, it is estimated that around 8,000 sub-national trade and investment promotion agencies exist and promote their constituencies' eco-nomic interests internationally. In the future, sub-national agencies (particularly those representing cities) will likely draw the most foreign direct investment, due to their attractive institutional spaces, while nationally oriented ones will generally work as policy designers and providers of political support (Lehmann and Tavares, 2017).[13]

On the other hand, the resistance to economic globalization among a coali-tion of activists, transnational social movements (such as those dealing with labor issues and environmental abuses), and groups whose interests were compromised has been rising, especially since the onset of the global financial crisis in 2008. Ikenson (2017)[14] describes two broad sets of interests in the US that affect its economic policy toward China: one belongs to the import-competing US indus-tries and organized labor, which seek to impede Chinese exporters' penetration of the US market; the other belongs to US-based multinational companies and exporters, which favor a more cautious and less antagonistic approach to China. The first group began to dominate over the latter in dictating US foreign eco-nomic policy since the Obama administration.

According to Haass (2008),[15] the traditional unipolar moment is over for the US. International relations in the 21st century will be defined by a lack of polar-ity, where power is shared among many state and non-state actors. With the rise of China, Russia, and other emerging powers, the complexity and dynamics of the global trading system created a necessity for a new perspective. Indeed, the global trading system appears to be in the middle of a transition from a unipolar order to a bipolar one, where the Soviet Union is now being replaced by China. China is seeking to organize its own bounded illiberal international order to enable competition and cooperation among its allies, while the US will move to-ward a more closed, power-based, protectionist trading system. This movement reflects the nationalist sentiment of the domestic nodes.

A serious problem in the multilateral trading system is the growing divergence between the interests and influences of leading countries in that system, espe-cially among the US, the EU, China, and India. However, this state of affairs has noticeably worsened in recent years as many leading countries simultaneously face a domestic challenge born of anti-globalization sentiments. When the strength of the nationalist inner network within a state's borders surpasses that of the liberal outer international network, a collapse of the existing global trading system is inevitable. A head-on collision between the inner and outer networks over the principles and future direction of the system will cause the liberal network to fall into ruin. The unipolar, liberal international order is falling apart into bipolar trading networks, one that is China-led and illiberal and another that is based on a set of power-based unilateral trading networks. Anarchic struggles among states on trade issues throughout the global community are unavoidable in the coming decades. The network structure of the global trading system is becoming increasingly fragmented, less centralized, and open-ended, which allows for additional domestic players from both within and outside of the network. From a realist perspective, the expanded influence of domestic actors on the state increases the uncertainty and unpredictability of the state's behavior within the global trading system.

Mearsheimer (2019)[16] observes that some nation-states are beginning to consider illiberal democracy and soft authoritarianism as an alternative to liberal democracy. This was not true in the 1990s but is now becoming more common. He places much emphasis on the rising level of nationalism, which thwarts the further improvement of the liberal democratization of the world. Within the current global trading system, as the inner and outer players continue to collide, it can be expected that there will be more policies that lean toward internal interests, as states and domestic concerns come to be seen as having greater importance than the external network interests.

2.2.2 Network Power and Standard

Three essential elements to better understand how network power is generated and exercised are *standard*, *leader*, and *entry barrier*.

A standard defines the particular way in which a group of people is connected within a network; it is a shared set of norms or practices that facilitates cooperation among members (Grewal, 2005).[17] It links members together, either by solving their coordination problems or by specifying the criteria necessary for admission or belonging. Network power especially depends on two characteristics of standards: first, the number of nodes that use the standards, and second, the effects of the coordination, which tend to progressively eliminate the alternatives over which free choice can be effectively exercised.

Leader can make a difference in establishing and operating a successful network, provided that they can effectively program the network and link the nodes. The reason why the leader matters is directly related to the concept of network-making power mentioned by Castells (2011).[18] According to Castells (2011), the network-making power is controlled by two types of players: the programmer, who constitutes and programs or reprograms the network according to set goals, and the switcher, who can link the nodes and ensure that all are cooperative in pursuing common goals. Only when a leader serves as an effective programmer and switcher, the network would thrive.

The third element is the entry barrier. The barrier can be made either by the cost/benefit structure of the network or by the power that insiders within the network can exert over outsiders. Cost/benefit structure implies the relative magnitude of the cost and benefit stemming from participation or non-participation in the network. The cost for those who did not join the network is pretty straightforward, as the devaluation that comes with the exclusion from the network increases rapidly (Castells, 2011).[19] But aside from the cost of non-participation, there is also that of participation. For example, the cost of participation increases when a major outsider retaliates against the nodes who join the network.

The World Trade Organization (WTO) and its former General Agreement on Trade and Tariffs (GATT)-based trade regime promote trade liberalization as a central principle by lowering tariff and non-tariff trade barriers. The WTO is the only legal and institutional entity that governs the multilateral rules of trade among sovereign states. The 164 members of the WTO account for 98% of world trade. As the size of the WTO expands, its members enjoy *network effects*, also termed *network externality*. Network effects can, in the given case, lead the value of a product or service to increase according to the number of those using it. Network effects are functioning for path dependence in the economy. This positive externality is generated from interdependent actions and/or positive feedback from the users of the same standard. However, with the excessive growth in the size of a network, its sustainability and usefulness begin to be questioned. *Reverse network effects* may also set in when an increase in scale damages the quality of the platform or service. As the scale of a network expands up to a point, the value of the network for users may begin to drop. In this case, the network may fail to manage the conflicts of interest among the members, adequately process the abundance of information from its members, or treat all sub-groups, such as later members, equally. The WTO shows symptoms of such reverse network effects. These effects turn powerful states back to bilateral or regional trade relations, away from the WTO. The US is already displaying a tendency to resolve trade disputes outside the global trading system. China is also seeking to develop new technologies through channels that are not possible in the WTO system. These actions challenge the sustainability of the WTO and require full-scale responsive innovations.

The power of the WTO to eliminate alternatives is also ebbing. The Doha Development Agenda (DDA) has been stuck in neutral for two decades, and no leading nodes have pioneered a major breakthrough. Multilateralism is failing not only to introduce the new rules required in a new round (for example, in digital trade) but also to maintain legal enforcement mechanisms. The Appellate Body of the WTO has been crippled since December 2019, when the US blocked appointments for new panelists to the settlement framework. These appointees would have ultimately made decisions over disputes between nations. Applying the network perspective, when a network (like WTO) becomes weaker in its intrinsic value, by which a standard simply functions better for a given node's purposes, that node will walk out and search for alternatives over which free choice can be effectively exercised.

Outside the WTO, countries have various options for pursuing trade liberalization, whether through bilateral or regional agreements. Alternatives to the WTO have proliferated over the past three decades. The WTO can be regarded as clearly in crisis if we consider the participation of key members. The former President of the US, Donald Trump, did not believe in the virtues of international institutions. He withdrew the US from the Trans-Pacific Partnership Agreement (TPP) in 2017, threatening to withdraw the US from the WTO, too. At WTO meetings, China complained about the US tariffs and quotas on Chinese products, while the US claimed these were put into place to penalize China for its unfair trade practices, such as intellectual property theft and forced technology transfers in ways not governed by the WTO's rules. While China continued to pursue economic reforms after becoming a member of the WTO in 2001, after witnessing the pandemonium of the global financial crisis in 2008, China changed its development trajectory and began to follow a retroactive authoritarian strategy. China's goal shifted from attaining the American Dream to realizing the Chinese Dream. State intervention in the market through massive subsidization of state-owned enterprises and aggressive industrial policies, as captured in the slogan Made in China 2025, became part of a road map to realizing the Chinese Dream. The EU is also suffering from strong anti-globalization movements, as seen by the Brexit vote. The leading nodes refuse to remedy the problems of the WTO, giving no regard to the continuing disintegration of the liberal global trading system.

The WTO offers a platform for member countries to negotiate trade disputes and communicate with one another. Because nodes join a network for either intrinsic or extrinsic reasons, and because extrinsic reasons tend to gain in importance as time passes, the future of the WTO depends in large part on whether new multilateral rules are introduced in a timely manner, successfully implemented, and effectively enforced. Although the WTO still possesses significant network power from the 164 nodes it connects, in the context of the power of the domestic players that are moving states toward protectionism and the nationalist behavior of the leading states that is the result of this, it is clear that the future of multilateralism is precarious.

Castells (2011)[20] divides the sources of network power into four categories: *networking power, network power, networked power,* and *network-making power.* Networking power is the type of power that nodes within the network can exert over outsiders. Within the network, nodes can accumulate power and exercise their gate-keeping power to control access to exclusive nodes within the network. Taking the WTO as an example, it is clear that the members of the WTO have certain rules that discriminate between members and non-members and determine whether to accept or reject a new member. Network power, which resembles the *power* concept of Grewal (2005)[21] noted above, is the power to generate coordinating standards to share among all actors in the network. These standards are usually discussed among the members before they are presented in the network, so network power cannot actually compensate for the bias toward members that hold more power than others. Networked power is defined as the power of nodes over other nodes in the network. In a network, we frequently observe that some nodes lead others in a variety of ways. Finally, network-making power is perhaps the most crucial. As was already mentioned above, it is controlled by two types of players: the programmer and the switcher.

If networked power is wielded by powerful nodes, the effectiveness of organizations like the WTO can be hampered by the coercion that occurs within a network among the constituent states. Grewal (2008)[22] identified two broad classes of concern that nodes, such as member states in the WTO in our example, can experience and contribute to anxiety about coercion within a network. The first one is called *distributional concern* – that the infliction of costs on different parties may be unequal or biased. During his presentation at the World Economic Forum, Khor (2000)[23] said that "tariff peaks (or high import duties on certain products) still remain in the rich countries for many industrial products that developing countries export." Some labor-intensive and farming products are heavily protected in the North. The second class is called *identity concern*, and it relates to issues of how cultural or historical identity is affected by a certain standard being raised to universality. It is easy to see this type of concern in many places at present. Notable examples of this can be seen in the EU. The EU is praised and criticized at once and has experienced this over time in different areas. Although the union closed gaps between countries, many expressed concerns over the free and easy movement of people and looser standards for immigration, which was felt by some to pose a threat to their national identity and culture. There has been a "rise of nationalist politics in some countries, either expressed by the rise of new parties, the electoral success of nationalist candidates or the shift of public discourse of established parties" (Bieber, 2018).[24] This trend may become linked to nationalism, which is the "most powerful political ideology on the planet," in Mearsheimer's (2019)[25] words.

In addition to these concerns regarding network power and the repercussions of hyper-globalization, international institutions, such as the WTO, face related problems of sustainability and relevance. It is yet to be seen how these questions will be addressed by networked power institutions as they attempt to regain their integrity and credibility.

Beyond the aforementioned characteristics of standards, leading nodes, and entry barriers, a network's power also depends on the character of domestic state structures. From the Asian context, Katzenstein and Shiraishi (1997)[26] draw the conclusion that regionalism gains strength in real markets rather than through formal institutions.

> *Asian regionalism presents an almost perfect case of the absence of successful regional institutionalization in economic affairs. EAEG (East Asia Economic Group)/EAEC (East Asia Economic Caucus) and APEC (Asia-Pacific*

Economic Cooperation) have either failed completely or seem to face uncertain prospects at best.

Haggard (1994)[27] argues that regional organizations in Asia "have played a role as a locus for the formation of transnational networks, but they have not graduated to the status of policy-making institutions, let alone a forum for consideration of the deep integration agenda." This may be considered an inevitable result of the difference between European and Asian contexts, as most of the Asian states were already struggling with their newfound sovereignty, poverty, and pre-industrial societies. On a smaller scale, the ASEAN is an important regional forum that allows regional integration, politically and institutionally, in Southeast Asia. Three main elements contribute to the institutional capacity and dynamism of the ASEAN. First, the ASEAN member states are respectful of one another's sovereignty, due to their shared colonial history. Second, all members have learned the lesson from the Vietnam War that national resilience is created through economic growth and domestic legitimacy. Third, all the ASEAN members subscribe to the ideology of capitalist growth. Thus, in the case of the ASEAN, the character of domestic state structures, especially state sovereignty, plays an integral role in the success of regional cooperation.

However, there is still the question of whether the power of a node is enhanced by the regional network in Southeast Asia. On the one hand, the ASEAN has successfully promoted the economic development of its member countries. The bloc has taken steps toward broad liberalization and is promoting globalization via a local FTA (AFTA). The AFTA offers preferential tariffs not only to members but also to non-members on a most favored nation (MFN) basis. One positive impact of the trade agreement is that more than 90% of the ASEAN countries' tariff lines have a preference margin of zero, where preferential tariffs are no lower than the MFN rate. And more than 70% of intra-ASEAN trade is also conducted at MFN rates at zero. Multilateralism has promoted rapid growth in overall trade and makes ASEAN the fourth-largest exporting region in the world, trailing only the EU, North America, and the People's Republic of China. As a result, nine of ten ASEAN countries experienced gross domestic product's (GDP) growth rates higher than 40% over 2010–2018, and Lao PDR, Cambodia, and Vietnam had growth of over 100% (ASEAN Integration Report, 2019).[28] On the other hand, ASEAN is not yet a powerful network on a global scale. As the ASEAN+1 bilateral FTAs were being negotiated, the ASEAN members sat together as a single party. The ASEAN-as-one approach is commendable for the way in which it increases external recognition for less powerful states, preventing divergence within the membership and enhancing bargaining power for all. Nevertheless, a look back at the ASEAN+1 FTAs reveals the limits to the bargaining power of the ASEAN countries. For example, the liberalization rate for trade in goods in the ASEAN–India FTA was 76.5%, but for others, it was above 90%. The ASEAN–Japan FTA contains more commitments than the ASEAN's internal economic agreements do (Mueller, 2019).[29] In addition, there is uncertainty as to the extent of the bargaining power exerted by the ASEAN states in the Regional Comprehensive Economic Partnership (RCEP), as the negotiations were significantly influenced by the preferences of regional powers like Japan and China.

2.2.3 Network Structure

Hocking et al. (2012)[30] present a framework for analyzing the changing diplomatic environment and suggest an integrative approach to diplomacy that takes into account the growing interconnectivity between various issues. The integration of agendas and arenas is related to the tendency of international negotiations to bring trade and non-trade agendas together as one package to the table. Non-trade agendas include security, diplomacy, and environmental and human rights issues. Karolina et al. (2018)[31] define this phenomenon as *issue linkage* and find that, while it is difficult to introduce non-trade issues into trade negotiations, once they are introduced, parties that are already committed to non-trade issues in the package agreement will demand similar commitments from successive partners. For example, the issue linkage between military cost-sharing and tariffs on automobiles based on Section 232 of the US 1962 Trade Expansion Act implies that global trading networks are vertically connected to other networks, such as those of international security and human rights. In other words, the trading network is only one of many within the multilayered network system of foreign diplomacy; furthermore, the nodes are interconnected both horizontally and vertically. If one link is disturbed by a leading node in one network, all interconnected networks may be disrupted.

Nation-states use trade agreements to make arrangements on non-trade issues, such as environmental questions, by adding either environmental provisions or entire chapters on the environment in RTAs, but the success of these measures in producing real environmental change depends on how the provisions and agreements are implemented by governments (George and Yamaguchi, 2018).[32] Some issues that are fairly common in RTAs include the promotion of trade in environmental goods and services, renewable energy, energy conservation, climate change, biodiversity, air quality, small- and medium-sized enterprises, gender equality, and women's empowerment. In a networked global trade system, all non-trade agendas are eventually either linked to or integrated with trade and investment issues.

A multilayered process of policymaking is one in which traditional distinctions among bilateral, regional, and multilateral agreements become less relevant. Hocking et al. (2012)[33] emphasize the importance of soft power as an integrating factor for different levels of diplomacy. They argue that all levels of diplomacy (international, regional, and national) tend to move in similar patterns and directions. Therefore, in a networked global trading system, it is less important whether the network is multilateral or bilateral. Instead, because policymaking activities are increasingly intertwined, the factors leading to the greatest differences are as follows: the strategic objectives of the states, the configuration of the nodes, the standards in the various networks, and the manner in which the nodes are linked. Because networks are multilayered and sometimes overlapping, the exact outcomes of negotiations are difficult to project accurately. Each node exhibits strategic behavior, especially when the leading node is absent; bilateral relationships between major nodes can affect the entire network.

According to Maluck and Donner (2015),[34] an international trading network necessarily includes two sub-networks, where the nodes represent countries in one and industrial sectors in the other. It has been suggested that, in both sub-networks, nodes with high trade volumes develop communities that are particularly closely connected. However, in national partitions, domestic trade will likely exceed international trade for randomly drawn nodes. In sectoral partitions, networks in the electrical and mechanical industry have stronger links, while those for financial services and business activities enhance the centrality of the nodes (mostly the US, Germany, and China) as mediators of the flow between nodes within a network. Furthermore, as a result of hyper-globalization, reciprocity in cross-country relations became saturated in 2000, while reciprocity in sectoral partitions decreased after 2000, which indicates that most emerging links are new one-way trade relationships between industrial sectors.

The global trading system is now more interconnected than ever before, and this necessitates structural changes. More importantly, neither the nodes nor the links in this network remain static or constant. There has been an increase in heterogeneity, changes in the average structural distance, and variations in the position of the countries in the world trade network (De Benedictis and Tajoli, 2011).[35] As the global trading system changes, its attractiveness as a multilateral network will depend not only on its standard but also on its influence on other connected networks. Only if the intensity and extensity of the links between the nodes from all dimensions are fully measured can the final impact of nodal moves upon the network be adequately understood.

2.2.4 Communication Pattern

Communication patterns reflect developments and changes in the ways that nodes communicate among themselves. Improvements in information technology require rapid responses and effective communication channels. Linkage patterns between nodes affect the means of communication among the vertices. An important study related to this analysis is cited in *Who Shall Survive* by psychotherapist Moreno (1978),[36] where relationship patterns among players in society are described and the practice of sociometry is developed as a quantitative method for studying interpersonal connections among individuals (Maoz, 2010).[37] Moreno (1978) writes,

> [S]ocial network analysts typically distinguish between two types of networks: relational and affiliational. Relational networks are characterized by rules that define the presence, direction, and magnitude of a relationship between any two units. For example, neighborhood, friendship, alliance, or trade networks are relational networks. Affiliational networks are those in which the

rule defines an affiliation of a unit with an event, organization, or group. Membership in professional associations, in social clubs, national membership in international organizations, or the distribution of states' population among different religions, all reflect affiliational networks.

Different network types lead to different communication patterns. In a multilateral trading system, communication networks are affiliational, in that all participants in the WTO debate and negotiate on an equal footing. However, as the US began to establish a hub-and-spoke system around themselves as the hub with other nation-states as spokes, the WTO's validity was undermined. Resulting from this, many states now find themselves part of relational trading networks. In the US-led hub-and-spoke system, relationships appear to be bilateral but are actually unilateral and asymmetric in their power distribution. Power began to flow unilaterally from one leading node, the US, to the others especially after Donald Trump took his office. That is exactly what has been observed in the US–Mexico–Canada Agreement (USMCA), the KORUS (Korea–US) amendment agreement, and the US–Japan (Digital) Trade Agreement under the Trump administration. China is also building a network in which a leading vertex (China) is bilaterally linked with many peripheral points. By utilizing its excess manufacturing capacity, China is seeking to establish a bounded, illiberal trading network to deter and counter the negative influence that the US has on China. With its own institutions, such as the Belt and Road Initiative (BRI) and the RCEP, China hopes to maximize its influence in the emerging new international order. These institutions seek to facilitate bilateral cooperation and provide the funds necessary to build sufficient infrastructure for the participating states. The patterns of dialogue between China and its allies are obviously *relational*, and the links between China's allies are non-existent. Overall, the communication pattern in the global trading system is rapidly shifting from an *affiliational* to a *relational* one.

Communication patterns within the inner network among the domestic nodes have also changed. The hierarchical character of the information flowing from state to non-state actors has been challenged by more interactive communication patterns. In this sense, the WTO has not adequately conveyed its goals and mission to its members. Many accuse free trade of taking away employment, damaging the environment, and even slowing economic growth. It is undeniable that globalization and international trade have been the causes of negative externalities; however, at the same time, opportunities and benefits have been achieved through this process. Tongia and Wilson (2007)[38] have shown that the cost of being excluded from a network increases at a much faster rate than the benefits of being included in it. Most of what is reported to the public are the negative impacts of being linked to the international trade network. At the same time, the benefits are often not recognized even as they are being enjoyed and shared among many, while losses are concentrated in a much smaller group of people. For these reasons, people blame trade for the economic drawbacks and shy away from being open to the rest of the world. Leaving aside whether this is a miscommunication, there is certainly a problem in conveying common goals among the nodes in the network and even within each node.

Both networks and resistance networks are powered by information and communication technologies. For example, the anti-globalization movement is a locally rooted, globally connected network that seeks to change the mind of the public as part of an initiative to influence policy decisions in favor of improving environmental governance or labor relations. The WTO should also secure a more effective communications channel for its members. It should pay attention to its relationships that go beyond other international organizations and national governments. It should consider the problem of coherence, which implies the potential for conflict between international organizations that have overlapping jurisdictions and that might encourage other countries to adopt conflicting policies (VanGrasstek, 2013).[39] Rapid developments in the speed and direction of communication require the WTO to build vertical and horizontal links with various nodes including civic groups in diverse networks in the global community.

2.3 Analytic Tools in Network Study

2.3.1 Positioning of a Node

A network consists of a set of nodes and ties between those. Nodes can be people, organizations, Web pages, or nation-states. According to Hogan (2017),[40] a network is developed from small to big scale: monadic (one node), dyadic (two nodes), triadic (three nodes), meso (clusters of nodes), macro (the entire network), and comparative (multiple networks). The positioning of a node is estimated by evaluating links attached to it, focusing on the existence of homophily, the appearance of community, and the types of network.

2.3.1.1 Degree and Direction

The study of node position enables us to estimate how valuable a particular node within a network is. Links between one node and the others play an integral role in defining the position and sphere of influence of one specific node in the network. Degree centrality of a node is defined as a score of links possessed by that node, where each link is considered *a degree*. Nodes with more links, in other words, higher degrees, are regarded as more central in a relational space; on the contrary, zero-degree nodes are seen as outliers of the network. Regarding the *direction* of node, we observe that there are two kinds of node-to-node relations: one is an undirected or symmetric relation, and the other is directed or asymmetric relation. Directed links are then classified into in-degree and out-degree links up to the direction of information flow between nodes. When links are represented as messages, nodes with a higher in-degree are more popular; meanwhile, nodes with more out-degree are more authoritative. For instance, considering the foreign direct investment (FDI) flows, the US is valued as a node with high out-degree links, as the country's FDI outflow in 2019 reached

5.96 trillion USD and was scattered in many countries around the globe.[41] The US has a strong sphere of influence over its FDI receiving partners. Meanwhile, Singapore becomes a popular FDI destination, as it obtains high in-degree links with FDI inflow from 38 nations and 2 institutional partners (the ASEAN and the EU).[42] The preferential attachment of links into a specific node also leads to the appearance of a hub-and-spoke network structure. Observing the connection of one node to the others, as the number of edges attached to a node becomes more numerous and abundant, it gains more degrees and becomes a hub in the scale-free network. Besides, as the connectivity shared among each other gets progressively stronger, it is likely that the hub can pull its spokes closer and form a more firm, concentrated network.

2.3.1.2 Homophily and Community

A network is developed from the micro level to the meso level of the community as an impact of *homophily*. Homophily is the terminology depicting a cluster of nodes of the like type that are particularly prone to linking up with one another, as in the proverb "birds of a feather flock together." Newman (2003)[43] also applied the theory of homophily in the network to explain the tendency that nodes of high degrees connect with others of high degrees and the low degree nodes to others of low degree. In simple words, homophily helps nodes associate and bond with ones of similar characteristics, eventually, to establish and expand a network.

The ASEAN is a perfect example of homophily resulting in a long-standing bloc. Similarities in history (colonial history), which constitutes the same 'feather,' of ten ASEAN countries; the common experience of national resilience from nationalist movements against imperialism; and the shared ideology of market-based capitalist growth are three pillars of the *ASEAN-ness*. Together with the geographic proximity, those similar characteristics attract Southeast Asian countries to link together and to cooperate for the goal of one vision, one identity, and one community.

However, in the network theory, the trick is not finding homophily but the right kind of homophily. Once various kinds of homophily co-exist within a network, it can induce polarization that leads to extreme fragmentation and even disruption of the network.

In the meso scale, the community appears when the homophily in the micro level leads to merging into a formation larger than a triad. Clusters of nodes with the same interests, concerns, or characteristics tend to group together. Where there are more nodes within a group than between groups, we consider it a community, which is described in the notion of *modularity*. High modularity implies clear groups; in contrast, low modularity means fuzzy groups. In addition, community detection is another important tool in network analysis besides node positioning. The technique can be illustrated by a node moving randomly until the movement makes it circle back to the original position; the area being traversed by that node in the random movement tends to be within the same community.

2.3.1.3 Four Types of Network

Regarding network collection types, Hogan (2017)[44] introduced four types of networks, namely, *whole network, partial network, ego network*, and *modal network*. A whole network implies a meaningful boundary that can provide us the rationale as to why these nodes and not others should be included. For instance, the WTO can be regarded as a whole network, while the world is not because no meaningful boundary exists. A partial network refers to a segment of the whole network. It is more common, compared to the whole network in the sense that collecting information of the whole network is difficult or, sometimes, impossible. A partial network also requires a meaningful boundary. Next, the ego network is another way to sample the population, in which we look at the connections around a specific individual and calculate differences among a number of ego networks. In the WTO, the US, the EU, and Japan, for example, are working on the issue of state-owned enterprises (SOEs) and subsidy as egos. The ego network, in this case, is the network of three economies with their FTA partners. Lastly, the modal network is considered the most theoretically tenuous type of network as nodes in that network are not linked directly but via their shared association. For example, the trading relationship between New Zealand and Angola is not noticeable, yet the two countries still possess a thin connection as members of the WTO.

2.3.2 The Role of Leading Nodes

As mentioned previously, leading nodes matter, as their role is related to the network-making power. The role of leading nodes can be classified into two types, the programmer and the switcher. Leading nodes utilize these networks and transform them into systems that will enable them to achieve and solidify either one or both roles. To better understand this, we will use some networking tools as examples in visualizing these networks.

2.3.2.1 Hub and Switch

The first two devices that we will talk about are similar to each other. Let us start with the *hub*, or sometimes called the Ethernet hub, network hub, multiport hub, etc. This is used to connect multiple devices in a network. All the computers plugged into the ports can receive data broadcasted through the hub.[45] The next device is called the *switch*. Like a hub, it has many ports where other computers can connect to. But it is different because, from the name itself, a switch can send data only to selected recipients within the network, switching data information to specified devices. Thus, with a switch, both unicast (sending to one recipient) and multicast (sending to multiple recipients) functions are available. In contrast, a hub is only capable of broadcasting data to all devices connected to the ports. A hub also has fewer ports, 4/12, compared to a switch with 24/48 ports.[46]

Also, it is worth noting that one of the most glaring differences between a hub and a switch is how collisions might occur in hubs as the transmission mode is only half-duplex, which means that both ends can send data but only one at a time, whereas through a switch, data is transmitted by both ends simultaneously, through a full-duplex transmission mode. Like in the previous part of this chapter, collisions also occur in global trading system networks, especially between the inner and outer networks. We can imagine that these networks are also like hubs and switches. Collisions between the nodes in a network are normal, but the ways that the collision is addressed vary from the type of system the network uses. In the next chapter, we will analyze the existing mega-FTAs, and it can be observed that the FTAs have varying transmission modes. On the one hand, some of them are like switches, wherein a full-duplex transmission mode is utilized, and that the parties in the FTA can send and receive data, hence negotiate, simultaneously. On the other hand, FTAs with hub-like features also exist. In this kind of network, the flow of data can only be processed one direction at a time, which shows the limitation of its negotiating system.

The process of negotiations in different trading networks greatly varies from one another. Some networks function like hubs, with a hub-and-spoke system, which was explained under the communication patterns part of this chapter. At first glance, it seems that hub-and-spoke is similar to a switch, as nodes communicate with other nodes directly. But it should be noted that a hub-and-spoke system is unilateral and asymmetric in its power distribution. Therefore, a hub only repeats the information from the source and transmits it to all connected devices. For a network with switch-like qualities, we can use the WTO as an example. In the WTO network, the communication pattern is affiliational, which means that members negotiate as equals. As discussed, switches have a full-duplex mode that allows simultaneous transmission of data from all parties. The same can also be mentioned in terms of the size capacity of the WTO, as switches can also accommodate more devices compared to hubs. Although, unlike a switch, we cannot say that collisions do not occur in the WTO. But the WTO system is an intelligent network or used to be one, as it has a dispute settlement system that parties can utilize to resolve issues.

The role of the leading nodes in these trading networks can also be compared with the function of a hub and a switch. We can look at the US, with its hub-and-spoke FTA networks, including the USMCA under Trump's administration, as examples. The USMCA network acts as a device used by the US to advance its interests. In contrast, the EU, being led by Germany, can be regarded as a switch-like network. The EU has an affiliational communication pattern, therefore, providing the members, in principle, equal negotiating abilities. These mega-FTAs will be discussed further in Chapter 3.

2.3.2.2 Modem and Router

The next two devices are *modem* and *router*. A modem literally modulates and demodulates electrical signals from phone lines, cables, and other types of wires.

This device is used to convert the data from the outside source to a format that the computer would be able to process and vice versa. A router is a device designed to route data between the devices connected to it and the internet network. It is normally connected to a modem that supplies the internet connection; other devices can connect to the router's port or wirelessly through WiFi to access the internet connection.[47] Normally, a modem connects to the phone line from the internet service provider, and it converts the connection to a format that the router can process. Similarly, the router then serves as the hub to which the devices can connect through both wired and wireless signals.

Going back to the network analysis of the global trading system, some nodes and trade networks act like modems and routers. China's BRI, unveiled by President Xi Jinping in 2013, is one such example. It is being used by China to expand its network of influence by providing infrastructure investments in different countries around the globe. In this scheme, we can think of China as the modem, which has access to the internet (financial resources/investments), and the BRI as the router. China, acting as both the programmer and the switcher of the BRI network, has the ability to set entry barriers, like how administrators of routers set up passwords before other devices can take advantage of the internet connection. Similarly, without the countries signing deals and connecting to the BRI, they will not be able to access China's resources through the said infrastructure investments. This puts the BRI in an important position as China's medium to connect to other nodes, thus increasing both its network and network-making power.

Trading networks do vary in their features, functions, as well as structure. And from the networking we have discussed, we can better understand these mega-FTAs and other trade networks and how they work. For some, a hub-like feature can be observed wherein the network only has a half-duplex function, which makes negotiation more difficult for the nodes within this network as the nodes cannot simultaneously and specifically transmit data within the network. These networks often use the hub-and-spoke system wherein the leading node has control over the network and usually has the role of both programmer and switcher, similar to both the American network created to oppose the development of the Eastern alliance under Trump's administration (for example, Economic Prosperity Network) and China's BRI. But for some, a more intelligent system, like a switch, can be considered. In these networks, nodes can utilize a full-duplex function of the network, wherein data can be transmitted simultaneously and specific destinations can be set. This opens the way to easier communication and negotiations. The WTO and the EU can be regarded as networks with switch-like features. And as mentioned in the previous part, China can also be compared to a modem connected to a router (BRI) that grants access to the resources for the nodes which are connected to this network.

These are just a few examples of how we interpret the global trading system using the network theory, especially the networking tools. Similarly, the collisions in networks occur for a variety of reasons, such as interlinking and overlapping connections. These phenomena will be discussed in the following chapters.

2.3.3 Multilayered Network

A *network*, as defined in the context of network theory, consists of a set of nodes that are tied together through linkages that define their relationship. As pinpointed by Borgatti and Halgin (2011),[48] the choice of the various sets of nodes and ties will eventually define the network itself. Considering these premises, we realize how broad and multilayered the networks can appear. Also, as defined by social network analysis (SNA), this theory is becoming increasingly popular and hence being applied to many different fields (from social psychology to international trade to computer science). Because of this, oftentimes, definitions and characteristics discovered in a specific field of study appear to be relevant for other fields as well.

2.3.3.1 Multiplex Networks and Network of Networks

Multilayered networks is one of such definitions, used in the context of social sciences but also to better represent the interaction between the fundamental nodes of the cerebral apparatus (Bianconi, 2015).[49] Multilayered networks are formed by several interacting networks, which work together in order to make the whole system function at maximum capacity. Without any of the internal components (here, networks) functioning, the multilayered system would not be able to thrive and perform. In a multilayered network, every linkage has a different connotation and property, which allows researchers to extrapolate more information from the network as a whole. Two major classes of multilayered networks can be distinguished: *multiplex networks* and *network of networks*. As written in the aforementioned paper by Bianconi (2015), "a multiplex network is a network formed by the same set of nodes interacting through different types of networks (also called layers) as, for example, a set of people interacting through different means of communication"; "a network of the networks is instead formed by networks that are interacting with each other but are formed by different types of nodes, such as the internet, the power grid, and other types of interdependent infrastructures…"

An example of a possible multiplex networks phenomenon could be represented by any subset of countries connected through links (interlinks) passing through different layers. The EU comes to mind, with its members connected with each other under different forums or environments (forum-like intergovernmental organizations like Organization for Economic Cooperation and Development [OECD], the EU's internal institutional seats, etc.), but similar examples can be found across the world. We can see this kind of connection between countries that agreed to sign RCEP, CPTPP (Comprehensive and Progressive Agreement for Trans-Pacific Partnership), and other agreements too. For example, Brunei, Malaysia, Singapore, and Vietnam share these regional trade agreements and are all part of the ASEAN (Association of South-East Asian Nations), interconnected under a number of different networks. Australia, New Zealand, and Japan are members of both RCEP and CPTPP. At the same time, Australia and Japan are key members of Quad, a strategic dialogue between the US, India, Japan, and Australia. Australia and New Zealand are also members of Five Eyes(FVEY), an intelligence alliance comprising Australia, Canada, New Zealand, the UK, and the US. Australia is another node of the Australia–UK–US network, which is a newly established trilateral security pact between Australia, the UK, and the US, designed to counter the influence of China in the Indo-Pacific region.

Therefore, a network of networks could be viewed as a macro environment in which other minor networks can remain connected. Following the previous example of the EU, if we consider each member country as a separate network, the Union as a whole could be considered a network of networks, which could in turn be considered a *node* from the point of view of the big players in the global economy. The concepts we have just introduced are somewhat abstract, but it is important to understand how, depending on the point of view, these interlinks could change how nodes interact with one another and how the global environment could be affected.

2.3.3.2 Interconnection and Issue Linkage

Interdependence (and interlinks) plays an important role while considering and studying multilayered networks. Indeed, cascading failures could be obtained as nodes become damaged and the system could undergo an avalanche of failures. Multilayered networks appear to be more fragile than single networks. Studies like the one carried out by Serrano and Boguná (2003)[50] and Schiavo et al. (2010)[51] give additional information about the topological structure of interdependent networks of countries, which are linked together to develop trading and financial ties. Specifically, in Serrano and Boguná's research, a high degree of correlation between the number of trade links and GDP per capita is discovered, providing what could be seen as a direct correlation in which countries seek to become trading hubs and to become closely interdependent with the global outer network. In this case, phenomena like the FTA hub-and-spoke system could arise, nurturing the creation of a *hub* in which trade creation would overcome trade diversion even while considering the network comprising *spokes* and the *hub* itself. To examine the motives behind a country's desire to become interconnected with the global trade system, Sopranzetti (2018)[52] focused on overlapping FTAs (or the networks created by the analyzed nodes in a global trading system). He concluded that countries that are better connected to other nodes end up exporting more, incentivizing the main players to further interconnect and create overlapping FTAs. It is also noteworthy in the study that an increase in the number of spokes that are not linked between them has, on average, a negative effect on the trade of the hub. In other words, while it is true that interconnection, FTAs, and additional interdependence between trading networks generally net positive results, connecting every single node might actually decrease the effectiveness of the consequent multilayered network (while being also, as we mentioned, more fragile and prone to cascading failures).

Schiavo et al. (2010) tackle the properties of ITN (International Trade Network) and IFN (International Financial Network) by discovering how "poorly connected nodes tend to connect to central ones and use them as hubs to access the rest of the network," creating a situation in which the core of the network is represented by richer countries and the periphery is defined by poor countries (in terms of GDP) that hold weaker links overall and among themselves. In this kind of situation, richer countries tend to become the center of the newly born *network of networks* and hence will end up maintaining significant networks and networking power. Poorer countries will end up having more interlinks with the *core* of the network and, overall, will grasp relatively smaller gains from the phenomenon.

Countries appear to become *interlocked* or *interconnected* much like the global system, and the *World City Network* (WCN) appears to be interlocked in Taylor's research (2001).[53] Derudde and Parnreiter (2014)[54] further explain the concept of *interlocking network model* (INM), according to which, in the context of the Globalization and World Cities (GaWC) research, uneven development results from a cluster of big cities that exert different kinds of power (geopolitical, ideological, etc.). Much alike cities, due to their centrality, that attract corporations and strengthen their inter-city relations, countries and other nodes that manage to become hubs see themselves as centers of developed, multilayered networks that eventually will become interconnected as did systems explained in the previous paragraphs.

Issue linkage is another important term that may be used to define connections between countries and the results of their ongoing international agreements. As explained by Maggi (2016),[55] issue linkage is a notion that contains three types of linkage: enforcement linkage, negotiation linkage, and participation linkage. The first one, enforcement linkage, involves a violation of an agreement and the consequent retaliation with sanctions; the second, negotiation linkage, involves a joint negotiation of an agreement instead of two separate negotiations; the third one, participation linkage, involves the threat of sanctions in area A to encourage participation in an international agreement in area B. Countries experience issue linkages everyday as they deal with many economic and non-economic problems such as human rights, security, environment, and labor issues. In general, there are many different examples of linkages depending on the nature of the areas involved (for example, the trade sanctions imposed on Russia for violating the territorial integrity of Ukraine would be considered a linkage between trade and security policies).

The issue linkage of trade and security is studied by Dorussen and Ward (2010)[56] by revisiting the classical-liberal arguments, which link trade interconnection to peacekeeping among the involved parties. By studying trade networks, direct internal trade, and indirect linkages involving external nodes, the authors conclude that a dyadic (as in, involving just two nodes) approach has to be improved by including external elements (the aforementioned indirect linkages and third-party trade connections). Indirect trade links appear to be of significant importance while considering the security and general peace of the nodes involved, and classical-liberal cosmopolitan arguments about trade and peace still appear to be relevant. Dorussen and Ward (2010)[57] mentioned that "we find general engagement with the international trade network to matter more than trade links with particular third parties." We can hence deduce that security, peacekeeping, and trade remain strongly interconnected even in the contemporary geopolitical environment and that components external to the relationships (or linkages) between two networks are still fundamental in defining the linkages themselves. Be it enforcement linkage, negotiation linkage, and participation linkage, all notions that mix economic and non-economic terms like security and evaluation of trade networks (like one could do with the ones revolving around the US and China) require a study that goes beyond mere economic analysis.

In this chapter, we were exposed to the concepts of network theory which have been applied in a wide variety of social science research fields. The theory is attractive due to its flexibility and its ability to actualize clearly structural patterns from a relational perspective with nodes and links. Through the geometric image, it is easier to observe the interaction and impact among nodes, as well as the strength and weakness of the links among those. Moreover, some new network devices are developed and applied to figure out the nature and pattern of trade networks.

To analyze the current situation and future prospects of the global trading system, we design the network theory to include the following four points: (1) collision between inner and outer factors within one node, (2) network power, (3) network structure, and (4) communication patterns among nodes within a network. In many countries, the conflict between inner and outer networks is conspicuous. In other words, social groups, labor unions, minority groups, MNCs, and local organizations are well able to promote or ruin a government's plan; thus, non-state factors play an integral part in the current and the future of the world trade network. Regarding network power, three elements of a standard, the role of leading node(s), and the extent of entry barrier are essential to measure how power is generated and exercised. On the other hand, network power is divided into four main sources, namely, networking power, network power, networked power, and network-making power. Network structure delivers concerns about trade and non-trade issue linkage as well as the multilayered process of policymaking. Lastly, relational and affiliational communication patterns are defined to provide us with a better insight into the relationship among nodes within a single network.

Network tools were developed to deal with the positioning of a node via its linkage and direction. When relations between two nodes are directed, a node can be in-degree or out-degree. Homophily is an important factor in forming a community and a consequent network. The coexistence of various types of homophily is expected to cause fragmentation or even a disruption in that network. Within a network, the role of a leading node is visualized by functions of four hardware equipment: hub, switch, router, and modem. Based on the characteristics of each piece of equipment, there are a diversity of leaders with different functions, such as information transmission, facilitation, gatekeeping, or programming. When observed on a larger scale, multiplex networks and networks of the networks appear. On the inside, we scrutinize the issues of interconnection and issue linkage that define the relationship and the result of mutual agreements among nodes. To illustrate the network theory better, in the next chapter, we will adopt four main points that we discussed above to interpret the four existing mega-FTAs, including the EU, CPTPP, USMCA, and RCEP.

Notes

1 Easley, D. and Kleinberg, J. (2010), *Networks, Crowds, and Markets: Reasoning about a Highly Connected World*, Cambridge: Cambridge University Press, p. 10.
2 Newman, M. (2003), The Structure and Function of Complex Networks, *SIAM Review*, 45, pp. 167–256, p. 169.
3 Diani, M. (2003), Introduction: Social Movements, Contentious Actions, and Social Networks: "From Metaphor to Substance"? in Diani, M. and McAdam, D. (eds.), *Social Movements and Networks: Relational Approaches to Collective Action*, Oxford: Oxford University Press, p. 6.
4 Castells, M. (2012), *Networks of Outrage and Hope: Social Movements in the Internet Age*, London: Polity Press, pp. 221–234.
5 Hamashita, T. (2001), Tribute and Treaties: East Asian Treaty Ports Networks in the Era of Negotiation, 1834–1894, *European Journal of East Asian Studies*, 1(1), pp. 59–87.
6 Degain, C., Meng, B. and Wang, Z. (2017), Recent Trends in Global Trade and Global Value Chains, in World Bank Group-IDE/JETRO-OECD-UIBE-WTO (eds.), *Global Value Chain Development Report 2017: Measuring and Analyzing the Impact of GVCs on Economic Development*, Washington, DC: World Bank. p. 51.
7 Goyal, S. and Joshi, S. (2006), Bilateralism and Free Trade, *International Economic Review*, 47, pp. 749–778.
8 Furusawa, T. and Konishi, H. (2007), Free Trade Networks, *Journal of International Economics*, 72, pp. 310–335.
9 Daisaka, H. and Furusawa, T. (2014), Dynamic Free Trade Networks: Some Numerical Results, *Review of International Economics*, 22(3), pp. 469–487.
10 Grewal, D. (2008), *Network Power: The Social Dynamics of Globalization*, New Haven: Yale University Press, p. 25.
11 Ibid., pp. 29–35.
12 Hufbauer, G., Cimino, C. and Moran, T. (2014), *NAFTA at 2.0: Misleading Charges and Positive Achievements*, Peterson Institute for International Economics (PIIE) No. PB14-13, p. 16.
13 Lehmann., A. and Tavares, R. (2017), *Economic Nationalism Is on the Rise, but the Future of Trade Lies with Cities*, Cologny: World Economic Forum.
14 Ikenson, D. (2017), Into the Abyss: Is a U.S.-China Trade War Inevitable? *Free Trade Bulletin*, No. 69, Washington, DC: CATO Institute.
15 Haass, R. (2008), The Age of Nonpolarity, What Will Follow US dominance? *Foreign Affairs*, 87(3), pp. 44–56.
16 Mearsheimer, J. (2019), Bound to Fail, *International Security*, 43(4), pp. 7–51, p. 30.
17 Grewal, D. (2005), Network Power and Global Standardization: The Controversy over the Multilateral Agreement on Investment, *Metaphilosophy*, 36(1–2), pp. 128–144, p. 131.
18 Castells, M. (2011), A Network Theory of Power, *International Journal of Communication*, 5, 773–787, p. 776.
19 Ibid., p. 774.
20 Ibid., pp. 779–784.
21 Grewal, D. (2005), Ibid., p. 128.

22 Grewal, D. (2005), Ibid., p. 142.

23 Khor, M. (2000), *Rethinking Liberalization and Reshaping the WTO*, Davos: World Economic Forum.

24 Bieber, F. (2018), Is Nationalism on the Rise? Assessing Global Trends, *Ethnopolitics*, 17(5), pp. 519–540, p. 537.

25 Mearsheimer, J. (2019), Ibid., p. 8.

26 Katzenstein, P. and Shiraishi, T. (1997), *Network Power: Japan and Asia*, Ithaca and London: Cornell University Press, 1–44, p. 12 and p. 22.

27 Haggard, S. (1994), Thinking about Regionalism: The Politics of Minilateralism in Asia and the Americas, presented at the American Political Science Association, pp. 8–12 and 60–66.

28 Jakarta: Secretariat (2019), ASEAN Integration Report 2019, p. 7.

29 Mueller, L. (2019), ASEAN Centrality under Threat – The Cases of RCEP and Connectivity, *Journal of Contemporary East Asia Studies*, 8(2), pp. 177–198, p. 184.

30 Hocking, B., Melissen, J., Riordan, S. and Sharp, P. (2012), Futures for Diplomacy: Integrative Diplomacy in the 21st Century (Report No. 1), Netherlands Institute of International Relations 'Clingendael', pp. 10–11.

31 Karolina, M., Hollway, J., Peacock, C. and Snidal, D. (2018), Beyond Trade: The Expanding Scope of the Nontrade Agenda in Trade Agreements, *Journal of Conflict Resolution*, 62(4), pp. 743–773, p. 746.

32 George, C. and Yamaguchi, S. (2018), Assessing Implementation of Environmental Provisions in Regional Trade Agreements, *OECD Trade and Environment Working Papers*, p. 8.

33 Hocking, B., Melissen, J., Riordan, S. and Sharp, P. (2012), Ibid., p. 11.

34 Maluck, J. and Donner, R. (2015). A Network of Networks Perspective on Global Trade, *PLoS ONE*, 10(7), pp. 2–3.

35 De Benedictis, L. and Tajoli, L. (2011), The World Trade Network, *The World Economy*, 34(8), pp. 1417–1454.

36 Moreno, J. (1978), *Who Shall Survive, Beacon House*, 3rd ed. (originally published in 1934).

37 Maoz, Z. (2010), *Network of Nations: The Evolution, Structure, and Impact of International Networks, 1816–2001*, New York: Cambridge University Press.

38 Tongia, R. and Wilson, E. (2007), Turning Metcalfe on His Head: The Multiple Costs of Network Exclusion, 35th Annual Telecommunication Policy Research Conference (TPRC), Washington, DC: TPRC, pp. 6–15.

39 VanGrasstek, C. and Pascal, L. A. M. Y. (2013). *The history and future of the World Trade Organization*. Geneva: World Trade Organization, p. 201.

40 Hogan, B. (2017), Online Social Networks: Concepts for Data Collection and Analysis, in Fielding, N., Lee, R. and Blank, G. (eds), *The Sage Handbook of Online Research Methods*, 2nd ed., Thousand Oaks, CA: Sage Publications, pp. 241–258.

41 The US' Bureau of Economic Analysis (2020), Direct Investment by Country and Industry, 2019.

42 Singapore Department of Statistics (2021), Foreign Direct Investment in Singapore By Investor Source (Stock As At Year-End), *Annual*.

43 Newman, M.(2003), Mixing Patterns in Networks, *Physical Review E*, 67, 026126, 1–13.

44 Hogan, B. (2017), Ibid.

45 Tutorials Point (2019), What are Hub and Switch in Computer Network? https://www.tutorialspoint.com/what-are-hub-and-switch-in-computer-network.

46 Ibid.

47 Wirecutter (2018), Modem vs. Router: What's the Difference? https://www.nytimes.com/wirecutter/blog/modem-vs-router

48 Borgatti, S. and Halgin, D. (2011), On Network Theory, *Organization Science*, 22(5), pp. 1168–1181.

49 Bianconi, G. (2015). Interdisciplinary and Physics Challenges of Network Theory, *EPL (Europhysics Letters)*, 111(5), p. 1.

50 Serrano, M. and Boguná, M. (2003), Topology of the World Trade Web, *Physical Review E*, 68(1), 015101.

51 Schiavo, S., Reyes, J. and Fagiolo, G. (2010), International Trade and Financial Integration: A Weighted Network Analysis, *Quantitative Finance*, 10(4), pp. 389–399.

52 Sopranzetti, S. (2018), Overlapping Free Trade Agreements and International Trade: A Network Approach, *The World Economy*, 41(6), pp. 1549–1566.

53 Taylor, P. (2011), The interlocking network model. *International Handbook of Globalization and World Cities*. Cheltenham: Edward Elgar Publishing.

54 Derudder, B. and Parnreiter, C. (2014), Introduction: The Interlocking Network Model for Studying Urban Networks: Outline, Potential, Critiques, and Ways Forward, *Tijdschrift Voor Economische en Sociale Geografie*, 105(4), 373–386.

55 Maggi, G. (2016), Issue Linkage, *Handbook of Commercial Policy*, North-Holland, Vol. 1, pp. 513–564.

56 Dorussen, H. and Ward, H. (2010), Trade Networks and the Kantian Peace, *Journal of Peace Research*, 47(1), pp. 29–42.

57 Ibid., p. 41.

3 Mega-FTAs –
A Reason for Hope?

The term *mega free trade agreement* (*mega-FTA*) refers to a trade deal that accounts for a considerable portion of the world trade, for instance, the European Union (EU), the Comprehensive and Progressive Agreement for Trans-Pacific Partnership (CPTPP), the US–Mexico–Canada Agreement (USMCA), and the Regional Comprehensive Economic Partnership (RCEP). The facts are clear that the establishment of the above-mentioned mega-FTAs has significant economic and geopolitical implications regarding the future of the global trading system. Several important questions can be raised in analyzing these extended FTAs. The questions are: Who are the leaders and what are their influences on the networks? Are these new trade pacts powerful enough to solve the existing problems of the multilateral approaches? What are the reactions of domestic nodes regarding their government's decision to join these mega-FTAs? Will mega-FTAs be effective substitutes for multilateralism in the future? To find appropriate answers to those questions, in this chapter, we will take a look at the EU and three additional mega-FTAs, analyzing their features and structures using a network perspective. We will begin with a brief history of each of these trade agreements to review the developments that each of them went through over time. Then, we will identify the leading node, analyze the network power structure, and categorize what communication mode each preferentially utilizes. Lastly, we will examine how the nodes interact with the inner and outer networks and how they react to the issues that such FTAs encounter and, for some, that are still facing.

3.1 The European Union (EU)

3.1.1 What's Inside the EU Network?

The EU, as the second-largest economy in the world, can be regarded as one of the most important players and powers in any global scenario. As a matter of fact, many scholars consider it a *superpower* due to its potential to exert both 'soft' and 'hard' power, making it possible for it to project international influence over a number of different contexts (Moravcsik, 2010).[1]

DOI: 10.4324/9781003305705-3

Nevertheless, the EU is also one of the most complex networks on the planet, with a system that tries to tie together different communities under common political and economic rules. More specifically, making a network analysis of the EU might prove to be a challenge due to the complexity, density, and ramification of its connective web. It is an entity that operates on different angles, considering the dichotomy between the Union's interests (and strategies) and the ones coming from each member country.

These countries, though, are tied by commonly shared values that can be defined as the standard of the EU. This standard represents a key element in the cultural integration of nations that could (and in some cases, do) have major differences in cultural values, identities, or systems. However, the newly joining members of the Union experienced "substantial cultural convergence with old member states after 1992, as did current candidates between 2001 and 2008" (Akaliyski, 2019).[2] This convergence can be explained by the adoption of the standard itself since more aspects of a country's political, cultural, and economic characteristics align with the ones from the EU, the longer they will stay intertwined.

In order to understand this standard, we can take a look at the EU's conditions for membership. According to the European Commission (2020),[3] a potential member can be eligible only if it will comply with all the EU's standards (which are the responsibility of the European Standardization Organizations, like the CEN, CENELEC, and ETSI). It also needs to have the consent of the EU institutions, EU member states, and the consent of their citizens. Moreover, other criteria were defined at the European Council in Copenhagen in 1993. Countries that wanted to join had to have

> *stability of institutions guaranteeing democracy, the rule of law, human rights and respect for and protection of minorities; a functioning market economy and the capacity to cope with competition and market forces in the EU; the ability to take on and implement effectively the obligations of membership, including adherence to the aims of political, economic and monetary union.*
> (Publications Office of the European Union, 2021)[4]

An extrapolation of the nine EU values reveals its constituents to be a hybrid polity. The nine values are *sustainable peace, social liberty, consensual democracy, associative human rights, supranational rule of law, inclusive equality, social solidarity, sustainable development,* and *good governance* (Lucarelli and Manners, 2006).[5]

Using Grewal's definition of *standard*, we can say that these criteria are what enable each member to cooperate and find a greater sense of belonging, which will ultimately make them part of the EU network. The EU's status and its political-economic success can be further explained by its growing network power. More specifically, by gaining more nodes (member states), the Union's reach managed to rival other superpowers like the US. Although the recent Brexit (Britain+exit) phenomenon made the Union lose an important member like the

UK (leaving it with 27 different constituents), the success in countries that chose to join the EU made it more appealing for other potential candidates to become involved in the system. Without such political and economic integration, average per capita income levels would have been 12% lower for newer member countries (Campos et al., 2014).[6] Not joining the EU (and other possible alternatives) became progressively less appealing for non-members, a phenomenon connected to the EU's increasing network power.

Obviously, there are exceptions for which the entry barrier gives an unfair advantage for a country's citizens. This has ramifications that go beyond economics, as it can lead to a clash between the individual identity of a member and the Union's values. A clear example would be Switzerland and its reluctance to join the EU, an unwillingness based on its historic identity and its neutrality-focused foreign policy (which would be undeniably threatened by aligning with the Union) (Morris and White, 2011).[7] As Grewal (2008)[8] highlighted in his book, nodes, both prior to or after joining a network, experience these issues due to the possible uncontrollable influence that the dominant standards might entail. He called this *identity concern*. For example, in case of Switzerland, it has been keeping a neutral identity throughout history. It even declined active participation in the two World Wars. Joining the EU would have affected its identity, placing it in a more burdensome position of taking sides shall conflict occur involving the Union.

From the perspective of EU standards, the provisions governing digital trade and green trade are the most renowned, as the EU is the pioneer in the field and their impacts are not limited to Europe but are worldwide in scope. The EU's General Data Protection Regulation (GDPR), including 11 chapters, came into force in May 2018 and applies to companies located in the EU countries or those located outside the EU but processing personal data of European residents. GDPR enlarged its scope to cover various types of private data, including basic identity information, web data, health and genetic data, biometric data, racial or ethnic data, political opinions, and sexual orientation.[9] Rights and obligations of individual users, data processors and controllers, and public independent supervisory authorities are strictly governed by the GDPR. The users' rights are enhanced as they can request the company to provide an answer regarding which personal data is being collected and for what purposes the data is used for. And should users do not consent the way their data is handled, they can ask the company to delete their personal data.[10] Besides, data controllers and processers are required to conduct data protection by design and default and to keep records of all processing activities; therefore, the periodic internal risk assessment and data protection officer (DPO) appointment are suggested in order to ensure the compliance of business to GDPR.[11] The Regulation also requires the establishment of one or more independent public authorities in each EU member state to monitor the application of GDPR and receive breach notification. The data safety regulations in the transfer process are also reinforced, especially for the process of transfer of data across borders and transfer of personal data to third countries or international organizations. Fines and penalties are set at an extremely severe level, up to 4% of a company's worldwide revenues or 20 million euros, whichever is higher. In the future, it is expected that businesses operating with the EU personal data will change the way of handling data in order to comply with GDPR and avoid strict penalties. And GDPR is believed to be "the new framework serving as a role model for other policy areas where the consequences of globalization and digitalization require a new regulatory approach in order to effectively safeguard values and standards" (Albrecht, 2016).[12]

Green Deal is ignited by the President of the European Commission, Ursula von der Leyen, through which she aims to create a climate-neutral and sustainable Europe by 2050 by cutting 100% of carbon emissions (compared to 1990 levels).[13] In accordance with Claeys et al. (2019),[14] the EU Green Deal consists of four parts, including carbon pricing, sustainable investment, industrial policy, and a just transition process. The latter three pillars focus on promoting eco-friendly investment, green innovation, and transition of coal-mining regions, support for technology switch of companies, and citizens' behavioral change inside the EU. Meanwhile, under the first pillar, the EU emissions trading system (ETS) is bolstered, and EU countries are pushed to increase the price for emissions not covered by the ETS. The EU carbon border tax is also prepared to ensure a robust mechanism against carbon leakage, which is expected to be legally enforced from the year 2026 (after a three-year grace period from 2023). Besides Green Deal, the EU Plastic Tax has been implemented since January 1, 2021, under the EU recovery package. The tax is calculated based on the weight of non-recyclable plastic packaging waste at an expected rate of EUR 0.80 per kilogram, the collection of which is an integral source of the EU revenue in the post-COVID era. From this perspective, while sustainable investment, industrial policy, and just-transition policies push for the intra-EU transformation, the carbon tax and plastic tax exert significant influence both inside and outside the EU borders. For instance, according to an estimation of BCG (2020), suppose that the EU levy on imports of $30 per metric ton of CO_2 emissions, profits of foreign crude oil producers would decline by 20%, while that of flat-rolled steel producers would be reduced by roughly 40%. The taxation mechanism based on waste footprint will alter competitiveness since it puts producers with high waste-intensive production processes at a strong disadvantage.[15]

3.1.2 Defining the Leader of the EU

The complexity of the EU requires a cautious approach to defining the leader of the network. More specifically, being a body composed of several institutions and 27 countries, finding a specific leader, with a focus on EU's network-making power, is something that should be done with discretion. As we have previously mentioned, an ideal leader should hold the roles of both programmer and switcher in order to reprogram its network and connect its nodes efficiently. It would be natural, then, to turn our attention to the biggest members of the EU. Germany, being the biggest economy in the Union, could be seen as a potential guide, but its pre-eminence in the European context and several growing constraints in the domestic political scene hampered a potential leading role and have raised international legitimacy concerns. Considered a *reluctant hegemon*, whose "economic leadership is recognized but politically contested," its influence on the EU's foreign policy decisions is clearly visible (Bulmer and Paterson, 2013).[16] Together with France and the UK, its involvement in many multilateral diplomacy forums gave them the capacity to shape important settlements, under a tacit agreement that the largest member states would take the lead (Lehne, 2012).[17]

According to Lehne, the influence of the biggest countries in Europe will be diminishing as the EU's common institutions get stronger and as their relative global relevance (measured in gross domestic product [GDP] and population) declines over the years. We can say that most of the EU's decisional power resides in these institutions, namely, the European Council, the European Commission, the Council of the European Union, the European Parliament, the Court of Justice of the European Union, the European Central Bank, and the European Court of Auditors (Treaty of the European Union).

As Castells (2011)[18] mentions, "...I suggest that in many instances the power holders are networks themselves, in fact, subnetworks of the networks that organize society"; this seems to be the case for the EU as well, where the role of programmer and switcher can be said to be shared among the most influential countries and the aforementioned EU institutions. At the beginning of its existence, the EU's values might have been upheld by powerful founding countries like Germany, which was considered a leading node in the newborn EU network. As institutions gained strength, more nodes were connected, and the influence from individual countries mattered less. We can imagine that the EU as a concept (represented by its institutions) gained the status of *leader* in this specific environment.

3.1.3 EU's Network Structure and Communication Pattern

EU consists of 27 members, excluding the UK. It is an obvious fact that the countries are not equal in terms of position. Depending on the interaction and relations among countries, some are more central, while some are relegated to the periphery of the network. For example, Germany is regarded as the central node in the EU, thanks to the rich linkage between it and other nation-states and international institutions, both inside and outside the EU – such as with Russia, the US, the G7, the OSCE, and NATO. The country also played an undeniably significant role in resolving the common issues in the EU, for instance, the Eurozone crisis in late 2009 and the refugee crisis in the summer of 2015. Through this, the out-degree tie between Germany–EU institutions and Germany–EU member states was bolstered. Virtualizing EU in a network, links attached to Germany are obviously more numerous and robust than those attached to Bulgaria, for example.

Furthermore, in the previous chapter, we discussed that nodes with more out-degree links tend to be authoritative. A survey of Aggestam and Johansson

(2017)[19] on European leadership role expectations revealed that 57% of the respondents ranked Germany as the most influential member state in the EU's Common Foreign and Security Policy (CFSP). If only member states' respondence is counted, the percentage goes up to 66%, which implies the primus inter pares position of the country. Therefore, though Germany is considered a reluctant leading node, via the strengthening of the out-degree linkage, the country has been engaged in a process of learning to lead in three main areas: diplomatic negotiations, politico-military crisis management, and EU sanction policy (Aggestam and Hyde-Price, 2020).[20] Nevertheless, the leadership of Germany is less likely to turn the EU into a hub-and-spoke network structure, because, besides Germany, there are other powerhouses such as France and intergovernmental institutions exerting their influence on the whole network.

As we mentioned at the start of the chapter, the EU is one of the most complex networks on the globe. Its exceptional singularity resides in the fact that the EU cannot be considered a federal system though having many of its characteristics (Kelemen, 2007).[21] Its structure involves not only the 'single market system' and trade-related sectors but also several horizontal and vertical layers that go beyond the supranational level. Each member country has its own interests, but at the same time, it has to comply with the EU's regulations. Although the EU is responsible for supervising foreign direct investment (FDI) projects involving its members following the 2009 Lisbon Treaty, due to many ambiguities surrounding the Union's authority, the block's cohesion might not be as effective as it should be, and member countries might take advantage by pushing their own agendas (Meunier, 2014).[22]

Under these assumptions, we can use Hocking et al. (2012)'s[23] framework to understand the EU's network structure, which can be classified as multilayered due to its complexity of connections. Examples of this reside in the EU's simultaneous focus on non-trade issues (NTIs) as well, like human rights or the environment. There are also several examples of success that highlight the European Network's effectiveness and its scope, which goes beyond national boundaries. One of these is the COREU network, which "allows member states to share important information about foreign policy" (Bicchi, 2011).[24]

The Union as a whole can also be described as a "system of authority fusion since governments responsible for policy-making at one level of government share responsibility with other governments of the same level at a higher, collective level" (Henning, 2009).[25] Henning takes a definition he previously introduced as a *multilevel system*, which goes hand in hand with a typical multilayered system (or network) in which multiple minor networks act as nodes that can be interconnected in different ways. Considering all the players involved – the political parties, the supranational system, and all the internal European institutions – we can use the definition of *network of networks* introduced in Chapter 2 to better represent the EU's actual network structure. At the same time, the 27 member countries are also intertwined under the umbrella of several international organizations, forums, and environments. Single nodes appear to be linked together over a set of different layers, creating an interconnected network that gives the Union its particular characteristics.

Regarding the EU's communication patterns, its very structure dictates an affiliational system in which every member country can contribute and influence the decisions of the Union. The presence of institutions such as the Council of the European Union and the European Parliament ensures that each country is represented fairly and in compliance with the EU's long-term objective of maintaining multilateralism as its preferred process. The Union's focus on regional integration aims to boost communication among its nodes. This general idea spills over even in the EU's foreign policy, which tends to maintain multilateralism as the ideal goal while dealing with external players (Renard, 2016).[26]

3.1.4 Brexit: The Collision of Inner and Outer Networks

The EU network appears to be complicated considering its inner and outer frameworks. Normally, we would have to consider the linkage between domestic players and other external nodes in order to understand a country's policy-making process. With the EU, there is an extra layer in between the interest of domestic actors and the interest of the Union itself, which is independent of the country's national interest. Most of the time, these three levels do not match, and priorities tend to be different for each player (Bevan et al., 2016).[27]

The *leave* result of the UK's referendum held in 2016 is the consequence of both the outer network's loophole in the adoption of common standards and the inner network's desire to protect national interests. According to Somai and Biedermann (2016),[28] among 28 countries, the UK was the member state that was granted the most exemptions from the Union's rules and regulations, even in key areas. For instance, the UK did not participate in the third phase of the economic and monetary union, kept its Great Britain pounds, and maintained its autonomy in monetary policies. It opted out of the Schengen Cooperation but ran a mini-Schengen with Ireland. The EU Charter of Fundamental Rights was not signed by the UK owing to its incompatibility with British labor law. The country also has the right to choose to join the justice and home affairs cooperation under the Treaty of Lisbon on a case-by-case basis and free from the EU's budget and the free movement of workers. Borrowing the network theory about the standard, the opt-out right indicates the flexibility of the network in the adoption of a common standard, which opens the room for the node to participate in the selective regulations that fit its own interests. The more nodes choose to exercise opt-out right for a specific provision, the weaker that provision becomes in governing the network members. Therefore, it can be said that the standard developed by the EU is not sufficiently strong to bind the UK tightly with the Union.

Furthermore, the referendum reflects the wish of the UK's internal constituents to pull the country out of the outer network. Concerns about immigration, globalization, and budgetary burden can be attributed to the negative attitude of the British toward the EU network. First, immigration is cited as one of the main issues that drove the UK to the decision of leaving the EU. Nickell and Saleheen (2017)[29] estimated that immigration has a huge impact on the wages of workers in the semi/unskilled services sector – wages decline by 2.6% in response to a 10%-point rise in immigrant-native ratio. However, Colantone and Stanig (2018)[30] stated that while there is no definitive relationship between Brexit and immigrant/total population ratio, they found one with respect to *new arrivals* from Eastern Europe. Regardless of the ratio being used in models of Nickell Saleheen (2017)[31] and Calantone and Stanig (2018), immigration has become a prominent impediment and an embedded feature in the relationship between the UK and the EU. Second, a strong correlation between the regional impacts of the China import shock and the Brexit referendum was discovered by Colantone and Stanig (2018). Utilizing the econometric model, they found out that *leave* votes were concentrated in the midlands and the north of England, where there was high exposure to globalization. Pushing for leaving the unified EU was, the voters felt, the first step to gaining back their economic sovereignty. This would be followed by building up new bilateral trade links, with nodes who are not current FTA partners of the EU, for instance, the US, Australia, New Zealand, South Korea, and CPTPP. In this situation, trade creation effects are expected to benefit the UK economy. Third, behind Germany, the UK and France are the second-third-biggest net contributors to the EU (European Commission, 2016)[32]; nevertheless, a large proportion of the common budget is distributed to the relatively backward regions rather than to the UK. Brexit is simply another manifestation of economic nationalism in Europe, which prompted the British to vote *leave*, to deliver their concerns and protect their interests.

The UK officially left the EU on January 31, 2020, yet a transition period of 11 months, till the end of 2020, was allowed, to give time to leaders to negotiate the future relationship between them. Agreed on December 24, the UK–EU Brexit trade agreement came into effect at 23:00 GMT on December 31, 2020, with some noticeable provisions. The UK maintains 'zero tariff, zero quota' free trade with the EU; however, the service businesses and individual professionals lost their automatic access to the EU. Regarding security and data, the UK no longer has automatic access to the EU's key security databases; nonetheless, data exchange will be conducted the same way for at least four months, with a condition that no change is made to the UK's data protection rules. Concerning fishing, the agreement stipulated that the UK gradually gains a greater portion of fish from its own waters over the next 5.5 years, meaning that the UK does not have sufficient control over its waters; thus, this provision was unsatisfactory to British fishermen.[33] From this point, it can be said that the trade deal successfully prevented the risks caused by a *hard Brexit*, including tariff slap and supply chain disruption between two parties, and minimized the negative economic impacts on both economies.

Brexit's case is a perfect example of how both *identity* and *distributional concerns* push a node to the edge and ultimately have it totally withdraw from the network. Although the UK benefited from the firstcomer benefits as it joined relatively early compared to other members of the Union, the reasons stated above were enough for its citizens to vote in favor of leaving the EU. The increase in immigration, especially from Eastern European countries, posed a threat to the UK's identity. In fact, in 2011, the share of foreign-born residents in England

and Wales increased to 13.4%, almost double the level in 1991.[34] This made the UK realize that the distribution of benefits and costs of remaining in the EU was totally undesirable.

To sum up, Brexit is proof of *intermediate networks* having a major impact on a country's policies, and when there is a significant difference between the three levels of interests – those of the Union, the nation, and the domestic elements – the collision between inner and outer networks is unavoidable.

3.1.5 Highlights in the EU Network

The EU was created to be the most sophisticated network in the world with the participation of both member states and intergovernmental institutions. Among member states, Germany is considered the leading node, *a reluctant hegemon*, and the Union's economic driver; however, as the institutions gain strength, the power of member states in the Union declines. Moreover, the conditions for entry are set clearly for all potential countries who want to join the EU – an examination of the countries' domestic situation, the consent of the EU institutions, EU member states, and citizens of member states. In terms of network performance, standards developed by the Union deal with both trade and NTIs. Especially, the EU is the world's pioneer in the Green Deal and digital deal, which are expected to have sizeable impacts both inside and outside the EU borders. The EU network operates based on a multilayered structure and affiliational communication pattern. However, as its rules allow member states to exercise opt-out rights, when combined with dynamics of inner factors, there are inevitable consequences such as the Brexit, causing a huge loss for the network.

3.2 Comprehensive and Progressive Agreement for Trans-Pacific Partnership (CPTPP)

3.2.1 Brief History

On February 4, 2016, a trade agreement was signed among Australia, Brunei, Canada, Chile, Japan, Malaysia, Mexico, New Zealand, Peru, Singapore, Vietnam, and the US, called the Trans-Pacific Partnership (TPP). Its roots can be traced to a trade agreement put in place in 2005 between countries surrounding the Pacific, including Brunei, Chile, New Zealand, and Singapore. Under Presidents George W. Bush and Barack Obama, this plan was expanded to a grander scale, and new countries joined it. The main goal of the TPP was to liberalize trade by lowering tariffs and other trade barriers among the 12 signatories.

However, the TPP, although the negotiation was completed, was never ratified and its benefits did not materialize. Donald Trump withdrew from the TPP soon after he became president in 2017. He has advertised his US-centric economic strategies, seeking to withdraw from involvement in global affairs. The absence of the US has led the remaining 11 members to adjust the agreement around the lack of its leading presence. In January 2018, the signatories reached an agreement and concluded their CPTPP.

CPTPP includes 30 high-standard chapters covering prominent issues of international cooperation, which is then used as a model for other trade agreements in the world. Among these, provisions on e-commerce, investment, rules of origin, cross-border trade in services and financial services, labor, environment, intellectual property, and state-owned enterprises (SOEs) are highlights of CPTPP. First, the electronic commerce chapter prohibits data localization measures, allows the cross-border transfer of information via the electronic method for business purposes, forbids customs duties imposed on electronic transmissions, and prohibits the requirement of access to source code of software owned by others as a condition for trade. Second, the investment chapter covers the core obligations of national treatment, most favored nation (MFN) treatment, expropriation and compensation, performance requirements and transfers, and the narrow-scoped Investor-State Dispute Settlement (ISDS) provisions. Third, the development of supply chains within the CPTPP region is supported by the allowance for production accumulation in more than one CPTPP country (the product is then to be treated as originating in the latter countries). Trade facilitation on self-certification of origin, advanced rulings, and customs clearance timelines are also provided in the chapter. Fourth, cross-border trade in services allows the existence of *negative lists* consisting of sectors that are exempt from MFN, market access, and/or local presence commitments. In the financial services chapter, a financial institution of one country can export new financial services to another country's financial institutions with that country's permission. Commitments, obligations, and a special dispute settlement are designed to fit the nature of financial services. Fifth, the labor provisions push for the freedom of labor association, elimination of forced labor, child labor, and employment discrimination. Sixth, in the environment chapter, CPTPP members are prohibited to enforce its environmental laws to promote or discourage trade or investment between countries. Certain types of fisheries subsidies that negatively influence overfished stocks are also forbidden (Corr et al., 2019).[35] Seventh, the intellectual property rules under CPTPP affirm the World Trade Organization's (WTO) TRIPS Agreement, yet add more provisions governing pharmaceutical products, cybersquatting of domain names, and trade secrets theft. Vis-à-vis TPP, patent delays, pharmaceutical patent test data, technology protection, and copyright term length, which were promoted by the US, were cut.[36] The common set of rules on intellectual property protection aims at not only preventing piracy and counterfeiting but also promoting the dissemination of information, knowledge, and technology (Australian Government, 2019).[37] Eighth, the issues of SOE are enhanced under CPTPP to ensure a fair business environment for all countries and firms. The SOE chapter indicates that SOEs engaging in commercial activities are to buy and sell goods and services in a non-discriminatory manner, and CPTPP country is not allowed to use non-commercial assistance to support SOEs, by which means, to harm other CPTPP countries. The country is also obliged to disclose certain information about SOEs to ensure transparency in international trade (Government of Canada, 2018).[38]

Overall, the goals of this agreement are similar to the previous incarnation, which are geared toward further trade liberalization and lowering trade barriers. Additionally, 22 TPP provisions prioritized by the US but not by other members were suspended or modified. At the current writing, the CPTPP has been ratified and is in effect in 7 of the 11 member countries.

3.2.2 Leading Node: From the US to Japan

3.2.2.1 US: The Leading Node of TPP until Its Withdrawal

During the early days of the TPP negotiations, the US was the central member. But after its decision to withdraw from the agreement in January 2017, it was Japan that emerged as a new leader. As mentioned in the brief history of CPTPP, the agreement was intended to be a forward development from the previous 2005 trade agreement of countries of the Pacific Rim, which was developed and nurtured by Presidents Bush and Obama. However, it was no surprise as to why Trump did not want continued US participation in this agreement because it was developed by his political rivals, the Democratic Party. Moreover, Trump, as a conservative nationalist, mainly focused on 'Making America Great Again' with his *America First* Policies, which meant withdrawing US support from international trade deals and agreements.

The prospect of the US rejoining CPTPP was proposed as Joe Biden became a strong candidate to become the 46th president of the United States. According to Cutler (2020),[39] four basic paths were suggested for US reengagement with CPTPP. The first option of returning to the original TPP means rolling back four years of progress in the trade bloc's negotiations, which the member countries are unlikely to agree as the current situation is far different from four years ago. Acceding to the CPTPP is a path that might gain the support of the CPTPP members; however, the US might not be satisfied since its leading role as the programmer, who configures and programs/reprograms the network according to set goals, will not be recognized. Third, renegotiating the CPTPP is suggested in light of the difficulties of the two options above. The standard would be modified to modernize digital trade, customs, and IPR provisions; to eliminate commitments that no longer represent US priorities such as ISDS mechanism and government procurement; and to reflect the concern of the US in rules of origin, labor, environment, and currency manipulation. While welcoming the US to rejoin, this option is time-consuming and causes domestic difficulties for the incumbent member countries. The last resort is pursuing interim sectoral deals, indicating that the US can offer plurilateral negotiation with CPTPP members on specific sectors before committing to a comprehensive one. The fourth option can open common trade talks to welcome not only CPTPP members but also countries having an interest in the bloc including the UK, Thailand, Korea, Taiwan, and other Association of Southeast Asian Nations (ASEAN) countries. This option seems realistic in that the Biden administration already started to build a new network, i.e. Indo-Pacific Economic Framework (IPEF), defining shared objectives around digital trade, supply chains, decarbonization and clean energy, trade facilitation, technology, and more. Ironically, however, the in-depth trade liberalization agenda is missing in the discussion of IPEF.

Each option has pros and cons that both the US and the CPTPP members need to consider thoroughly. Nonetheless, achieving consensus in sectoral negotiations is not easy, as is meeting the WTO requirement of covering 'all substantial trade' and including 'substantial sectoral coverage.' Even the Biden administration decides to reengage with CPTPP, unlikely though, the re-participation will not be decided as quickly as Trump's withdrawal since it takes time for Biden to "invest in Americans and equip them to succeed in the global economy."[40]

3.2.2.2 Japan as the New Leading Node

Japan has the largest GDP among the 11 signatories of the CPTPP. It is the third-largest economy in the world, behind the US and China, respectively. Abe, the former Japanese prime minister, first reacted poorly to the US exit, making his remarks that the trade pact was meaningless without its leading player. However, it is astonishing to see how Japan, previously a mere member, although un-deniably a significant one, has become the leading node of this promising trade agreement. It was hard to tell whether Japan sought out the role, as it would not have been possible had the US remained part of the agreement.

However, it is worth noting that if not for Abe's effort to salvage the TPP, it would have been a very tedious task to bring this trade agreement into reality. The question then is, why did Abe step up and take the lead? As Trump pulled America back and retreated from the global stage, China was doing the opposite, launching its Belt and Road Initiative (BRI) to amplify the connections in its networks. This combination put Japan in a difficult spot as it sought to balance the regional order and serve its own interests at the same time. Abe's so-called Abenomics was launched to re-awaken Japan's stagnant economic growth. By utilizing a multilayered, multilateral regional strategy through the CPTPP, Abe tried to stimulate the economy and also keep Japan's balance between the US and China.

Even before the CPTPP, Japan played an active role, acting as a leader, follow-ing the flying geese paradigm. It depicts Japan's position as the lead goose in a flock, followed by the four Asian Tigers, the larger ASEAN countries, and the least-developed major nations in the region. In the 1980s, Japan and Australia coordinated to help advance the APEC and the ASEAN Regional Forum. The roles that Japan took in these contexts were motivated by the fact of decreas-ing US' presence in the Asia-Pacific region along with the growing threat that China is posing with regard to the balance of regional power. Looking past the atrocities once perpetrated by Imperial Japan, modern-day Japan appears more than capable of serving as the leading node for the CPTPP. It would also seem to be worthwhile for others if Japan were to take the lead. First, as the leader of the CPTPP, Japan will have additional negotiating power to deal with the US and other potential members like Korea, Taiwan, and the UK. Second, like the

US, Japan considers containing China a top priority, which can best be achieved through the use of the advantage offered by the strategic multilateralism of the CPTPP to generate collective pressure of member states vis-à-vis China.

However, with the inauguration of Prime Minister Yoshihide Suga, Japan's position toward power balancing seems to have changed somewhat. Japan seems to be aiming at expanding the CPTPP, catering to potential member states like Britain. Recently, China, Taiwan, and the UK all expressed interests in joining the deal. Japan will not find it easy to negotiate a new FTA with China under the influence of the US, but having China join the CPTPP can be still considered a smart move as China's inclusion in the CPTPP will also put the country under the rules of the network. Japan has also been persuading the US, as it believes that Washington's return to the CPTPP has strategic implications that can further improve the bilateral economic cooperation of the US in the Indo-Pacific region.

3.2.3 Network Power

The CPTPP is a representative mega-FTA in the Asia-Pacific region, with 11 member states, producing a combined 12.9% of the world's GDP and 14.9% of world trade volumes, with a total population of 500 million people. Although its network power depends on many factors, such as shared standards and the effects of coordination, these figures show that in terms of sheer size, the CPTPP is clearly one of the largest trade networks in the world.

Again, the issue of standards in a network and how it affects network power cannot be understated. In the context of the CPTPP, the comprehensive agreement contains 30 chapters that legally bind its 11 member states. We can say that the CPTPP has a clear set of shared norms and practices, backed up by its dispute settlement system, which has the advantage of encouraging its members to conduct themselves more cooperatively and transparently. Unlike the WTO, whose relevance has been questioned, especially regarding the closure of its Doha negotiations and the concerns over the Appellate Body, the CPTPP is all the more timely, as the agreement seeks to go beyond the commitments made through the WTO, including the opening of more service sectors to CPTPP member firms, increasing business mobility by allowing the travel of skilled workers between CPTPP markets for business purposes, and incorporating criminal procedures and remedies into questions of intellectual property rights.[41]

The CPTPP entered into force on December 30, 2018, with Australia, Canada, Japan, Mexico, New Zealand, and Singapore as the initial ratifying parties. On January 14, 2019, Vietnam also ratified the agreement. This leaves four signatories – Brunei Darussalam, Chile, Malaysia, and Peru – which have yet to ratify the agreement. Beyond the original signatories, several countries, such as Indonesia, South Korea, Thailand, and the UK, have expressed their intent to join the agreement. Recently, China also expressed its positive and open attitude toward joining the CPTPP. It is quite apparent that the more members subscribe to the common standard, the stronger the trade pact becomes. However, should both G2 countries, the US and China, engage in the CPTPP, members will worry about the reverse effect. Some members of CPTPP, including Japan, Canada, and Mexico, would find it difficult to negotiate a new FTA with a non-market country (China) due to their respective trade agreements with the US.

Though the full effect of this coordination has yet to materialize, it is believed that it will have a greatly positive impact on trade among the members. Petri and Plummer (2020) expect that the CPTPP and RCEP 15 will more than offset global losses caused by the US-China trade war.[42]

3.2.4 Network Structure

The analytic framework provided by Hocking et al. (2012)[43] includes the idea of *integrative diplomacy*. This concept relates to several issues in a network and its nodes, specifically in relation to both trade and non-trade agendas. For the CPTPP, many cases of issue linkage were observed by Karolina et al. (2018).[44] With these in mind, we can see that the CPTPP, as a trading network, is multilayered, but overall its nodes share strong standards ranging from the importance of digital trade to the value of democracy and human rights. Some chapters of the CPTPP cover provisions related to the declaration of the International Labor Organization (ILO) calling for the elimination of forced labor, the abolition of child labor, and the elimination of employment discrimination. There are also binding and non-binding commitments that prohibit the parties from waiving or derogating their environmental law in favor of pursuing trade and investment.[45]

3.2.4.1 CPTPP vs. WTO

The WTO is the inevitable comparison to any multilateral trade agreement. In the context of the emergence of newer RTAs, such as the CPTPP and RCEP, the WTO's continued relevance is a natural question. For sheer size, the WTO has the advantage, with 164 members and 24 observer governments, easily dwarfing CPTPP's 11 members. For the same reason, however, the WTO is weighed down by the complex demands of its members, especially the developing economies. In addition, the enforcement mechanisms for both agreements must be compared. The WTO was founded upon the old General Agreements on Tariffs and Trade (GATT), and even though this was a solid base, which paved the way to trade liberalization, it leaves much to be desired in terms of the results that the WTO can achieve. The fact was that the Doha negotiations, which began in 2001, still remained without any conclusion. Nineteen years is a long span, and much modernization that has already become necessary at the beginning of the process is now long overdue. The CPTPP, being the product of a more recent process, contains more up-to-date provisions better suited to current questions in the trading world at present. As mentioned previously, these include additional commitments in terms of digital trading, service industry, human rights, and environmental protection.

The mechanisms of the CPTPP could become the basis of how the WTO responds to rapidly changing trends in the global trading system. As its members reap the benefits of the CPTPP, the world will certainly keep an eye on the agreement's best practices and include them in new or existing trade agreements.

3.2.5 *The Interaction of Inner and Outer Networks*

In any examination of inner and outer networks, such as those of the member states of the CPTPP, as contrasted with their domestic nodes, we must consider many factors, such as the current economic condition of the state, its global trade activities, and how its people perceive the changes entailed by globalization as a whole. As the CPTPP is bringing significant changes that favor trade liberalization, added inflows of foreign products could be expected. These may hurt domestic suppliers, and implementing protectionist measures will become almost impossible, as it would defeat the purpose of joining an FTS. For example, we can look at the changes to the Japanese beef market entailed by the CPTPP's preferential tariff treatment. Effective December 30, 2018, Japan lowered its tariff on chilled/frozen beef imported from CPTPP members from 38.5% to 27.5%. The second round of tariff cuts went into effect the following April 1, with rates lowered to 26.6% (GAIN Report, 2018).[46] The Japan Livestock and Products Annual Report for 2019 stated that cattle production continued on its decades-long decline. Declining domestic cattle production and consequent high domestic prices make imported beef more appealing for domestic consumers. Of course, even if this favors those Japanese who like to eat beef, it may also be a flashpoint for opposition from domestic cattle farmers. Anti-globalization movements can form in such circumstances, and this is the most likely point for a clash between inner and outer networks. The outcome of this process will entirely depend on how the government assesses the situation and its plans for future domestic policies.

Japan makes an interesting case for how inner and outer networks interact. As we have mentioned, domestic networks have a strong influence on the outer networks, often fueled by a strong sense of nationalism and anti-globalism. The case of Japan marks a contrast, however, as newer strategies appear to have had the opposite effect, as inner networks are greatly influenced by the outer ones. Japan's agricultural reforms are an example here. Japan's agricultural sector is heavily centralized under the Central Union of Agricultural Co-operatives, also known as JA-Zenchu. Thanks to the influence of this cooperative, the Japanese farming sector enjoys subsidies from the government to support the price of rice and other agricultural products. Protectionism even goes so far as to maintain high trade barriers through tariffs and technical barriers. This situation is currently undergoing changes, which are the result of several different factors. Former Prime Minister Abe introduced a Revitalization Strategy for Japan in June 2014, which included further development of agricultural policies as a part of a larger Abenomics reform package.[47] These reforms include curbing the influence of JA-Zenchu, although the administration considers it to be a bedrock institution.

What are the reasons for these actions, which seem to be curbing the inner networks in favor of outer ones? First of all, we must look at the agricultural sector of the country. Japan's rural population has been declining since the 1970s. Currently, only 8.5% of the population lives in rural towns or villages, a fraction of the rate of 36.7% from the 1960s and even of 21.3% from 2000. This decline has had a seriously negative effect on the level of agricultural production. To make things worse, the shrinking rural population meant the ballooning of Japan's urban population. This makes it essential for Japan to open up its agricultural sector to foreign suppliers because of a larger urban population to feed. In addition, Japan is under a high degree of pressure from its commitments to the CPTPP and other international trade agreements. Japan also has an FTA (not full-fledged) with the US that may be a contributing factor as to why it wants to open up its market. Trump used coercion, such as the threat of imposing national security tariffs on Japanese car imports. Trump also pressured Japan to sign the said US–Japan FTA, which is expected to balance trade in favor of the US. The combination of all these factors places Japan in a tight position, forcing its government to exert its influence on its inner networks to meet the expectations its trading partners.

3.2.6 Communication Mode

Almost all signatory countries of the CPTPP have separate bilateral and multilateral agreements in place with seven or more of their co-members, with the sole exception of Canada, which only has individual trade agreements with Chile, Mexico, and Peru. This means that changes or even new communication patterns may emerge, especially among members without prior agreements with others. The existing FTAs among the members of the CPTPP also show the characteristics of the linkages and the ways in which the nodes communicate with one another.

Like the WTO, the CPTPP is a small-scale multilateral trading system, which means its communication network is affiliational. The nodes, or the member states, discuss and make arrangements together as equals. The CPTPP Commission is the decision-making body of the CPTPP, and each of the 11 signatories has a representative in the commission who participated at both commission meetings, which were held in Tokyo and Auckland. In this type of network, the rules determine the connection that a member has with the group.[48] The 584 pages of legal text in the CPTPP are legally binding, and their contents dictate the roles of each member of the network.

3.2.7 Highlights in CPTPP

The CPTPP has huge potential for promoting economic growth via expanded trade and investment among its members. The agreement also contains more relevant commitments that may have been included in the WTO, had the Doha negotiations been successfully completed. The CPTPP commitments address some of the loopholes in the current WTO system, making the CPTPP appealing to other non-member countries. Even though the CPTPP is still young, many other outside countries have already expressed an interest in joining the agreement. Increased numbers of nodes can be expected to benefit the network, as Metcalfe's law postulates.[49] However, like any multilateral trading network, CPTPP is vulnerable to several potential challenges. Conflicts between the inner and outer networks, between states and non-state actors, and between international and domestic players can be expected. Recognizing this returns us to Mearsheimer's discussion of the rise and fall of the international liberal order. Promising as the network may seem, the CPTPP must still balance the positive and negative effects of hyper-globalization. If the opportunities brought by the CPTPP cannot improve the lives of its member states' people, safeguarding job markets and wage equality from hyper-globalization, those issues can cause domestic forces to arise and oppose the agreement. This is why some member states have yet to ratify it.

The CPTPP is a network that is still in its early stages. This fact can be interpreted as good or bad. It is good because there are only 11 members, which make issues related to a novel or updated commitments easier to manage should they arise. On the other hand, the agreement likely has important challenges that are as-yet unknown, waiting in its future. Whatever comes to pass, while there may be pitfalls, the CPTPP, like a toddler, can only learn from falling and getting back up.

3.3 US–Mexico–Canada Agreement (USMCA)

3.3.1 *From NAFTA to USMCA*

The USMCA was ratified by all three countries before March 13, 2020. Before entering office in early 2017, the US President Donald Trump denounced the 25-year-old NAFTA as "the nation's worst trade deal." Taking a mercantilist approach to trade policy and attempting to make the US the keystone of every possible deal, Trump pulled the US out of NAFTA and several other trade agreement discussions, after which he initiated rounds of renegotiation with Mexico and Canada to modernize NAFTA. The finalized agreement, termed USMCA, included chapters on topics that were not addressed under the previous agreement, such as digital trade and corruption, as well as the sunset clause. Other important revisions included enhanced environmental and labor regulations, increased regional value content (RVC), labor value content (LVC) for auto manufacturing, updated intellectual property protections, and an updated dispute-settlement mechanism. The deal also opened Canada's well-protected dairy and beverage industry by allowing additional access for exported products from the US.

The major changes in the USMCA from NAFTA, its predecessor, can be briefly summarized as follows. First, regarding the RVC under the rules of origin provision – to qualify for zero tariffs, 75% of automobile components and

70% of a vehicle's steel and aluminum must originate in North America. Concerning LVC, by 2023, about 40%–45% of automobile parts must be made in high-wage factories where workers are paid at least $16 an hour. Second, labor provisions are strengthened as Mexico committed to conduct legal changes to get rid of forced labor and violence against workers and give allowance for independent unions and labor courts. The abovementioned wage level of $16 per hour for automotive workers also presents a challenge for domestic reform in Mexico. Third, Canadian dairy market barriers are lowered so that American milk, cream, butter, and cheese can have better access to the Canadian market. In exchange, the US adopts reciprocal treatment for Canadian dairy and sugar exports to the US. Next, in terms of intellectual property, the term of copyrights is extended from 50 years to 70 years beyond the life of the author. New criminal penalties for theft of trade secrets and cybertheft are also stipulated in the agreement. In the investment aspect, the ISDS can no longer be used in disputes between the US and Canada and will be limited to conflicts between Mexico and the US in several industries such as petrochemicals, telecommunications, infrastructure, and power generation. Moreover, a sunset clause is added, indicating that the agreement will expire after 16 years. USMCA is also subject to a review every six years, at which point the US, Mexico, and Canada can decide to extend the agreement.[50] Furthermore, the USMCA's digital trade provisions, which were not governed under NAFTA, forbid the imposition of customs duties and ensure non-discriminatory treatment of digital products. The requirement of the disclosure of the source code and the algorithm expressed in that source code, as conditions of market access, is strictly prohibited in the USMCA. The prohibition of data localization measures is extended to the financial service sector. And the digital trade provision also promotes cross-border transfers of information. Besides, Article 32.10 is considered a special article in USMCA, the intention of which is to prevent its members from trading with 'non-market countries' (including China). The clause stated that if any USMCA party undertakes to negotiate an FTA with a 'non-market economy,' that party must notify other parties of its intention and provide others with an opportunity to review the full text of the agreement. In case that party chooses to enter into an agreement with non-market economies, other parties can terminate USMCA.

The renegotiation of NAFTA to USMCA was carried out as an important act under the *America First* strategy of President Trump, to address trade deficits and job loss in the US caused by NAFTA. According to USTR Lighthizer (2020),[51] 176,000 new jobs for Americans are projected to be generated within the next five years, and in the agriculture sector, a $2.2 billion increase in export value is expected, as a result of the USMCA. From the vantage point, USMCA was negotiated to enhance the welfare gains of the US from trade rather than the entire region.

3.3.2 The USA's Leading Power

In 2016, Donald Trump campaigned with a nationalist and protectionist vision, expressed in his promise to 'Make America Great Again.' Among his first actions as president was to withdraw the US from the TPP, and he even threatened to withdraw from the WTO. In his mercantilist view of the global trading system, summarized by 'making every transaction zero-sum and with clear winners and losers,' there is no such thing as a win-win situation.[52] The Trump administration had accused the multilateral trading system of undermining the US leverage in negotiations and letting other nations gain where the US loses. In reference to the WTO, the US also questioned the fundamental principle of nondiscrimination, in particular the MFN treatment, as they claimed that this has been hurting its national interest. Bilateral trade negotiations, in which countries that are engaged in the negotiation agree to drop trade barriers in a reciprocal and mutually advantageous manner, impose potential free-rider problems, as many nations abuse this format to demand lower tariffs without giving up their own high trade barriers in return.[53] Perceiving that a multilateral setting cannot yield the ultimate benefits for the American national interests, Trump embarked on bilateral negotiations believing that one-on-one deals will grant the US greater leverage. After four years of his leadership, Trump's approach to trade achieved limited success, as we can see in the renegotiation of NAFTA into the USMCA, the US–Japan trade agreement, and the US-China Phase One agreement. The US has also amended its FTA with Korea and initiated trade talks with many other countries and entities, such as the UK, the EU, India, and Brazil.

3.3.3 Why Must It Be USMCA?

To discuss the USMCA a bit further, we should first look back at the old NAFTA, negotiated in 1994, and enumerate the characteristics of this trilateral trade agreement. Originally, NAFTA was two separate bilateral trade interactions between the US and Canada and between the US and Mexico. The US and Canada had already signed a bilateral trade agreement in 1988 before Mexico proposed an FTA with the US. Fearing that Mexico would gain an advantage and that the US-Mexico deal would undermine the advantages Canada had gained through direct negotiations with the US, Canada joined the talks and proposed a trilateral arrangement.[54]

In mid-May 2017, the Trump administration notified Congress of its intention to begin the renegotiation of NAFTA and its desire to begin renegotiations on a trilateral basis; however, the US made it known that it would be open to bilateral negotiations if the attempt at a trilateral agreement did not succeed. In August 2018, Trump notified Congress of his opening of trade negotiations with Mexico, and he also expressed that he would do the same for Canada if it was willing to enter negotiations in a timely manner.

Within this trading system, it is undeniable that the US played the leading role. Both in the entire world and within North America, due to the economic size, market size, military power, and political influence of the US, it is always the dominant party in any negotiation (Condon, 2019).[55] Because the Canadian and Mexican economies rely more on exports and due to their relatively small trading volumes, exports to the US account for 70% to 80% of their total export value, while the US exports to its neighbors are at a much lower level – only 15%

to 25% of total exports. The US used its political and economic power to intimidate Canada and Mexico, forcing them to agree to a trade deal that clearly meets the demand of and is more beneficial to the US rather than its two partners. It is possible to ask why Canada and Mexico agreed to the deal if it was unfavorable to their interests. As Grewal (2005) noted, there are intrinsic and extrinsic benefits of joining a network. The intrinsic benefit of inclusion in such a system may become less significant and even less desirable over time, but the extrinsic benefit can increase over time.[56] For Mexico and Canada, not to deny the benefits that USMCA may bring to the two nations' economies, the possibility of trade restrictions imposed by the US, or even worse, retaliation against them, would be far more significant in inducing them to join the USMCA. Far from being willing to join as such, they were likely in part coerced to join this trilateral network.

Moreover, the *networked power* of the US, defined by Castell (2011)[57] as the power of one node over the others within a network, is depicted vividly in the agreements on the rule of origin, labor, and digital trade under USMCA. The one-sided deal was negotiated to serve the US goals of generating jobs and promoting business expansion for the Americans. Rule of origin in USMCA is upgraded to a higher standard; in comparison with NAFTA, for instance, RVC is raised from 62.5% to 75%. Evident is the fact that the minimum wage level of $16 per hour is excessively high for a developing country like Mexico. The increase in both RVC and LVC under USMCA is referred to as a tactic of pooling manufacturing jobs to the US. On the one hand, the labor provisions in the trade deal ignited domestic reforms to improve the working conditions for Mexican workers and mitigate the wage gap between them and the American counterparts, but on the other hand, it would erode the competitiveness of the Mexican workers by making it more expensive for their American employers to hire foreign labor force. Furthermore, in terms of digital trade, the prohibition of customs charges on digital products, proscription of data localization barriers, and the promotion of cross-border transfers of data are paving the way for US tech giants, including Google, Apple, Facebook, Amazon, etc., to expand their business to the region without the fear of intellectual property theft, cyber espionage, or regulatory impediments to data transfers. Aside from this, the provision also welcomes recognition of the enormous importance of the global sale of digital products made in the US. Therefore, it is clear that the deal on the rule of origin, labor, and digital trade supports the US to solve its current problems and promote the thriving path for its conglomerates. From this viewpoint, it can be said that the US had exerted its networked power over the USMCA negotiation process, to make it a unilateral deal serving the American interests.

3.3.4 Network Structure

As mentioned, the US trade policy under the Trump administration sought to resolve its trade issues by negotiating country-by-country and sector-by-sector deals that focused on bilateral and quid-pro-quo agreements rather than depending on traditional multilateral negotiations. The USMCA is an update of

NAFTA with some enhancements and new provisions. These provisions bundle trade and NTIs together into a single package for negotiation among the three nations. However, the US approach to the renegotiation of NAFTA can be understood as state-centric, with the sole objective of resolving domestic trade issues, rather than being a cooperative partnership with its two neighbors. The trade agenda, as outlined by the USTR Office, focuses on breaking down unfair trade barriers imposed by other markets, promoting reciprocal trading relationships, opening foreign markets by increasing all possible sources of leverage, and so on.[58]

The linkage of trade and NTIs in the USMCA shows the connection of enforcement and participation with Trump's favorite tactic of imposing higher tariffs and economic sanctions. As already explained in Chapter 2, a study by Maggi (2016) shows three types of issue linkages: enforcement linkage, negotiation linkage, and participation linkage. The US has successfully used its power to coerce and threaten its trading partners to sign trade agreements that are asymmetric and more beneficial to American interests. Mexico and Canada do not have equal standing to negotiate the deal, and their leverage is further undermined by their dependence on US markets for their exports.

Regarding the positioning of nodes within a network, Hogan (2017)[59] stated that the preferential attachment of links into a specific node leads to the creation of a hub-and-spoke network structure. Observing the ego network of the US on a North American scale in terms of export/import, the US accounts for a remarkably high proportion of exports (approximately 80%) and imports (about 50%) of Canada and Mexico. Meanwhile, in Canada and Mexico, each country covers less than 20% of US exports and less than 15% of US imports. The bilateral trade between Canada and Mexico is also unremarkable compared to the trade volume between each country and the US. Hence, if links are referred to as flows of goods and services, it becomes obvious that US-Canada and US–Mexico relations are directed, or asymmetric, in favor of the US. In this ego network, the US gains degree and becomes a hub, with Canada and Mexico as spokes. However, the renegotiation of NAFTA to USMCA together with the implementation of trade remedies by the Trump administration, for the purpose of winning at the other's expense, seriously hurt the relationship between the US and its long-term allies. Therefore, even when the USMCA was signed and came into effect, it is less likely that the USMCA can help the hub to pull its spokes closer and form a truly firm network.

3.3.5 *Inner vs. Outer Networks*

Under the revised standards for auto and auto parts manufacturing in the USMCA under the terms *RVC* and *LVC*, the US is seeking to increase its comparative advantage of producing parts for the domestic market and preventing domestic producers from moving their production to Mexico to take advantage of the lower cost of production.[60] For example, the LVC requirement for the USMCA is that auto component pieces, for example, must be made by workers who earn $16 per hour on average. While this particular requirement may not pose a challenge to the US or Canada, as the wages in their auto industries are already above that level, it does disadvantage Mexico, where minimum wage laws remain lax and the average hourly wage for an autoworker is approximately $4, only one-fourth of the requirement. This could be seen as the more developed nations within the USMCA are seeking to apply their laws on the other member (a case where an inner network is attempting to apply an inner standard onto the outer network). Together with increasing RVC, USMCA seeks to strengthen the performance of the auto industry, equalize the cost of production, and improve working conditions in the labor force over the entire North American region.[61]

USMCA incorporates both trade issues and NTIs (such as environmental concerns and labor). These provisions are now in force and may lead to extensive changes in the inner systems of the three countries. For example, in relation to labor regulations, the USMCA requires Mexico to pass legislation to improve the collective bargaining capacity of labor unions (specifically, to follow ILO's Convention 98 on freedom of association and collective bargaining). Unlike many countries, workers in Mexico do not have the freedom to form unions. Instead, unions are normally formed by groups of employers, who use them to put downward pressure on wages, making them a major element in why labor conditions are poor in Mexico. Within the USMCA, the US also mandated certain provisions that may be related to countering unfair practices on the part of China, such as curtailing state-owned enterprises, currency manipulation, and the dealings with non-market countries, to indirectly discourage its trading partners from entering into a future deal with China or nations that have similar practices (for example, Vietnam).

Like the *leave* result of the UK's referendum held in 2016, USMCA is the consequence of both the outer network's loophole in the adoption of *American standard* and the inner network's desire to protect domestic jobs and national interests. In North America, a disruption of the existing trading system seems inevitable since the strength of the protectionist inner network within the US border surpasses that of the liberal outer trilateral network.

3.3.6 Communication Mode

Observing the recent patterns in the US trade negotiations, it seems clear that the US under the Trump administration was backing away from multilateral deals and turning toward unilateralism with more bilateral deals. The US is pursuing a hub-and-spoke system where it is the hub and other allies are the spokes. The bilateral agreements between the US and other countries are founded on a set of standards and defined lists of commitments that determine the direction and magnitude of the relationship between the parties. This characteristic appears in the USMCA as well. Network analysts often distinguish between two types of networks: a *relational* type and an *affiliational* type, where the relational network, also called a one-mode network, is characterized by rules that define the presence, direction, and magnitude of the relationship between any two units, and an affiliational network, or a two-mode network, in which a rule defines the affiliation of a unit with an event, organization, or group (Maoz, 2010).[62] Under this understanding, the USMCA would be an asymmetric relational network, which the US establishes by negotiating trade deals that are clearly more beneficial to itself than to its partners. This asymmetric relational network prevails in other trade agreements and negotiations undertaken during the Trump administration, indicating the aggressive approach the US is taking to international trade and with its firm intention to strike the deal that will benefit itself the most. It would be extremely difficult for America's trading partners to enter talks on an assumption of equality. In discussions of transportation networks, a hub-and-spoke structure has one fundamental advantage over other types of networks – greater flexibility through a concentration of flows. The Trump administration has completed a trade deal with Japan and renegotiated agreements with major traditional allies, including Korea, Canada, and Mexico. The US government hopes to complete other deals in the near future with the EU and the UK, and it is actively pursuing trade deals with India, Brazil, and Kenya to expand its influence over international issues, including reforming the WTO and finding new ways to counter China. Trump hoped to make the US a central hub with a broader range of spokes orbiting around it. Undermining the validity of the multilateral trading system, Trump tightened his grip on the economic benefits that could be expected from bringing more FDI and reshoring production back to the country after it had lost it to the comparative labor advantage held by many developing nations across the globe and ultimately bringing more jobs to the domestic market and enabling higher levels of economic growth. As long as trade and foreign policies are concerned, *America is not back yet*. Joe Biden inherited the *America First* Policies of Trump's and, indeed, has reinforced them from the moment he took office.

3.3.7 *Highlights in USMCA*

This clear change in emphasis from the long-standing US preference for regional and multilateral trade relationships to a set of purely bilateral deals will necessarily alter the dynamics of American trade relationships, not only with its current trade partners but also with all potential trade partners that the nation may enter into talks with in the future. Donald Trump and his administration firmly believed in the need to increase leverage to guarantee a better deal for American interests, by changing all deals to being negotiated on a one-on-one basis. With success in these deals (e.g., the updated KORUS, USMCA, and US-Japan trade agreement), there is no sign under the Biden administration that the US will stop using this tactic. Of course, simple bilateral relationships cannot explain how contemporary international trade operates, as world production and consumption cannot be confined to only one or a few countries, as these activities are divided and carried out among multiple countries across the globe. In other words, changes in the global economic environment have direct and indirect implications on the GVC. Certain preferential treatments and requirements that are possible in bilateral agreements, such as LVC and RVC, to satisfy tariff reduction, will be a threat to the GVC. The open US preference for bilateral trade talks will likely have a disruptive impact on the GVC. While it is possible to argue that the WTO is in decline and far less effective in managing the world trading system, we cannot deny that the WTO has helped harmonize standards and regulations and shaped a predictable trading system for all participants. However, in a trading world where most relationships are bilateral, there will be few common regulations, and everything will be up to the power-based agreement between pairs of partners.[63]

To say that the USMCA and America's novel negotiation approach will have an impact on the WTO might be an overstatement. However, all the same, these developments may be the start of a trend of general infringement of rules-based trading and multilateral trade relations under the WTO. Not in the short but in the medium-long term, the US will continue to pursue the negotiation structure with future partners, and the picture of the global trading system will change eventually. Further, China, the second great power, is also creating its own trading network.[64] These trade agreements can speed up the fragmentation of the world trading system into trading zones with overlapping memberships, trade preferences, and requirements, as well as their own dispute settlement mechanisms. This will naturally increase the complexity of doing business abroad and decrease the efficiency of multinational production and trade. Above all, emerging and developing countries are most likely to suffer if the situation prevails. Apart from the framework of a transparent multilateral system, their bargaining power will be substantially weakened with reference to the great powers, and it will be impossible for these countries to ever negotiate a beneficial trade deal.

3.4 Regional Comprehensive Economic Partnership (RCEP)

3.4.1 ASEAN+3 or ASEAN+6?

The RCEP is a mega-FTA network, consisting of 16 nodes, initially, including 10 ASEAN members and 6 bilateral FTA partners of ASEAN (China, Japan, South Korea, Australia, New Zealand, and India). The RCEP was endorsed after the ASEAN leaders considered the proposals of the East Asia FTA (EAFTA) and the Comprehensive Economic Partnership of East Asia (CEPEA). EAFTA was recommended by the East Asia Vision Group in a report to the ASEAN+3 (CJK; China, Japan, and Korea) leaders in 2001. China regards the ASEAN+3 as a natural grouping for East Asia's trade and investment cooperation, and its proposal of EAFTA echoes that perspective. The scope of the EAFTA includes foreign affairs, economy and trade, macroeconomics and finance, environment, energy, health, labor, science and technology, and social welfare. CEPEA was proposed by Japan, based on the East Asia Summit or ASEAN+6 (CJK + Australia, New Zealand, and India) in 2006. The East Asia Summit is still larger and focuses on broader questions, including the avian flu, education, energy, finance, and natural disasters. From Japan's perspective, the ASEAN+6 is more appropriate for East Asian integration, in that it provides a more effective platform than ASEAN+3 for countering and balancing the influence of China and increasing the bargaining power of traditional allies (Japan, Korea, Australia, New Zealand) of the US.

After considering both recommendations and reviewing a series of studies and reports, in November 2011, the ASEAN leaders endorsed a framework for the RCEP to replace CEPEA and EAFTA.[65]

RCEP negotiations, launched in November 2012, would eventually involve 31 rounds of negotiations, a series of ministerial meetings, and four summits over eight years. In the third summit, held in Bangkok, Thailand, on November 3, 2019, India decided to withdraw from RCEP to protect its domestic production, and the remaining 15 countries (as known as RCEP15) agreed on a text-based conclusion. A year later, on November 15, 2020, RCEP was signed in the fourth summit, which was held in the format of an online conference, forming the largest trade agreement in the world. The trade deal will come into effect 60 days after at least six ASEAN member states and three non-ASEAN member states complete the ratification, which would take several months to years.

The objective of the RCEP is to achieve a modern, comprehensive, high-quality, and mutually beneficial economic partnership among member countries. The agreement is finalized in 20 chapters, containing provisions that go beyond the current ASEAN+1 FTAs and covering diverse aspects of economic integration in the East Asia region, including trade in goods, trade in services, investment, economic and technical cooperation, intellectual property, competition, dispute settlement, e-commerce, small- and medium-sized enterprises (SMEs), and other issues.

To briefly summarize some notable contents of the RCEP agreement, trade in goods chapter covers both tariff and non-tariff measures, stipulating schedules to reduce or eliminate customs duties, export subsidies for agricultural products, and quantitative restrictions, as well as pushing for greater transparency in the import license granting process. The rules of origin chapter specify product-specific rules for all tariff lines at the HS 6-digit level and allow the cumulation in origin declaration. In terms of trade remedies, safeguards, anti-dumping, and countervailing duties are allowed, according to relevant WTO agreements; however, no RCEP members can have recourse to dispute settlement under the RCEP for disputes arising on anti-dumping and countervailing duties. Next, trade in services chapter includes details about three specific service sectors: financial services, telecommunications services, and professional services. Temporary movement of natural persons forms a special chapter of RCEP, which aims to mitigate unjustified impediments in immigration processes, freeing the movement of human resources among RCEP countries. Chapter 10 of RCEP contain four pillars that govern investment procedures: protection, liberalization, promotion, and facilitation, which are regarded as an upgrade and enhancement of investment provision of existing FTAs. The intellectual property chapter of RCEP affirms WTO's TRIPS but is more expansive and covers technological protection measures and enforcement in the digital environment.[66] Furthermore, RCEP is expected to become a modern FTA, vis-à-vis current ASEAN+1 FTAs, as it would supply businesses and customers with markets in an online platform with well-protected privacy and more business information available, higher economic efficiency from fair competition, transparent government procurement process, and better economic technical cooperation activities across the RCEP region.[67]

3.4.2 The Leadership of Three Powerhouses

ASEAN, Japan, and China are all trying to exert leadership over the RCEP. According to Fukunaga (2014),[68] one of the primary motivations for proposing the RCEP was ASEAN's desire to be central, as declared in the ASEAN Framework for RCEP in 2011. ASEAN's centrality was sought in order to solve the noodle bowl phenomenon caused by the coexistence of multiple ASEAN+1 FTAs, to enable a balance to be struck with non-ASEAN initiatives. The author indicated that ASEAN has done well to prioritize functional centrality as the 'facilitator of the process,' which is seen in the Trade Negotiation Committee (where ASEAN has taken the chairmanship role without any co-chairmanship among partner countries). Furthermore, seven RCEP working groups and four sub-working groups are chaired by ASEAN member states. However, the second function of centrality, to be "the driver of substance," who "sets directions, engineers compromises, and provides leadership,"[69] is less clear in the RCEP.

Japan is another candidate for the leading role in the RCEP network. The original proposal for the structure of the current RCEP, formerly known as CEPEA (ASEAN+6),[70] was presented by Japan. During negotiation rounds, the country pushed for customs reform issues and sought to take the lead in the RCEP to resolve outstanding issues that would allow India to rejoin the RCEP.

Viewing from the past, the integral position of Japan in Southeast Asian economic integration has been apparent since the second half of the 20th century. Being aware that Asian regional economic dynamism is market-driven and open, Japan has actively pursued cooperation by providing funds and aids, both official and private, to ASEAN countries and China in order to pull those economies closer to Japan and to each other simultaneously, to encourage US and European corporations to invest and do business in the region, through which regionalism in Asia and SEA is kept open. Nowadays, with the appearance of Japanese branches and factories spreading out in Southeast Asia, Japan's GVC is tied closely with the supply chains in the region.

Therefore, the signing and implementation of RCEP as ASEAN+6 are as meaningful as a development level of East Asia regionalism for Japan. RCEP Article 3.4 about cumulative rules of origin stipulates that the components and parts produced in a factory in Vietnam, for example, which are used as materials for production of a finished good or material in Japan, shall be considered as originating in Japan. Japan has been successful in making use of tariff elimination and cumulative rules of origin under existing FTAs to maximize export enlargement effects.[71] The two provisions continue to be enhanced in RCEP, and the terms and conditions of all separate FTAs are expected to be unified into one RCEP. When implemented, tariff elimination and cumulative rules of origin would turn RCEP countries to become a huge manufacturing factory for Japanese companies and boost the value of Japanese exports. Second, from Japan's perspective, the RCEP is an effective tool for halting the protectionist trend and sustaining the free and open trading amid the crisis of multilateralism caused by the US economic nationalism. Third, the significant involvement of Japan in RCEP is regarded as an active confrontation, given the dominance of China in the East Asia economy, especially in terms of intellectual property protection and the operation of digital trade.

In addition to ASEAN and Japan, China is also seeking to become a powerful leading node in the negotiation rounds and the network as a whole. Due to the enormous and continuous growth of its economy, China has developed important links in the regional production network. Moreover, the Asian Infrastructure Investment Bank, officially established in 2015, intended to boost infrastructure connectivity in Asia and beyond, was pioneered by China.

China's strategy, as exhibited in its FTAs, is to take advantage of its important position in the region. According to Sampson (2019),[72] Beijing pushed for agreements that were initially narrowly scoped. It involved limited liberalization and subsequently expanded over many years in numerous rounds of negotiation. As a result of this expansion, China and its partners will shape the region and guide it to become more economically interdependent. China is already the most important export destination for other members, especially of the agricultural products and natural resources of ASEAN countries. Chinese mechanical and electronic components account for a large proportion of partner countries' imports. Taking advantage of the heavy dependence, China improved its bargaining position over time. For example, it negotiated with Pakistan, which is not a member of the RCEP, to extend the scope of Chinese exports that could be imported with zero tariffs from 35% to 90%. Moreover, China is also utilizing its economic clout regarding issues beyond trade, such as security and diplomacy. For example, the Chinese government pushed an anti-Korean campaign, halting tour groups to Seoul and boycotting Korean products imported from Korea or even made in China. Hyundai and Lotte Mart took the brunt of China's economic offensive, and the latter finally left China, liquidating all its assets there. The net loss amounted to almost $2 billion. It all happened because the Korean government installed the US Terminal High Altitude Area Defense system (THAAD) at a South Korean Air Force base in Seongju County in 2017. Beijing strongly objected to the deployment of this US missile defense system, with a radar that could see deep into the Chinese territory.

Although the structure of the RCEP at present is different from China's initial proposal, China has two major incentives to support the RCEP. First, China is hoping to develop the RCEP as a bounded order to deter and counter the influence of the US in the world trading system, especially after the US signed USMCA, which contains a clause that seems to discourage trade with the so-called non-market countries.[73] USMCA intends to prevent US partners from signing any new trade agreements with China. Second, the RCEP is a complementary network to the BRI of China. Most of the members of the RCEP are part of China's belt of overland corridors and/or the maritime road of shipping lanes; however, several are voicing negative attitudes toward the 21st-century silk road, namely, Australia, India, Myanmar, Malaysia, and Japan – all RCEP members. Japan, Australia, and India have expanded their own regional development plans to compete with the BRI. The BRI is, in each case, negotiated bilaterally between China and the host-state; therefore, Chinese investment relies heavily on the regulations of the foreign states. The negotiation of RCEP, which includes investment and competition chapters, together with some commitments on the free movement of people, may open new opportunities for strengthening economic relationships, which, by the same token, may ease the difficulties involved in the negotiation and implementation of the BRI process between China and its partners. As can be seen from the example mentioned above, China uses its economic power strategically as leverage for altering its partners' diplomatic or military stance on issues where Chinese interests are at stake.

After eight years of negotiation, RCEP was finally signed on November 15, 2020, in the Fourth RCEP Summit as part of the 37th ASEAN Summit in Hanoi, Vietnam. The special event was claimed as a victory for China and ASEAN, but *a painful choice* for Japan, in the word of Kawashima (2020).[74] With ASEAN, the successful signing of RCEP is unequivocal evidence of ASEAN's leadership and the bloc's ability to mediate between the regions' great powers. Moreover, the event opened a new chapter for China's influence on economic flows in the Asia-Pacific. While the US opted out of TPP and followed state-centric economic strategies, China made its way to become "the leading protector of regional free trade."[75] Though not stated explicitly by Chinese leaders, the signing of RCEP is the triumph of China over US leadership in Asia. In contrast to other countries' eagerness, Japan seems to hesitate to sign the agreement in the final stage. From Japan's viewpoint, the appearance of India in RCEP has not only economic but also political meaning. As allies in Free and Open Indo-Pacific Initiatives (FOIPI; with the US and Australia), Japan and India together can have sufficient power and bargaining position to counter China under RCEP. Nevertheless, India decided to withdraw from RCEP to protect its domestic economy, and Japan is trying to solve the outstanding problem of tariff liberalization in order to persuade India to rejoin. Furthermore, the concerns of the US on the isolation of non-market economies (including China) were conveyed through the negotiation of the US-Japan Trade Agreement under Trump and Abe. Should Japan sign an FTA with a non-market economy, the agreement would be subject to US vetting, and Japan's trade agreement with the US would push it to the verge of collapse. The article's main aim is to prevent the US allies and partners from signing FTAs with China. However, the situation has changed since then. The US–Japan Trade Agreement had been concluded without the non-market economy provision in the text. Abe resigned from office, and Trump lost the US presidential re-election. Despite its hesitation, Japan signed the RCEP as the other 14 countries have.

3.4.3 Network Power

There are both extrinsic and intrinsic reasons for member states to participate in the network, which will define the magnitude of the power of the RCEP. The sheer size of the network, including all of ASEAN, the second- and third-largest economies of the world, and another prominent emerging economy (India), make it an attractive trading partner. The bloc (including India) is the largest regional trading network worldwide, accounting for half of the world's population, over 30% of global GDP, and over a quarter of the world's exports.[76] The expected economic boost, job creation, and new opportunities for both large and small businesses are intrinsic reasons for member countries to be part of the RCEP. For instance, from Australia's perspective, the RCEP is of great importance, as it includes 10 of its top 15 trading partners in 2018. Australia's exportation of goods and services to RCEP countries in 2018 totals $311 billion, accounting for 76% and 51% of the country's total exports of goods and services, respectively. The RCEP will remove tariff and non-tariff barriers and thus create significant new trade and investment opportunities for Australian businesses in the Asia-Pacific region. By the same token, the RCEP will also establish a common set of rules to minimize regulatory differences among countries and provide greater certainty and easier access to regional production chains. Over the long term, RCEP is expected to mitigate the potential emergence of discriminatory trade blocs that would harm its members' economic and security interests.

Nonetheless, the RCEP is considered to have low standards and lower levels of FTA, leaving it somewhat behind the WTO. Clearly, the standards the WTO adheres to have far greater pressure on its 164 members than those of the RCEP on its member states. WTO's 164 members and 24 observer governments account for 99.95% of world trade, 99.98% of world GDP, and 99.35% of the world population.[77] Second, the coordination capacity of the RCEP is limited, as illustrated by the comparison between RCEP and the CPTPP. While the CPTPP contains 30 chapters, the RCEP has only 20 and fails to cover the two prominent issues of environment and labor standards. The RCEP 15 takes account of 90% of tariff lines for goods (maintaining carve-outs for agriculture products) and a small list of service-sector businesses. (The liberalization rate for RCEP 16 was only 85%.) Not all of the tariff lines drop to zero, even at the end of full implementation. On the contrary, the CPTPP covers trade in goods, services, and investments at a high level, and tariff lines for all goods and more than 160 service types are addressed in detail. Once fully implemented, the CPTPP would reduce tariffs to zero on 99% of tariff lines. Furthermore, a settlement provision for investor-state disputes is included but is not likely to be used, unless members decide to activate it in three years when it will be revisited. The competition chapter also does not include discipline related to SOEs. Moreover, in relation to the e-commerce chapter, the RCEP fails to allow for free cross-border movement of information or to include customs duties on electronic transmissions.[78] Overall, the RCEP standard does not fully and strictly cover all aspects of economic integration, which may push its members to search for alternative solutions.

Furthermore, the inability of RCEP standards to resolve problems or harmonize interests among its network nodes resulted in the withdrawal of India. This decision was made because it feared that a flood of cheap Chinese manufactured products would harm its domestic production, in which case, India would be the loser. China, which accounts for 50% of the trade deficit in India in 2017–2018, would be the winner in a free trade scenario. India thus has an incentive to keep its low rate of liberalization with RCEP members through existing bilateral FTAs. India's action has had an impact on the direction of the RCEP, which seeks to open a huge integrated market for all 16 countries by promoting free trade and minimizing tariffs and non-tariff barriers. In the future, if the network continues to fail to satisfy the interests of its member countries, others might follow India's lead. Thus, the momentum for the completion of the RCEP negotiation may be lost in the near future.

Despite all drawbacks of network standards, together with CPTPP, RCEP plays an important role in the global trading system amid the COVID-19 pandemic. Petri and Plummer (2020)[79] suggest that the implementation of CPTPP and RCEP will "offset the global losses caused by US–China trade war, but not the individual losses of the US and China." In particular, via computable general equilibrium model under trade-war conditions, the US-China trade war will lead to an annual $301 billion worth of economic losses for the world, whereas CPTPP and RCEP will raise the global national incomes in 2030 by $121 billion and $209 billion, respectively, $330 billion in total. Furthermore, CJK are expected to be the biggest beneficiaries from the trade networks, because these countries account for 80% of RCEP 15's GDP, and RCEP is the sole FTA that all of them have joined. The successful implementation of RCEP (the big network) might form a good base for the development of CJK FTA (a smaller network) in the future. However, the US (left TPP) and India (left RCEP) are expected to suffer losses caused by the elimination of trade diversion, a cost of non-participation in the networks.

3.4.4 Network Structure

Asian-Pacific regional trading networks display multilayered and overlapping structures, due to the coexistence of various schemes and initiatives, such as the East Asia Economic Caucus (EAEC), the ASEAN Economic Community (AEC), the CPTPP, the RCEP, the BRI, and the Indo-Pacific. Each network shapes its own economic and diplomatic order. For instance, the CPTPP and the RCEP are multilateral FTAs directed toward a liberal international economic order that facilitates cooperation among member states, whereas the BRI is a hub-and-spoke network (i.e., a bounded network), built on bilateral negotiations between China and its partners. In the international economic structure of the RCEP, China, a great power in the network, has exerted its influence on the RCEP, hoping to produce an effective device to counter TPP in the early 2010s. Once the US retreated from the TPP, China lost its momentum to conclude the RCEP and instead moved its policy priority to the BRI. Japan, another leading node, has insisted on a high-quality trade agreement that would cover prominent issues beyond China. Japan is seeking to resolve the outstanding issues in the RCEP and persuade India to rejoin because India's participation would have both economic and political significance. Japan believes that together with India, it can counter the influence of China on the RCEP network and make it a truly comprehensive, high-quality, and mutually beneficial FTA for all 16 nations.

The memberships of the RCEP and the CPTPP are not mutually exclusive. In particular, among the 16 original members of the RCEP, there are 10 bilateral and trilateral FTAs already in force, and an additional three FTAs are under negotiation (Japan–Korea since 2003, India–Australia since 2011, and China–Japan–South Korea since 2015).[80] While the ASEAN+1 FTAs are regarded as the basis for RCEP negotiations, the linkages among non-ASEAN countries represent a challenge for ASEAN's influence on the RCEP discussion, especially the CJK–FTA, which includes two of the world's top three economies.

When we imagine the initial RCEP as a network consisting of ASEAN and its six FTA partners, ASEAN will occupy the central spot, with other members in the corners. The number of trade deals in force among RCEP countries helps us to draw the connections within that network where each FTA signed represents one edge or one degree. The ASEAN and Australia gain the highest number of six degrees; meanwhile, China has four degrees, and Japan is the lowest degree node with three edges only. Among the six partners, Japan and China stay closer to the ASEAN as the trading value between ASEAN and them is larger than with other partners. Referring to our previous discussion on leading nodes of the network, it can be said that though ASEAN acquires degree centrality, thanks to the largest number of edges attached to it, the bloc is not yet a powerful leader of the network; in contrast, despite low degree, China and Japan are exerting enormous influence on RCEP. Hence, the position and degree of a node do not significantly represent its power within the network.

For further discussion on ASEAN's positioning in RCEP, the bloc is a cluster of homophilic nodes, a popular high in-degree node, in case we consider links as investment flows, especially from the BRI of China and FOIPI of Japan. Southeast Asia is the strategic area in BRI in both mainland and maritime routes. Many ASEAN countries, which are located on mainland China–Singapore Corridor, maritime China–Indochina Peninsula Corridor, and Bangladesh–China–India–Myanmar Corridor, have been receiving huge investments from China for infrastructure development. This includes Thailand, Myanmar, Cambodia, Malaysia, Singapore, the Philippines, and Indonesia.[81] However, Japan, together with the US, India, and Australia, is making a great effort to counter the dominant power of China by proposing FOIPI. In that initiative, all ten countries of ASEAN are the strategic investment destinations. With FOIPI, ASEAN is given a golden opportunity to develop port facilities, ensure maritime security and safety, reduce disaster risk, clean mines, and strengthen counterterrorism and counterpiracy systems.[82] In the past, ASEAN has attracted FDI and ODA from developed countries. With the signing of RCEP, and the development of BRI and FOIPI, it is expected that ASEAN countries will receive much more investment from China, Japan, and other RCEP partners.

3.4.5 RCEP Citizens: For or Against RCEP?

India's decision to pull out of the RCEP in the third summit in November 2019 illustrates the power of the inner network on the outer network. Among the ASEAN+1 FTAs, the India–ASEAN agreement has the lowest degree of liberalization, at 76.5%, while other FTAs show a liberalization rate above 80%. Additionally, in 2017, India's trade deficit with the RCEP nations was $105 billion, of which China accounted for $54 billion. Therefore, India was extremely reluctant to join the RCEP and produce levels of liberalization that would go beyond its current FTAs. The elimination of trade barriers in the RCEP is considered detrimental to India's economic interests and policy priorities, including the *Make in India* initiative. Due to fears of Chinese manufactured and heavy machinery goods, steel from Japan and Korea, dairy products from New Zealand, and cheap agricultural goods from South Asian nations flooding in, the Indian government opted to pull out of the deal. This withdrawal reduced the scale of the RCEP to 2.2 billion people (down from 3.6 billion) and 29% (down from 33%) of the world's GDP. It may also influence the positioning and direction of other members as it develops as a single market.

The Korean government has persuaded its own inner network of the benefits expected by joining the RCEP. It is hoped that the membership will improve the export environment for Korean companies by facilitating market access and diversifying trade in the region. The RCEP will also enhance the chances of Korean firms entering the emerging ASEAN e-commerce market and will boost major manufacturing sectors, including electrical, electronics, and automobile manufacture. As the ten ASEAN countries are emerging as the center of a GVC, along with China and India, Korean firms will find it costly not to ride on the RCEP bandwagon. Moreover, many large-scale factories of Korean brands, including Samsung Electronics and LG, are located in the ASEAN countries, especially Vietnam. The majority of Korean chaebols support the signing of the RCEP deal, although its impact on the Korean economy is limited. Once it is signed, the RCEP likely cements the foundation of the China–Japan–Korea trade bloc, although the negotiations here have been slow in recent years, notably in relation to Korea–Japan export boycotts. Through RCEP and CJK FTA, Korea can take advantage of Japan's technologies and technological intermediate products, as well as cheap labor and the huge market of China. Overall, the Korean government believes that the inner network can obtain potential benefits from the trade pact, despite its loose standard; therefore, the country pushed for the successful conclusion of RCEP.

3.4.6 Communication Mode and Highlights in RCEP

As a network, the RCEP operates on an *affiliational* communication pattern. Though China is seeking to increase its influence as a leading node, it cannot make the RCEP function as part of its hub-and-spoke system, due to the presence of other members, such as Japan and (potentially) Korea. The RCEP is a forum for fair negotiation among a diverse membership. The 15 participating members in the RCEP, in spite of the large gaps in their development levels, have equal bargaining positions in negotiation, allowing them to promote regional integration and protect their own interests simultaneously. However, the differences in opinions among ASEAN countries, China and other countries like Korea and Australia, could be the likely source of future conflicts over sensitive issues. Overall, the RCEP has maintained affiliational dialogue channels, even though China and Japan have played an important role as leading nodes.

The RCEP is a mega trade pact including 15 countries in the Asia-Pacific area, which is intended to form a comprehensive, high-quality, and mutually beneficial FTA. The RCEP does not seek a unipolar economic order but a multipolar one, with leading roles played by China, Japan, and the ASEAN. The RCEP contains both extrinsic and intrinsic reasons for its members to engage in the network. It is hoped that it will resolve the noodle bowl phenomenon in the Asian market and build up a common set of regulations to facilitate trade among its members. However, the RCEP standard is not a strong one, in terms of its power to eliminate alternatives. Though the scope of the RCEP is huge, it does not cover all important issues in sufficient depth. Additionally, it has failed to harmonize the interests of all members, as seen in the withdrawal of India. That decision was a result of the collision of the inner network (the domestic market) and the outer network (the RCEP). The RCEP is currently functioning in an affiliational communication mode, in which all countries bargain from equal positions. They are free to make decisions, vote for or against any proposal, and stay or leave the network for the sake of their own interests.

In this chapter, we focus on the four largest trading areas of the world through the lens of network theory. The EU, CPTPP, USMCA, and RCEP are interpreted individually through a set of features: a brief history, leading nodes, network power, network structure, inner-outer network collision, and communication pattern. First, the EU lies in the higher level of economic integration; thus, its standard and structure are more sophisticated than the others and governed by a number of institutions. The tight standard and high entry barrier (based on the EU member criteria) are cited as major reasons for EU members staying intertwined for such a long period of time. Next, the CPTPP, also known as TPP11, was concluded in 2018 without the participation of the US – the network's one-time leader. Similarly, 15 countries decided to sign RCEP – the world's largest trade accord – in 2020 without India. CPTPP is regarded as Japan-led, while the RCEP is regarded as a China-led network; nonetheless, in RCEP, it would not be right to downplay the influence of Japan and ASEAN. A comparison of the CPTPP and RCEP reveals clearly that CPTPP standards are tighter and have more success delivering prominent issues in international trade regarding labor, environment, intellectual property, and SOEs. CPTPP commitments address some of the loopholes in the WTO system and, together with RCEP, are expected to generate a total of $330 billion annually to offset the negative impact of the US-China trade war and benefit its member states. As for the network structure, the two trade pacts overlap in terms of members and suffer the spaghetti bowl effect owing to the existence of FTAs among members. The initiation into CPTPP led to a domestic upheaval in Japan, while the RCEP in India floundered in the face of strong reaction from the country's domestic factors. In both trading networks, affiliational communication method was adopted. Lastly, the USMCA is the trade agreement that well reflects the US President Trump's *America First* strategy. The leading position and power of the US in the North American economic network are enhanced, once again, by the success of NAFTA renegotiation to USMCA, in which terms and conditions were negotiated for the ultimate goal of protecting US interests. The communication within USMCA is asymmetric relational, which helps to form a hub-and-spoke network structure for the trade pact.

The EU, CPTPP, RCEP, and USMCA are existing mega trade agreements that have huge impacts on the world's economy. In the future, which networks will lead the global trading system amid the US-China trade war? Can the G2 confront each other with the consolidated power of its FTA network? The questions will be answered in the next chapter.

Notes

1 Moravcsik, A. (2010), Europe, the Second Superpower, *Current History*, 109(725), pp. 91–98, p. 91.
2 Akaliyski, P. (2019), United in Diversity? The Convergence of Cultural Values among EU Member States and Candidates, *European Journal of Political Research*, 58(2), pp. 388–411, p. 388.
3 European Commission (2020), European Standards. European Commission. Retrieved from https://ec.europa.eu/growth/single-market/european-standards_en
4 Publications Office of the European Union (2021), Accession criteria (Copenhagen criteria). EUR-Lex. Retrieved from https://eur-lex.europa.eu/legal-content/EN/TXT/?uri=LEGISSUM:accession_criteria_copenhague
5 Lucarelli, S. and Manners, I. (2006), *Values and Principles in European Union Foreign Policy*, London: Routledge, pp. 201–215.
6 Campos, N., Coricelli, F. and Moretti, L. (2014), Economic Growth and Political Integration: Estimating the Benefits from Membership in the European Union using the Synthetic Counterfactuals Method, *IZA Discussion Paper*, No.8162, p. 21.
7 Morris, K. and White, T. (2011), Neutrality and the European Union: The Case of Switzerland, *Journal of Law and Conflict Resolution*, 3(7), pp. 104–111, p. 104.
8 Grewal, D. S. (2008). Network power. In *Network Power*. New Haven: Yale University Press, pp. 153–155.
9 Nadeau, M. (2020), *General Data Protection Regulation (GDPR): What You Need to Know to Stay Compliant*, CSO. Needham: CSO. https://www.csoonline.com/article/3202771/general-data-protection-regulation-gdpr-requirements-deadlines-and-facts.html
10 He, L., Lu, Y. and Wu, H. (2019). The Impact of GDPR on Global Technology Development, *Journal of Global Information Technology Management*, 22(1), pp. 1–6.
11 Tankard, C. (2016), What the GDPR Means for Businesses, *Network Security*, 6, pp. 5–8.
12 Albrecht, J. (2016), How the GDPR Will Change the World, *European Data Protection Law Review (EDPL)*, 2(3), pp. 287–289.
13 Harvey, F. and Rankin, J. (2020), What Is the European Green Deal and Will It Really Cost €1tn? *The Guardian* (March 9, 2020).

14 Claeys, G., Tagliapietram S. and Zachmann, G. (2019). How to Make the European Green Deal Work, Brussels: Bruegel Policy Contribution, No. 14 (November 2019), pp. 2–6.
15 Aylor, B., Gilbert, M., Lang, N., McAdoo, M., Öberg, J., Pieper, C., Sudmeijer, B. & Voigt, N. (2020), *How an EU Carbon Border Tax Could Jolt World Trade*, Boston: Boston Consulting Group. https://www.bcg.com/publications/2020/how-an-eu-carbon-border-tax-could-jolt-world-trade
16 Bulmer, S. and Paterson, W. (2013), Germany as the EU's Reluctant Hegemon of Economic Strength and Political Constraints, *Journal of European Public Policy*, 20(10), pp. 1387–1405.
17 Lehne, S. (2012), *The Big Three in EU Foreign Policy* (Vol. 5), Brussels: Carnegie Endowment for International Peace.
18 Castells, M. (2011), A Network Theory of Power, *International Journal of Communication*, 5, pp. 773–787, p. 776.
19 Aggestam, L. and Johansson, M. (2017), The Leadership Paradox in EU Foreign Policy, *Journal of Common Market Studies*, 55(6), pp. 1203–1220.
20 Aggestam, L. and Hyde-Price, A. (2020), Learning to Lead? Germany and the Leadership Paradox in EU Foreign Policy, *German Politics*, 29(1), pp. 8–24, p. 19.
21 Kelemen, R. (2007), Built to Last? The Durability of EU Federalism, *Making History: European Integration and Institutional Change at Fifty, The State of the European Union*, Oxford: Oxford University Press, 8, pp. 51–66, p. 52.
22 Meunier, S. (2014), Divide and Conquer? China and the Cacophony of Foreign Investment Rules in the EU, *Journal of European Public Policy*, 21(7), pp. 996–1016.
23 Hocking, B., Melissen, J., Riordan, S. and Sharp, P. (2012), Futures for Diplomacy: Integrative Diplomacy in the 21st Century (Report No. 1), Netherlands Institute of International Relations "Clingendael."
24 Bicchi, F. (2011), The EU as a Community of Practice: Foreign Policy Communications in the COREU Network, *Journal of European Public Policy*, 18(8), pp. 1115–1132.
25 Henning, C. (2009), Networks of Power in the CAP System of the EU-15 and EU-27, *Journal of Public Policy*, 29(2), pp. 153–177.
26 Renard, T. (2016), Partnerships for Effective Multilateralism? Assessing the Compatibility between EU Bilateralism, (inter-)Regionalism and Multilateralism, *Cambridge Review of International Affairs*, 29(1), p. 15.
27 Bevan, S., Jennings, W. and Wlezien, C. (2016), An Analysis of the Public's Personal, National and EU Issue Priorities, *Journal of European Public Policy*, 23(6), pp. 871–887.
28 Somai, M. and Biedermann, Z. (2016), Brexit: Reasons and Challenges, *Acta Oeconomica*, 66(Supplement1), pp. 137–156.
29 Nickell, S. and Saleheen, J. (2017), The Impact of EU and Non-EU Immigration on British Wages, *IZA Journal of Development and Immigration*, 7(15).
30 Colantone, I. and Stanig, P. (2018), Global Competition and Brexit, *American Political Science Review*, 112(2), pp. 201–218.
31 Nickell, S. and Saleheen, J. (2017), Ibid.
32 European Commission (2016), EU Expenditure and Revenue. European Commission. Retrieved from https://ec.europa.eu/info/strategy/eu-budget/long-term-eu-budget/2014-2020/spending-and-revenue_en
33 Edgington, T. (2020), Brexit: What Are the Key Points of the Deal? *BBC* (December 28, 2020).
34 Hutton, R. (2020), The Roots of Brexit, *Bloomberg* (January 31, 2020).
35 Corr, C., Rosenzweig, F., Moran, W., Scoles, S. and Solomon, M. (2019), The CPTPP Enters into Force: What Does it Mean for Global Trade? *White&Case* (January 21, 2019).
36 Caporal, J. and Lesh, J. (2019), *The CPTPP: (Almost) One Year Later*, Washington, DC: CSIS.

37 Australian Government (2019), CPTPP: Intellectual Property, Fact Sheet. Department of Foreign Affairs and Trade. Retrieved from https://www.dfat.gov.au/trade/agreements/in-force/cptpp/outcomes-documents/Pages/cptpp-intellectual-property

38 Government of Canada (2018), What Does the CPTPP Mean for State-Owned Enterprises? Government of Canada, Gouvernement du Canada. Retrieved from https://www.international.gc.ca/trade-commerce/trade-agreements-accords-commerciaux/agr-acc/cptpp-ptpgp/sectors-secteurs/state_owned-appartenant.aspx?lang=eng

39 Cutler, W. (2020), Reengaging the Asia-Pacific on Trade: A TPP Roadmap for the Nest U.S. Administration, New York: *Asia Society Policy Institute Report*. Retrieved from http://asiasociety.org/sites/default/files/2020-09/A%20TPP%20Roadmap%20for%20the%20Next%20U.S.%20Administration.pdf

40 Biden, J. (2020), Why America Must Lead Again: Rescuing U.S. Foreign Policy after Trump, *Foreign Affairs*, 99(2), pp. 64–76.

41 Corr, C. et al. (2019), Ibid.

42 Petri, P. and Plummer, M. (2020), East Asia Decouples from the United States: Trade War, COVID-19, and East Asia's New Trade Blocs, Peterson Institute for International Economics, *Working Paper* 20–29.

43 Hocking, B., Melissen, J., Riordan, S. and Sharp, P. (2012), Ibid.

44 Karolina, M., Hollway, J., Peacock, C. and Snidal, D. (2018), Beyond Trade: The Expanding Scope of the Nontrade Agenda in Trade Agreements, *Journal of Conflict Resolution*, 62(4), pp. 743–773.

45 Corr, C. et al. (2019), Ibid.

46 USDA Foreign Agriculture Service, (2018), CPTPP Changes to Japanese Beef Market, Global Agricultural Information Network, Report No. JA8109, p. 2.

47 Honma, M. and Mulgan, G. (2018), Political Economy of Agricultural Reform in Japan under Abe's Administration, *Asian Economic Policy Review*, 13(1), pp. 128–144.

48 Moreno, J. (1978), *Who Shall Survive*, Beacon House, 3rd ed. (originally published in 1934).

49 Metcalfe's Law states that the value or utility of a network is proportional to the number of users of the network.

50 Swanson, A. and Tankersley, J. (2020), Trump Just Signed the USMCA. Here's What's in the New NAFTA, *The New York Times* (January 29, 2020).

51 Lighthizer, R. (2020), USMCA, Replacing NAFTA Today, Is the Model for All Future Trade Agreements, *Triblive* (July 1, 2020).

52 Bown, C. and Irwin, D. (2019), Trump's Assault on the Global Trading System, *Foreign Affairs*, 98(5), pp. 125–136.

53 Bown, C. (2017), Trump's Attempted Takedown of the Global Trade Regime? *The Future of the Global Order Colloquium*, Fall 2017. Philadelphia: The University of Pennsylvania, Perry World House.

54 Condon, B. (2019), From NAFTA to USMCA: Two's Company, Three's a Crowd, *Latin American Journal of Trade Policy*, 1(2), pp. 30–31.

55 Ibid., p. 32.

56 Caldwell, C. (2008), Network Power That Works Too Well, *Financial Times* (May 23, 2008).

57 Castells, M. (2011), Ibid.

58 Office of the United States Trade Representative USTR (2017), *USTR Releases Updated NAFTA Negotiating Objectives*. Retrieved from https://ustr.gov/about-us/policy-offices/press-office/press-releases/2017/november/ustr-releases-updated-nafta

59 Hogan, B. (2017), Online Social Networks: Concepts for Data Collection and Analysis, in Fielding, N., Lee, R. and Blank, G. (eds), *The Sage Handbook of Online Research Methods*, 2nd ed., Thousand Oaks, CA: Sage Publications, pp. 241–258.

60 Condon, B. (2019), Ibid.

61 Johanson, D., Williamson, I., Broadbent, M., Schmidtlein, R. and Kearns, J. (2019), U.S.-Mexico-Canada Trade Agreement: Likely Impact on the U.S. Economy and on Specific Industry Sectors, United States International Trade Commission (USITC). *RVC* is the requirement used in rules of origin. It requires a good must contain at least a minimum amount of originated material from one or more of the parties of the agreement. *LVC* is a terminology involved in the USMCA rules of origin. LVC, consisting of three components, must account for 40% of the total manufacture cost for passenger vehicles and 45% for light trucks. Three components are (1) high-wage material or manufacturing costs (25%–30% of net cost of the vehicle), (2) high-wage R&D and IT expenditures (10%), and (3) qualifying plant credit (5%).

62 Maoz, Z. (2010), *Network of Nations: The Evolution, Structure, and Impact of International Networks, 1816–2001*, NY: Cambridge University Press.

63 Karolina, M., Hollway, J., Peacock, C. and Snidal, D. (2018), Beyond Trade: The Expanding Scope of the Non-trade Agenda in Trade Agreements, *Journal of Conflict Resolution*, 62(4), 743–773. The authors define POWER as the ability to compel or attract others to accept NTIs. They tested the hypothesis: powerful states are more likely to include NTIs in their preferential trade agreements. The conclusion drawn is that while dyadic POWER is insignificant in all networks, states' monadic POWER (EGO) has significant impact in both bilateral and plurilateral NTIs; this effect is positive in the former but negative in the latter. Irrespective of partners, powerful states prefer bilateral NTIs, and weaker states prefer plurilateral NTIs. This makes sense since bilateral arrangements make it easier for major states to exert power.

64 Brewster, R. (2019), The Trump Administration and the Future of the WTO. *Yale Journal of International Law* Online, 10, p. 8.

65 Department of Foreign Affairs and Trade, Australian Government, Background to the Regional Comprehensive Economic Partnership (RCEP) Initiative. Also see Kawai, M. and Wignaraja, G. (2018), EAFTA or CEPEA: Which Way Forward? *ASEAN Economic Bulletin*, 25(2), pp. 113–139.

66 ASEAN (2020), *Summary of the Regional Comprehensive Economic Partnership Agreement (RCEP)*. Retrieved from https://asean.org/summary-of-the-regional-comprehensive-economic-partnership-agreement-2/

67 Foreign Affairs and Trade of New Zealand (2020), *RCEP: Summary of Outcomes*. Retrieved from https://www.mfat.govt.nz/assets/Trade-agreements/RCEP/RECP-Agreement-112020/RCEP-Summary-of-Outcomes.pdf

68 Fukunaga, Y. (2014), ASEAN's Leadership in the Regional Comprehensive Economic Partnership, *Asia & the Pacific Policy Studies*, 2(1), 103–115.

69 Petri, P. and Plummer, M. (2013), ASEAN Centrality and the ASEAN–US Economic Relationship, *Policy Studies*, 69, p. 13.

70 Oba, M. (2016), TPP, RCEP, and FTAAP Multilayered Regional Economic Integration and International Relations, *Asia-Pacific Review*, 23(1), pp. 100–114, p. 102.

71 Kim G., Lee, H. and Kim, E. (2014), A Study on Japan's FTA Strategy and Its Policy Implications for Korea, Korea Institute for International Economic Policy (KIEP), *Policy Analyses*, 14-13.

72 Sampson, M. (2019), The Evolution of China's Regional Trade Agreements: Power Dynamics and the Future of the Asia-Pacific, *The Pacific Review*, 33(6), pp. 259–289.

73 The clause stated that if any USMCA party undertakes negotiations for an FTA with China or other non-market economy, that party must notify others of its intention and provide others with an opportunity to review the full text of the agreement. In case that party chooses the agreement with non-market economies, other parties can terminate USMCA. (Agreement between the United States of America, the United Mexican States, and Canada 12/13/19 Text. Article 32.10, https://ustr.gov/trade-agreements/free-trade-agreements/united-states-mexico-canada-agreement/agreement-between).

74 Kawashima, S. (2020), Japan's Painful Choice on RCEP: Tokyo Faces a Major Conundrum with the Proposed Free Trade Agreement, *The Diplomat* (August 3, 2020).

75 Kurlantzick, J. (2020), The RCEP Signing and Its Implications. New York: Council on Foreign Relations. Retrieved from https://www.cfr.org/blog/rcep-signing-and-its-implications

76 Australian Government (2022), Regional Comprehensive Economic Partnership, About the Regional Comprehensive Economic Partnership Agreement (RCEP). *Australian Government, Department of Foreign Affairs and Trade.* Retrieved from https://www.dfat.gov.au/trade/agreements/in-force/rcep

77 WTO (n.d.), Accession in Perspective, *Handbook on Accession to the WTO.* Geneva: WTO. Retrieved from https://www.wto.org/english/thewto_e/acc_e/cbt_course_e/course_index_e.htm

78 Reinsch, W. and Caporal, J. (2019), At Last, An RCEP Deal, Critical Questions, Center for Strategic and International Studies (CSIS). Also see Elms, D. (2017), TPP11 and RCEP Compared, *Asian Trade Centre Policy Brief,* No. 17–12.

79 Petri, P. and Plummer, M. (2020), Ibid.

80 Mueller, L. (2019), ASEAN Centrality Under Threat – The Case of RCEP and Connectivity, *Journal of Contemporary East Asia Studies,* 8(2), pp. 177–198, p. 185.

81 Oxford Business Group (2018), China's Belt and Road Initiative reshaping Southeast Asia, The Report on Myanmar. London: Oxford Business Group. Retrieved from https://oxfordbusinessgroup.com/analysis/road-china%E2%80%99s-belt-and-road-initiative-reshaping-south-east-asia

82 Ministry of Foreign Affairs of Japan (2021), Japan's Efforts for a Free and Open Indo-Pacific. Retrieved from https://www.mofa.go.jp/policy/page25e_000278.html

4 Networking Strategy in Competition
The US vs. China

Free trade agreements (FTAs) are treaties created between two or more countries and are focused on reaping economic benefits by reducing or eliminating tariffs, quotas, subsidies, or prohibitions to promote trade and investment liberalization. FTAs also facilitate stronger trade and commercial ties between participating countries. Thus, they are a good tool to widen a country's network of influence in the global community. At present, the global trading system is dominated by two contrasting poles, the US and China. Aside from playing active roles in the mega-FTAs that were discussed previously, both superpowers are constantly pursuing ways to counter each other's efforts by establishing their own networks and expanding their sphere of influence. How are FTAs and networks evolving among the US, China, and their respective allies? In this chapter we are going to analyze the main trade agreements supported by the two contrasting blocs, the reasoning behind their development, and, thanks to the network theory, we will be able to define their main strategies and the related implications.

4.1 The USA's FTA Network

4.1.1 A Closer Look

According to the Office of the US Trade Representative (USTR),[1] the US has 14 FTAs in force with 20 countries to date, namely, FTAs with Australia, Bahrain, Dominican Republic-Central America (CAFTA-DR), Chile, Colombia, Israel, Jordan, Korea (KORUS), Morocco, Oman, Singapore; trade promotion agreements (TPAs) with Panama, Peru; and a mega trade agreement with Mexico and Canada (US–Mexico–Canada Agreement [USMCA]). Besides, there is a lengthy queue of countries seeking to negotiate bilateral FTA with the US, including Uruguay, Egypt, New Zealand, Pakistan, the Philippines, Sri Lanka, and Taiwan.

Since President Trump took office in the White House, the renegotiation of NAFTA to USMCA, KORUS 2.0, withdrawal from the Trans-Pacific Partnership (TPP), and the US–Japan trade agreement (including a separate digital trade agreement) are the four prominent points of the US FTA network.

DOI: 10.4324/9781003305705-4

Trump signed the USMCA into law on January 29, 2020, which was the revised version of the North American Free Trade Agreement (NAFTA). Noteworthy changes of the USMCA are explained in the previous chapter, among which, the new standards on the rule of origin (especially for automobile products), labor, and digital trade are the most visible. The renegotiation of NAFTA to USMCA, characterized as a one-sided deal, was a part of the wave of US economic nationalism – the *America First* strategy of President Trump, aiming at reducing the trade deficit and job loss in the US caused by NAFTA. With such modifications, 176,000 new jobs for Americans are estimated to be generated within the next five years, and in the agricultural sector alone, a $2.2 billion increase in export value was expected.[2] President Trump, who called NAFTA a nightmare, believed the USMCA to be a *colossal victory* for the US.[3] It received bipartisan support, and even the new US President, Joe Biden, admitted that USMCA is better than NAFTA.

KORUS 2.0 came into force at the beginning of 2019 with unfavorable modifications for Korea.[4] In the renegotiated deal, Korea agreed to impose the voluntary export restraint on steel, which limits the Korean steel exports to the US at 70% of the average volume for years between 2015 and 2017 (about 2.68 million tons). Additionally, the import quota for US automobiles doubled under KORUS 2.0, from 25,000 to 50,000 vehicles annually per manufacturer. And the US safety standard is the only compulsory regulation needed to pass. The 25% US tariff on Korean light trucks would be extended for two decades until 2041, in order to further postpone the invasion of US markets by Korean manufacturers. In the pharmaceutical field, the new agreement forced Korea to amend its Premium Pricing Policy for Global Innovative Drugs to ensure non-discrimination, fair treatment, and avoidance of infringement of American intellectual property. Despite considerable modification in trade conditions, based on the current import-export status, KORUS 2.0 is expected to bring only a slight change in the trade value between the two countries but will have a significant impact on the opportunities for Korean exports in the long term.[5]

TPP was one of the largest regional trade pacts negotiated by the US; however, the country decided to opt out from that right after President Trump took office in 2017. The reason was, as discussed in the previous sections, the shared value of trade liberalization in TPP was strongly opposed to the *America First* strategy of Trump's administration. It was criticized that the withdrawal of the US from TPP led the country to lose the opportunity to lead the Pacific Rim regional integration and contain China in international trade. However, new ideas for breaking China's dominance were developed, such as the Free and Open Indo-Pacific Initiative (FOIPI) (vs. China's Belt and Road Initiative [BRI]) and the already-mentioned 'Anti-China' US-led network (former Economic Prosperity Network [EPN] and recent Indo-Pacific Economic Framework [IPEF]).

Those actions not only protect the US welfare from free trade but also amplify the US networked power over the others within networks. Together with the establishment and implementation of IPEF, and a network of like-minded nations, the US is trying to re-exert its leadership and its network-making power in forming the sectoral and plurilateral networks excluding China.

Regarding the US–Japan Trade Agreement (USJTA) signed on October 7, 2019, we have to consider its dual form since it implements standard measures with liberalization of commerce as in many other agreements and also tackles several 'digital issues' that were bothering both the governments in Tokyo and Washington. Indeed, the first part of the agreement either eliminates or lowers tariffs on US agricultural products while providing special country-specific quotas that will further liberalize trade between the two parties (USTR, 2019).[6] All in all, more than 90% of the American agricultural products imported by Japan will face preferential tariffs or will be imported at a 0% tax rate. Adding to this, safeguards used by Japan on products like beef, pork, and whey will be phased out, and the US will cut tariffs on several agricultural and industrial imports from Japan, but the deal doesn't include cars, one of the most contentious topics in the US-Japan trade talks. The second part of the agreement, the US–Japan Digital Trade Agreement, aimed to reach a high-standard digital accord that could ease the safe transfer of data between the countries' industries while providing homogeneous standards and rules, similar to the deal negotiated within USMCA's framework (CRS, 2020).[7] The aforementioned deal was labeled as 'stage one' of possible further ease in trade relations between Japan and the US. However, as mentioned in the Congressional Research Service's report on the USJTA (2020), this kind of *partial and relatively non-comprehensive* deal might not be pursued by both the administrations that followed the departures of Trump and Abe, and indeed several approaches could be instead chosen by Kishida and Biden. Further regional talks could be pursued (especially considering a possible extension of CPTPP, which is Comprehensive and Progressive Agreement for Trans-Pacific Partnership), or a unique comprehensive agreement could replace the original USJTA. Nevertheless, the problems brought by the COVID-19 pandemic appear to have interrupted the talks on the matter, pushing the US–Japan trade agreement to the sidelines and probably postponing additional negotiations by both parties.

4.1.2 *Chronological Evolution*

The evolution of the US FTAs started after World War II (WWII) when the US led the establishment of the multilateral General Agreement on Tariffs and Trade (GATT). At that time, the US administrations only focused on the pursuit of global comprehensive trade agreements, which enhanced US leadership in the global trade system. A series of negotiation rounds were conducted to lower trade barriers among countries, and as a result, US average tariff rates declined significantly from 60% in 1930 to 5.7% in 1980 and even dropped to 2.7% in 2013. Non-tariff barriers were also lowered.[8] The creation of the World Trade Organization (WTO) under GATT's Uruguay Round (UR; 1986–1994), which marked the biggest reform of international trade since the end of WWII, was the evidence of American efforts to lead the world's trading system.

From the mid-1980s, the forms of US trade agreements shifted toward bilateral or regional accords. The US–Israel FTA was the very first bilateral FTA of the US, which was negotiated in 1974 and then signed and implemented in

1985. NAFTA was among the most important trade deals of the US since it includes Canada and Mexico, the second- and third-biggest trading partners of the country. The US and Canadian leaders already signed CUSFTA in January 1988 (after two years of negotiations). Then at the behest of Mexico, NAFTA negotiation was launched in 1991, received congressional approval in 1993, and was implemented in January 1994. The trilateral NAFTA marked an unprecedented integration of two developed countries and Mexico, the developing one, and formed the largest FTA at that time.

The change in US attitude from multilateral to bilateral and regional trade reflected the effects of the Uruguay Round and the US policy toward Europeans. The multilateral negotiation for UR was remarkably lengthy, as it took eight years (from 1986 to 1994) to conclude. The postponement of UR was due to lack of effort to break the deadlock between the Europeans and the US. Moreover, the power of GATT in spurring trade encountered the challenge, prompted by the recovery of European countries after WWII in the form of the establishment of the European Commission (EC). In Europe, to boost import-export activities, Britain adopted preferential trade deals with former colonies, while France applied preferential treatment of certain trading partners. Hence, the US needed to form an alternative network to further enhance its power and counter newly emerging powers in the global trading system. The country entered bilateral FTAs with allies and neighbor states in the region, as well as hosting commercial agreements with countries around the globe.

Noticeably, eight years of the George W. Bush presidency witnessed the highest number of FTAs signed and implemented. From 2001 to 2009, FTAs with 17 countries from FTA with Jordan to that with Panama were concluded or ratified, in which the agreement with 13 countries (from FTA with Jordan to that with Costa Rica) came into force. Thanks to the FTA network generated by Bush's administration, the export value of US goods and services grew rapidly by 79% from 2001 to 2008, accounting for a salient portion of 12.49% of total gross domestic product (GDP) in 2008 (World Bank data).[9] In 2014, the US merchandise trade with FTA partner countries comprised 70% of all US exports in goods and services and more than 80% of all US imports of goods and services (Council of Economic Advisors).[10]

In the subsequent period, the American FTA network continued to be bolstered with two mega-regional trade agreements, initiated by the Obama administration, the TPP with 12 Pacific Rim nations, and the Transatlantic Trade and Investment Partnership (TTIP) with the European Union (EU). The US commenced TPP's negotiation in 2008 as an expanded version of the Trans-Pacific Economic Partnership Agreement among the Pacific-4, including Brunei, Chile, New Zealand, and Singapore. After 19 official rounds of negotiation and many separate meetings, all 12 countries, including the US, agreed to the conclusion of the TPP in October 2015 and signed the agreement in early 2016. However, as a newly elected president, Trump withdrew the US from TPP only days after taking office in January 2017. On the other hand, the negotiations of TTIP between the US and the EU began in 2013. In three years and 15 rounds of negotiations, 27 chapters were discussed, covering a wide range of issues, from anti-corruption measures and intellectual-property protections to market access and trade barriers. However, in 2016, Germany admitted that the trade pact 'has de facto failed' without a single chapter being concluded. Trump also announced to halt TTIP further. All in all, the two mega-regional FTAs initiated by the Obama administration became stalled under Trump's regime.

Nowadays, with the resumption of the Quadrilateral Security Dialogue (Quad 2.0), the FOIPI is carried out by the US, Japan, Australia, and India. A network of 'free, fair, and reciprocal trade' was promised in the US outline; however, it was not clear whether a free trade area would be established or not. The Trump administration also initiated the EPN, which consists of 'like-minded' countries, companies, and civil groups and operates under a set of 'trusted principles'; nevertheless, the shared value of 'free trade' has never been mentioned in those principles. And since Trump lost the presidential election in November 2020, the termination of EPN in its original form was inevitable, making way for a possible alternative network. More recently, the Biden administration is teeing up its IPEF to launch in 2022. The framework is reported to include topics such as technology, supply chains, infrastructure, climate change, taxation, anti-corruption, and more. The scope of the deal is not comprehensive, but partial and sectoral. Critics argue it could be a merely recycled and rebranded EPN unless the White House provides a more detailed road map for the project.

4.1.3 FTA Partner Selection Strategy

According to the US Government Accountability Office Report (2004),[11] the number of factors guiding the FTA partner selection process declined from 13 to 6 only, including country readiness, economic/commercial benefits, benefits to the broader trade liberalization strategy, compatibility with US interest, congressional/private-sector support, and US government resource constraints. The above criteria were determined under the presidency of George W. Bush, some of which have remained until recently, whereas some others were modified in the Biden era to fit the current trade policies.

Country readiness evaluates the partner country's political will, trading capacity, and a system to ensure the rule of law. Since the FTA partner selection process involves both Congress and the private sector, depending on issues of concern for each agency, country readiness can be expanded to other aspects of adherence such as trade obligations, leaders' commitment, macroeconomic stability, and strength of its financial and banking system.

Economic and/or commercial benefits are thoroughly reviewed by the interagency group. They take into consideration the benefits to FTA partners as a result of America's macroeconomic impacts and also potential impacts on specific products and sectors. The FTA goals of the US are twofold: expand export opportunities for 'Made in America' goods and services and protect the interest of US stakeholders, including intellectual property, labor, environment, etc.

The criteria for 'benefits' in the broader trade liberalization strategy are closely tied to the prospective FTA partner's support for US trade goals and key positions in international institutions, for example, FTAA (FTA of the Americas) and WTO. Nevertheless, the WTO has been stagnant for two decades without a breakthrough in the Doha Round, and no leading nodes, including the US, have found a way out. Additionally, trade liberalization was not America's trade goal during Trump's tenure. Liberalization was replaced by the desire for national welfare protection and 'making America great again' in the global trading system.

Compatibility with US interests suggests an examination of whether the interests of the FTA partner will accord with broad US interests, including its support for US foreign policy positions. This criterion is highlighted in every single FTA partner of the US. For example, the US–Israel FTA was signed with the purpose of countering the discrimination against US exporters that resulted from the bilateral Israel – EC FTA (signed in 1975, final tariff cut in 1985). The sign of US–Israel and CUSFTA in the late 1980s broadly aimed at putting pressure on partners of the US to move multilateral negotiations forward under the US-led GATT. Nowadays, the idea of a network of free and reciprocal trade in the FOIPI does require diplomatic compatibility, as the network will contain only 'like-minded' partners who support US policies in the Indo-Pacific region.

Due to the growth in power of internal factors, support from Congress, business groups, and civil society is also scrutinized as a part of FTA partner selection. Otherwise, the collapse of the negotiation process or the difficulty in ratification is unavoidable.

Constraints on US government resources are the last criteria. According to the USTR, human and time resources are the constraints to FTA's negotiation and post-negotiation activities. Freud and McDaniel (2016)[12] reviewed the USA's 20-FTA summary and found that the average period from the first round of negotiations (launching date) to the signing date is 18 months, while that from the launching to implementing date takes 45 months (with extensive variation owing to small sample size). Thus, it is necessary to estimate resource hindrance in the FTA partner selection process to prevent the FTAs from any disadvantages derived from the shortage of funds.

4.1.4 The Viability of the Current FTA Network

After selecting, negotiating, and implementing, the viability of the FTA network is determined by the interdependence among parties and the satisfaction of each party regarding the common rules and regulations.

That US FTA partners are interdependent with the US economy is an advantage in evaluating the viability of the current US FTA network. Interdependence is evaluated via shares of trade and income elasticity. In accordance with Jackson (2018),[13] 20 FTA partner countries made up $677 billion, or 47% of total US goods exports, and $749 billion, or 34% of total US goods imports in 2016. The USA's FTA partners, including both developed and developing countries, have substantially smaller economies, compared to the US, and the US is among the top five biggest trading partners of all FTA partners. US trade with these countries is focused on a limited number of items, mostly, raw materials, intermediate processed goods, and agricultural commodities. In most countries, the top ten export and import commodities comprise 90% of total bilateral trade. Furthermore, following the estimation of income elasticity, every 1% growth in US GDP will increase US imports by 2.11%. Similarly, should US partners' GDP rise by 1%, consumers in those countries would increase their consumption of US goods by 1.86%. Overall, the data indicate a close tie in trading relations between the US and its FTA partners.

However, the excessive power of the US over other countries within an agreement might lead to dissatisfaction among countries in the long term. The revised version of USMCA and KORUS 2.0 is evidence of Trump's pressure on US partners. Trump criticized the old agreements as *horrible deals* and pushed for renegotiation, forcing partners to share the costs of free trade. Most of the renegotiated terms would have had an adverse effect on the partners' welfare within the agreement. For example, the extremely high minimum wage of $16/hour for workers in the automobile sector, which is three times higher than the existing wage level, is a burden on the developing economy of Mexico. The VER on Korea's steel exports and the prolongation of the tariff period on light trucks aim to constrain the export growth of spearhead economic sectors of Korea. The renegotiation is beneficial to the US workers and investors but harmful for other countries. Therefore, FTA is no longer a win-win game, which would be less appealing to US partners. Considering both strength and weakness in the linkage between the US and its partners, the viability of the network is maintained, thanks to the intertwined trading relations; however, it was being undermined by the aggressive and protectionist policy of the US.

4.1.5 The Voices in the Inner Network

The current direction of the US government's trade policies reflects the forcing of change in the outer network for the sake of the inner network. Trump's administration considered WTO an impediment to his *America First* Policies, which aim to protect US workers and farmers and exert its leadership in the world economy. The supranational institution was also blamed for the incredibly fast growth of China, as it did little to stop China from unfairly subsidizing its products. Hence, limiting WTO was deemed necessary for the success of US protectionism.[14] In addition, regarding TPP, seven years after President Obama's commitment to the TPP, over 1,500 US advocacy groups urged opposition to the trade pact by signing a letter in January 2016.[15] They criticized the negative impacts of TPP on the US economy and American living standards. First, opening trade with countries like Vietnam and Malaysia, i.e. low-wage countries, would raise the trend of offshoring, thus driving down domestic wages. Second, the TPP's Environment Chapter only fulfills one of the seven policies specified in the 'May 10th' agreement between congressional Democrats and President Bush. It even fails to include climate change. Third, food safety is undermined as TPP allows massive food exports to the US and gives foreign exporters the right to challenge the port inspection determination in case of quality problems. Fourth, the extension of medical intellectual property rights would promote patent monopolies, postpone the introduction of low-cost generic medications, raise health care prices, and reduce access to medicine. Lastly, foreign firms would be given preferential rights through the TPP's Investment Chapter and investor-state dispute settlement system, at the expense of domestic firms. They could skirt domestic laws and courts to challenge US federal, state, and local decisions. Based on the impetus provided by internal actors, Trump made a withdrawal from the TPP his first action in the office, an act he regarded as a 'great thing for the American workers.'

The collision between the inner and outer networks is one of the reasons that lead to the inevitable stagnation of TTIP, the free trade initiative between the US and the EU. Hundreds of thousands of people throughout the EU took part in mass protests on the streets, signed petitions, and formed coalitions against this FTA.[16] The European demonstrators waved the banner of 'People over Profits,' arguing that open trade with the US will result in a flood of genetically modified food. The American food safety standard does not comply with that of the EU; for example, 82 pesticides are being used in the US that are banned in the EU for horticulture and cattle production. TTIP is thus seen as undermining the European public health standards since the US negotiated to abolish the UK's National Health Service. In addition, the open trade between the US and EU is expected to cause a rise in outsourcing and, eventually, job losses. As the interests of the inner factors, consumers and workers, are not protected, the TTIP faced difficulties in negotiation and ratification. In 2016, Germany's vice-chancellor announced that the trade pact had 'de facto failed.' In 2017, Trump decided to halt it altogether.

The US–Colombia FTA had pushed small-scale farmers to the brink, as they are unable to compete with giant agricultural corporations receiving subsidies from the US. A series of protests in Colombia occurred during the negotiation, where students joined farmers in solidarity, fighting against the trade policy between the two countries. The tension generated from Colombia's domestic factors led to the advent of a special article named 'Labor Action Plan' (LAP), a guide for the Colombian government to protect worker rights, in the final agreement. According to LAP, the establishment of a separate labor minister as corps of labor inspectors is required; the role of the International Labor Organization, governed by the UN, should be strengthened in Colombia to monitor and support plans related to labor rights. The country also launched programs on multi-media to inform the workers of their rights. All in all, Colombia had changed its inner network to align itself with the outer network's policy and, in particular, with the very first criteria for FTA partners of the US: country readiness.[17]

4.1.6 Network Power

Network power is measured by three elements: standard, leading node, and entry barrier. A standard includes norms and practices that govern how members connect and cooperate in a network. The US FTA network comprises 14 regional and bilateral FTAs with 14 agreements accordingly, and the texts are all similar in spirit. Scrutiny of the USA's FTAs reveals that a common format was designed and has been applied for different accords. USMCA contains the highest number of chapters (34 chapters) in the final text, while other FTAs consist of 22 to 24 chapters with similar core contents. The contents of the agreements (i.e. standard) cover various issues of cooperation regarding both trade and non-trade, widely ranging from tariff elimination for specific lines of goods, services trade to trade remedies or safeguards, from rules of origins, sanitary and phytosanitary (SPS), technical barriers of trade (TBT) to intellectual property rights, labor, and environmental standards. Though the negotiation results are different depending on the FTA, the basic set of goals for all US free trade accords is clearly defined and followed. Among 14 FTAs, the USMCA is the one consisting of the most modern and high-standard provisions, which replaces NAFTA to become the model set of rules and disciplines for future FTAs. The parallel in USMCA's digital trade provision and US–Japan Digital Trade Agreement[18] is a typical example of cohesion in the US FTA network. The two agreements' key outcomes are similar, including the prohibition of customs duties on digital products, ensuring non-discriminatory treatment, ensuring cross-border transfer of data, facilitating digital transactions, forbidding data localization, bolstering cooperation in addressing cybersecurity challenges, protecting against forced disclosure of source code and algorithms, and guaranteeing for enforceable consumer protections. Digital trade both in USMCA and in US-Japan Digital Trade Agreement is designed with the ultimate goal of making information free and available for business expansion. All in all, since every aspect of the cooperation is coherently considered and negotiated under FTA, the standard effectively eliminates the possibility of finding alternatives. And thanks to the cohesion among US FTAs, the US would find it more convenient to exert their network power.

As a leading node, the US holds four key sources of the FTA network power: networking power, network power, networked power, and network-making power (the concept was introduced by Castells (2011)).[19] First, networking power gives the members a strength over outsiders. The stringent FTA partner selection process is utilized as a gate-keeping tool to control access to the exclusive network. Second, network power to generate coordinating standards to share among all actors in the network is exercised in this network, evidenced by the common format and spirit of all 14 FTA final texts. Third, the networked power, or the power of one node over the others, is owned only by the US, thanks to its substantially larger economy and vigorous diplomatic and military power to exert its leadership in the network of 14 FTAs. Fourth, the network-making power of the US is performed when it plays the integral roles of both programmer and switcher in the network. The programmer is defined as the node that constitutes and programs or reprograms the network according to set goals. And switcher refers to the actor who provides linkage between nodes and makes certain that all are cooperatively pursuing the common coal. Except for USMCA, and

CAFTA-DR, the other 12 FTAs are bilaterally negotiated; hence, the most important link in this network is between the US and each partner. The US stands a significant role in forming and reforming the standard, as well as establishing and maintaining the bilateral cooperative relationship between countries. The US owns the power to prompt the enactment of domestic policy and economic reforms in partner nations, which will make it easier for them to pursue further liberalization at the multilateral level (Schott, 2004).[20] Considering the US FTA network in the Americas, the US expedites reforms that make its partners comply with American values and standards, for example, the reform of labor rights in Colombia and Central America, and the reform of minimum wage in Mexico. In Korea, the FTA is believed to strengthen transparency and efficiency, improve legal procedures, and boost other systems in dynamic ways. By supporting other countries in policy and economic reforms, the US bolsters linkage with partners, as well as makes cooperation among them become more effective.

The entry barrier in the US FTA network is built on the basis of the cost-benefit structure of the network. Regarding the benefits of joining the FTA, as the US withdrew from the TPP, the bilateral FTA seems to be the only feasible way to obtain trade liberalization with the country. By signing FTAs with the US, partners get opportunities to conduct economic and social reforms as well as stimulate productivity improvement. By the same token, they can make their domestic conditions and standards become more developed and suitable for multilateralism on a larger scale. On the other hand, undeniable is the fact that opening trade with substantially great power is a challenge for partner countries owing to the power asymmetry. The growth and jobs in the home country might be endangered because of the invasion of big corporations and high-quality products at reasonable prices. Additionally, with increasing tensions between the US and China, excessively close relations with the US might deteriorate the economic relations of that country with China. China's retaliation against the products including coals, dairy products, iron ores, and wines from Australia is a case in point. However, in case a country does not join the FTA to protect the domestic market, the cost might be even more severe, as the country might face retaliation, or even risk a trade war with the US.

4.1.7 Network Structure and Communication Pattern

A glance at the current FTA network of the US reveals a hub-and-spoke[21] model where the US is the hub and its partners are spokes located around it. Since the inauguration of President Trump, it is observed that the country is seeking unilateralism via bilateral trade deals with asymmetric power distribution. In the network, except for two regional accords of USMCA and CAFTA-DR, the links between US partners hardly exist. Yet even when economic relations do exist, it seems not as valuable and vital as the relation between those partners and the US. Therefore, the US can place itself in the central spot with the highest degree of centrality, where it is the sole great power that exerts its sphere of influence on the whole system.

An interpretation of American power within its FTA network in the previous section, in combination with a glance at the new terms and conditions of US-MCA and KORUS 2.0, reaffirms the existence of the power asymmetry; in other words, the possession of networked power by the US over the others within its FTA network. The US is exploiting the advantages of its networked power to make its FTAs one-sided trade deals that focus more on the interests and concerns of the US. Regarding links as trade flows, the US aims to promote itself to be an out-degree rather than an in-degree node, which means that the US wants its imports to be limited (by high tariff and non-tariff barriers) and exports to be encouraged (by government support and subsidies). To complete that goal, Trump was aggressive in implementing economic nationalism via the use of trade remedies, FTA renegotiations, global value chains' decoupling, and immigration limitations. Biden inherited this protectionist legacy of Donald Trump. Though the goal of avoiding becoming the in-degree node in terms of trade and immigration is still maintained, it is expected that Biden's economic strategies will treat the US allies and partners better than Trump's. When mutual benefits are ensured, the stronger connectivity shared among nodes will help the hub tie spokes closer together and form a more firm network.

The communication pattern within a network is categorized into relational and affiliational types. The former defines the presence, direction, and magnitude of the relationship between any two units, while the latter governs an affiliation of a unit with an event, organization, or group. Based on this insight, the US FTA network is defined as a relational trading network, in which, the dialogue is limited to the scale of each sub-network. In the future, even if the Indo-Pacific Economic Framework supports a free, fair, and reciprocal trade as promised, the same pattern of relational dialogue will be exercised between the US and its allies since the links between US allies are relatively weak or even non-existent.

4.1.8 Characteristics of the USA's FTA Network

Through the scrutiny of US FTAs with the application of network perspective, two distinct characteristics of the network emerge, including strategic positioning and the participation of private sectors.

After the end of WWII, the US has been playing the role of the world leader, and FTAs were considered its tool for managing both commercial interests and security objectives. The US sought to amplify its power base deeply in various regions of the world via bilateral or regional FTAs. For example, together with US–Israel and US–Jordan FTAs, the free trade accord between the US and Morocco is viewed as a key to a broader Middle East integration. The US officials expected Morocco to become a hub for sub-regional integration and to serve as one of several sub-regional centers that eventually would be built into the Middle East FTA. Recently, the US had renegotiated USMCA, KORUS 2.0 FTA, and US–Japan Trade Agreement. Together with attempts toward the FOIPI and EPN, the US wants to enhance its trading, diplomatic, and military power in the

Indo-Pacific region. And by linking countries in the region into a firm network, the US aims its ultimate goal to counter China and contain its growing multi-faceted dominance.

The US set up a detailed list of criteria for the FTA partner selection process, in which the consultation with business and public interest groups is appreciated. The process of assessing potential FTA partners has improved since 2003 by way of expanding the number of interagency groups involved in the assessment. Before the negotiations of the US-Singapore FTA, it was not the US official negotiators but the business community that performed a key role in the FTA initiative. Twenty-two US business executives paid a visit to Singapore to discuss with the prime minister about the feasibility of establishing an FTA and bolstering the US–Singapore ties. The participation of private sectors in FTA partner selection would reflect the agreement and satisfaction of the inner network; by the same token, it would minimize the possibility of an inner-outer network collision. Furthermore, the cooperation of the business sector is especially important in the development of the alliance-based networks, as the government is calling upon the US firms and corporations to reshore or relocate their supply and production chains out of China.

4.1.9 Assessment and Prospects

The US FTA policy has changed over time. In the post–WWII period, the US acted upon its global trading interests and bore its responsibilities as the leader of the multilateral trading system and the burden of all nine rounds of GATT and WTO (Schott, 2004).[22] From the late-1980s, the US FTA policy changed toward bilateralism owing to the sluggishness of the UR and the emergence of the EC in spurring global trade. The current US FTA network consists of 2 regional and 12 bilateral agreements, of which the effective date ranges from 1985 to 2009. Since the inauguration of President Trump, he concluded the trade agreement with Japan and renegotiated NAFTA to USMCA and KORUS to KORUS 2.0. The US turned to protectionism by adopting a limit on WTO operations, withdrawing from the TPP, and a halt in TTIP. Besides, the formation of the FOIPI was carried out to attract 'like-minded' parties to join the US in challenging the multifaceted dominance of China.

The country adopts a specific FTA partner selection process including six criteria, namely, country readiness, economic/commercial benefit, benefits to the broader trade liberalization strategy, compatibility with US interests, congressional/private-sector support, and US government resources constraints. The viability of the FTA network is built on interdependence in the trade of the US and its partners. However, this interdependence is being threatened by the excessive asymmetric power of the US in bargaining (the failure of TTIP is a typical example).

The alternation of the US FTA policy leads to a change in the number of partners. At first, the selected FTA partners are the US allies (e.g. Israel, Australia, Korea) or those located in the strategic location for regional integration (e.g. Jordan, Morocco for the future Middle East FTA, CAFTA members for FTA of Americas). However, according to the goal of FOIPI, the more *like-minded* nations, firms, and civil societies join the networks, the more powerful the networks become. Thus, the network scale is not limited to the US allies, but to open it around the world, and seeks the countries that comply with the most important partner criterion of 'compatibility with US interests.'

As a programmer and as the holder of four key sources of the FTA network power,[23] the US designed a clear set of commitments (in other words, standard) that is included in every FTA final text. By playing the role of the switcher, the country assisted reforms in partner counties that comply with American values and standards, in order to ensure their linkage with the US and cooperatively strive for the same common goal. The US FTA network is now being operated in a hub-and-spoke structure and relational communication pattern where the US is the unipole that exercises leadership throughout the whole network.

Considering Mr. Biden's campaign pledges and his success in the presidential election of 2020, we expected a different kind of approach in the upcoming years, more similar to the one pursued during the Obama administration, in vain. The US needs to play a more active role in writing high-quality international trade rules that do not confine its interest to green and labor issues (and, supposedly, better relationships with likely minded countries, i.e. Europe). Aiming to take back the world leader position, however, Biden will not rush to enter into a new trade agreement until he is certain that inner strength gives it a decisive advantage in the global economy.[24] About the existing trade pacts created by the Trump administration, since FOIPI is the only initiative that promises a 'free, fair, and reciprocal' trade, the network would have been utilized for pursuing tight cooperation with its allies. The characteristic of strategic positioning and the criterion of 'compatibility with US interests' in FTA networks could be upheld to attract more Indo-Pacific countries to the US-led value-oriented network and hopefully counter China's sphere of influence in the region.

4.2 China's FTA Network

4.2.1 *China in the Global Trading System*

China's continuous rise in the global trading network is undeniably noteworthy. With the stagnation of the multilateral trade process, the number of FTAs has been increasing as it is relatively easier to negotiate for a smaller number of parties based on their shared interests and collaboration. This phenomenon can be well observed in China. Aside from its own BRI, which is being assertively promoted by President Xi Jinping, China also has a wide FTA network that further strengthens its sphere of influence. According to the Chinese government,[25] China regards FTAs as a new way to further open up its domestic market, integrate itself into the global economy, and strengthen its ties with other countries through economic cooperation.

Beijing seems to have learned how to strategically position itself when creating such agreements. This made China cement its status as the world's manufacturing hub and expand its access to more economies in the world. China has a total of 17 FTAs that have been signed and implemented already and 12 FTAs under negotiations and 8 FTAs under consideration. Once all of these are finalized, China will have a total of 37 FTAs. This number dwarfs the US, with 14 existing FTAs in terms of the number of FTAs.

As of 2021, the FTAs already signed and implemented are:

RCEP, China–Mauritius FTA, China–Maldives FTA, China–Georgia FTA, China–Australia FTA, China–Korea FTA, China–Switzerland FTA, China–Iceland FTA, China–Costa Rica FTA, China–Peru FTA, China–Singapore FTA, China–New Zealand FTA, China–Chile FTA, China–Pakistan FTA, China–ASEAN FTA, Mainland and Hong Kong Closer Economic and Partnership Arrangement, Mainland and Macau Closer Economic and Partnership Arrangement

The FTAs under negotiations are:

China–GCC (Gulf Cooperation Council) FTA, China–Japan–Korea FTA, China–Sri Lanka FTA, China–Israel FTA, China–Norway FTA, China–New Zealand FTA Upgrade, China–Moldova FTA, China–Panama FTA, China–Korea FTA second phase, China–Palestine FTA, China–Peru FTA Upgrade, China–Cambodia FTA

The FTAs under consideration with joint feasibility study are:

China–Colombia FTA, China–Fiji FTA, China–Nepal FTA, China–Papua New Guinea FTA, China–Canada FTA, China–Bangladesh FTA, China–Mongolia FTA, China–Switzerland FTA Upgrade

Let's look at three FTAs to have a better picture of China's FTA network. First, let us start with one of the latest FTAs signed between China and Mauritius. The China–Mauritius FTA was signed on October 17, 2019. The negotiations started in 2017, and it is the first trade agreement between China and an African country. It includes the zero imposition of tariffs on trade in goods, which reached 96.3% for China and 94.2% for Mauritius in the proportion of tax items. China mainly exports steel products, textiles, and other light industrial products, which will all benefit from this agreement. Mauritius will also be able to enter the Chinese market through its special sugar. For trade in services, both countries committed to open more than 100 sub-sectors. And regarding investments, both parties agreed to upgrade this FTA compared to the 1996 China–Mauritius bilateral investment protection agreement. This includes upgrades in terms of protection level and scope and dispute settlement mechanisms.

Second, we can look at the China–South Korea FTA, which was signed in 2015. It is regarded as more comprehensive compared to the other FTAs of China, but according to Wang (2016),[26] it still remains "relatively shallow" from a global perspective. This characteristic of China's FTA network will be further discussed in the latter part of this chapter. The China–South Korea FTA, upon entry into force of the agreement, eliminated tariff lines from 50% and 20% to 79% and 71%, within ten years. Since then, both countries became close trading partners, with China being the largest destination of export goods from Korea and Korea being the fourth-largest destination of Chinese export products. The trade agreement in the East Asia region is currently being pushed to greater heights through the China-Japan-Korea (CJK) FTA. In November 2019, the 16th round of negotiation was held in Seoul, but progress is slower than expected.

Lastly, there is the China–ASEAN FTA (CAFTA). CAFTA was the very first FTA signed by China, together with the ASEAN leaders, in 2002. It progressed to the signing of the Agreement on Trade in Goods of the CAFTA in 2005, the Agreement on Trade in Services in 2007, and the Agreement on Investment in 2009. The first stage with six signatories engaged in the elimination of tariffs on 90% of their goods by 2010. Aside from the fact that all ASEAN members are also part of the BRI, China's transformation into a global economic superpower led to an increase in foreign investment within the so-called bamboo network, which is the link between businesses operated by the overseas Chinese community in Southeast Asia. In 2015, CAFTA was upgraded; the upgrade covers goods, services, investment, and economic and technological cooperation.

4.2.2 Chronological Evolution

With China's accession to the WTO in 2001, its sense of regionalism greatly improved as it had closer access to the other nodes within the WTO network. The first trade agreements were signed in 2002 and 2003, with ASEAN, and its outlying regions, Macau, and Hong Kong, respectively. China's initial FTA strategy focused on local areas, as mentioned recently, and relatively smaller economies. Except for ASEAN, the first 12 FTAs by China are all with small trading partners. From 2005 onward, China concluded FTAs with more countries such as Chile in 2005; Pakistan in 2007; New Zealand and Singapore, respectively, in 2008; Peru in 2009; Costa Rica in 2010; Iceland and Switzerland, respectively, in 2013; Korea and Australia, respectively, in 2015; Georgia and Maldives in 2016; and the latest one, Mauritius, in 2019.

In the early stages of negotiating its FTAs, China started with goods and then services and investment. This strategy was used in the negotiations of the China–ASEAN FTA, CPFTA, and the China–Chile FTA. Both CAFTA and CPFTA started from an Early Harvest Scheme, which is a precursor to an FTA between two trading parties. This stage helps build confidence between the trading partners as they pinpoint the products for tariff liberalization before finalizing the terms of the FTA.

4.2.3 FTA Partner Selection Strategy

While it is difficult to identify the specific criteria that China looks for in an FTA partner, there are certain features that its FTA partners have in common: resource-rich, strategically important, and small countries but with open economies. First, China tends to establish partnerships with resource-rich countries. Australia, exporting a total of 53.7% of the world's iron ore supply, is a good example. Its iron ore trade with China, despite the tensions regarding Australia's call for the investigation of the origin of the coronavirus in April 2020, continues to expand as China's demand for steel increases due to its new infrastructure projects. Another example is Chile, which exports copper ore to China, making Beijing its largest export destination with a total value of $19.2 billion. This criterion can also include the cases of Georgia and Peru, as these countries are significant suppliers of other mineral ores to China. With these examples, we can see that even though China is known to be a major exporter and producer of the world, it also imports lots of primary inputs and raw materials.

The second criterion is the openness and strategic importance of a country. Mueller and Seabra (2019)[27] conducted research on the model determining the possibility of signing an FTA with China based on variables, namely, GDP, distance, Asian or non-Asian countries, number of RTAs (regional trade agreements), commodity imports, and foreign direct investment inflows and outflows. After testing the hypothesis with that model, the two authors suggested that the higher the number of existing FTAs a country has, the higher the likelihood of that country concluding an FTA with China. In reality, those having a big network of FTAs seem to be open economies that are willing to lower tariffs and non-tariff barriers to liberalize trade. Being an outsider of significant trade agreements in other regions, such as the EU, USMCA, and CPTPP, China has little or even no chance to join the trade pact or acquire market access preference; therefore, the country tends to partner with countries that have a high number of existing FTAs. Looking at the existing FTA partners of China, most of them participate in more than 10 FTAs. For instance, Chile has 11 FTAs, Australia and Costa Rica have 14, Korea has 15, Singapore has 25, and Switzerland has 31 free trade pacts with 41 partners. In other words, China tends to make FTAs with countries ready and willing to liberalize trade.

The last criterion is the smaller size of a country, with an open economy that can serve as a hub. Overall, we can see the nominal GDP of China's FTA partners is not huge. But if we look closely, most of these economies are also the most open in the world. Five FTA partners of China are also in the top five of the 2020 Index of Economic Freedom released by the Heritage Foundation, which are Singapore, Hong Kong, New Zealand, Australia, and Switzerland.[28] The effects of the FTAs are amplified in terms of market access and infrastructure, investment environment, enterprise conditions, and governance. This perfectly fits China's expansionary policies of spreading its industry and investments all over the world.

Three abovementioned selection criteria are demonstrated vividly in the China–Mauritius FTA. Mauritius is a small country located off the east coast of the African continent. The country has an advantage in such exports as sugar, fish, and clothes, while its main imported products are petroleum products, frozen fish, cars, medicaments, and radio transmission equipment. Trading relationship has been established between Mauritius and many partners over the world, namely, the EU, the US, India, China, and South Africa. Especially, China is the third-largest source of imports, accounting for 16.5% of the country's total imports in 2018.[29] There are three rationales that can be invoked for the signing of the China–Mauritius FTA in 2019. First, Mauritius possesses huge natural endowments for sugar and fishing, which makes the country a source of cheap primary products for China. Second, the country is a small but open economy proven by its open trading network with a variety of big countries. Third, Mauritius is a strategically important bridge between China and African countries. China–Mauritius FTA is just the beginning of the cooperation between China and the Africa Union, as well as the African Continental Free Trade Area (AfCFTA) spanning 55 nations with a combined GDP of US$3.4 trillion and about 1.3 billion consumers.[30] The huge Chinese investment in Africa under the BRI and the FTA signing with Mauritius, if successful, would be good examples of cooperation that drives other African countries' demands for having an FTA with China (an effect of the domino theory of regionalism developed by Baldwin [1997]).[31] Going back to the network theory, the more nodes attend in a network, the more powerful that network becomes. Trade and investment in the region would make China a significant partner for African countries and empower China's FTA network in the African continent.

However, besides the aforementioned three factors in the trade side, the political side of selecting FTA partners should be considered as well. It is obvious that China, the same as the US, is forming its own network to counter the influence from Washington. If we look at the countries within China's FTA network, none are strongly aligned with the US, with Australia being the only exception. Of course, it will be tough for China to forge an agreement with a country that is heavily leaning toward the US as there might be conflicting interests and political pressures that can hinder the process of reaping the benefits of an FTA.

Although these factors are not conclusive and do not apply to all FTA partners of China, it is undeniable that in some cases, these hypotheses make perfect sense. This is not surprising as it is rare for a market to sign into agreements with only unilateral benefits. Reciprocity is the number one factor as to why two countries would want to sign a trade agreement with each other. Without the mutual benefits that they will reap out of that deal, it is pointless to even think of starting one.

4.2.4 *Spaghetti Bowl Effect*

There are OTHER issues that need to be addressed to ensure the viability of China's FTA network. Eleven FTA partners are all in the Southeast/East Asia region. Although the trade costs might be low due to close proximity, this region is known to have overlapping trade agreements, which then results in a 'spaghetti bowl' effect. This is a side effect of any FTAs that might result in underutilization and inefficiency of the FTAs within the region.

According to Zhang and Shen (2013),[32] many companies might not even use these FTAs due to the differences in schedules of tariff phase-out, conflicting standards and rules of origin, and other inconvenient documents and red tapes. These FTAs, which were created to facilitate a stronger economic and commercial relationship between signing countries, are not being used to their maximum potential. The China–ASEAN FTA, with the highest usage rate out of all China's FTA networks, was only utilized by 29.6% of the 232 Chinese firms that were surveyed.

This underutilization of FTAs within China itself leads us to the next issue that might affect the viability of China's FTA networks. The failure of identification and application of these FTA preferential treatments often results in higher tax overhead cost that is much more than what the companies should have shouldered had they properly negotiated with the customs and tax offices in China. It was also mentioned that some of the consulting agencies purposely hide relevant data to keep those investors from acquiring interests outside of China's domestic markets.

These two issues can be regarded as the main roadblocks that challenge the viability of China's FTA network. We will talk more about it as we proceed with the overall assessment and future prospects of this FTA network.

4.2.5 Lack in Inner Networks?

The Chinese government is known for its strict media censorship, and that makes it difficult to know whether there are conflicts between the state and non-state actors within the country and how the domestic nodes respond to the growing FTA network of China.

There is an obvious asymmetry within China as the Chinese Communist Party (CCP) holds the monopoly of power in the country. According to the article written by Ball (2020),[33] the threats from ethnic, religious, and economically motivated groups make the CCP wary. Any economic disturbance or downturn could affect the public's trust in the party, and that might lead to political insurgencies. Through the years, Chinese leader Xi Jinping was able to concentrate power in the CCP, and this will make it difficult, if not impossible, for other domestic groups to form an inner network and express their sentiments against the negative impacts of some China's FTA agreements.

This lack of inner networks also causes China to have asymmetry problems with its current and possible trading partners. We can take China–South Korea FTA as an example. In 2014, a protest was widely reported in Seoul involving 5,000 farmers against the FTA, and at that time two parties were under FTA negotiation.[34] These farmers, mainly growing chili peppers, onions, and garlic, voiced their opposition to China's demand for the removal of tariffs on the said items. The possible surge of cheap farm goods grown in China definitely threatened the local farmers, especially the farmers in South Jeolla Province in Korea, as their major products were those included in this FTA. Although the FTA was eventually signed and implemented in 2015, the same concerns are present in other trading partners within China's FTA network.

This asymmetry in the internal consensus cultivating process was suggested by Heo (2013),[35] who stated that China and Korea are in opposite situations due to their different political systems. Compared to China's centralized government, Korea often faces difficulties with its internal nodes when the government tries to negotiate on external networking. Severe conflicts with domestic nodes can hinder the progress of FTAs that the government pursues and sometimes governments can end up withdrawing from the negotiation process altogether. However, the government can also utilize the local voices as an effective leverage in external negotiation to increase its bargaining power. In the future, the Chinese government will also inevitably face the growing pressures of domestic nodes on its policies. When the seemingly non-existent inner network of China and its inside nodes start to raise their own voices, the conflict between CCP and inner nodes can reach a new level of intensity.

4.2.6 Network Power

In this section, we will examine the standards of Chinese FTA networks, leading node, and entry barrier to properly assess the network's power. To identify the standard, let us look at the shared set of norms or practices that facilitates cooperation among the parties in these FTAs. On the one hand, although China is often believed to be only serving its self-interest, the USCC report (2020)[36] shows that China's cooperation and concession with its FTA networks have been quite positive. For example, China allowed each ASEAN member to set individual tariff schedules inside the FTA. China also opened up its agricultural imports and liberalized farm products despite possible opposition from domestic nodes. On the other hand, China usually starts its FTAs with a smaller scope and expands them when necessary. This makes its FTAs low in quality and narrow in scope. While the standard of China's FTA network is flexible enough to accommodate certain requests of its trading partners, Beijing also tends to stick with a narrower scope of product categories and carefully analyzes the situation to find out whether certain expansions are needed or not. It is also noted by Sampson (2019) that China's gradualist and minimalist approach with its FTAs allows the country to apply sticks and carrot based on the flows of negotiations or the strategic implications of the FTA itself.

When it comes to the leading node, out of all of its signed FTAs, it is obvious that China holds the upper hand. We cannot deny the fact that China's economic prowess gives it an advantage in negotiating with its trading partners. China also has the BRI that it can also use to further emphasize its role as the programmer and switcher within the network. It should be noted that out of its 16 FTA partners, only four countries are not members of the BRI, namely, Australia, Iceland, Mauritius, and Switzerland. Therefore, it is easy for China to influence the other FTAs and incorporate the strategies it has under the BRI.

As mentioned in the previous chapters, the entry barrier can be made either by the cost-benefit structure of the network or by the power that insiders within the network can exert over outsiders. China, being the world's largest exporter of goods since 2009, can be considered an inevitable trading partner. Therefore, being outside China's FTA network comes with several disadvantages such as limited access to Chinese market, retaliation on domestic firms operating in China, and military threat to FTA-defying countries.

China holds vast networking, network, networked, and network-making powers, as outlined by Castells (2011).[37] First, China's growing FTA network expands its networking power and thus increases the cost of exclusion, especially if we consider the synergistic effect of its own BRI. Second, China's network power is also strong, considering the fact that it has much influence that drives the direction of the FTA and also decides the rules of the agreements. Third, its networked power, at least in relation to its domestic nodes, is also quite exceptional that it often acts regardless of the opposition of other social actors, such as the case of the imports of agricultural goods from ASEAN that negatively affected the local farmers in China.

All of these easily make China a powerful node in its FTA networks. China has a vast supply chain with which it can easily push its FTA partners, and this gives it the ability to play the role of both the programmer and the switcher.

4.2.7 Network Structure and Communication Pattern

While China appears to hold a central position in most of its extended deals, in reality its *network of networks* would be considered complicated, due to the *spaghetti bowl* effect of its overlapping FTAs. As examples, we could use the coexistence of the China–ASEAN FTA (came into effect in 2005), China–Singapore FTA (came into effect in 2009), and the RCEP (signed in 2020). The sophistication of overlapping FTAs creates discrepancies in rules and regulations, which might confuse potential workers and executives.

Concerning the degree of centrality in Chinese networks, since the BRI started to cast its influence on foreign markets, China has become a high outdegree node when links are referred to as investment flows. BRI is estimated to add over 1 trillion USD of outward funding for foreign infrastructure in ten years from 2017 to 2027. Most of the Chinese funding for BRI projects comes from state-directed development and commercial banks, multilateral development banks, and private-public partnerships.[38] As of January 2021, BRI investments from China have reached 140 countries all around the world. Among the 140 countries, there are 40 countries in sub-Saharan Africa, 34 in Europe and Central Asia (including 18 EU countries), 25 in East Asia and Pacific, 18 in Latin America and the Caribbean, 17 in the Middle East and North Africa, and 6 Southeast Asian countries.[39] The BRI's history and development and other related issues will be discussed in more detail later in this book; however, a fact that needs to be emphasized is that China's BRI investment has become an irreplaceable source of not only infrastructure development but also economic and social development in many countries, especially in low- and middle-income economies. Through BRI projects, the relations between China and BRI partners have been improving and strengthening substantially.

On the other hand, China is also qualified as a high in-degree node in the FTA network, referring to one of the FTA partner selection criteria of rich resources. Since natural resources are essential for many pivotal emerging industries, China is increasingly dependent on imports of some minerals, for instance, 95% of chrome, 90% of cobalt, 79% of gold, 73% of copper, 73% of iron ore, and 67% of oil. Especially, China is the largest consumer of iron ore in the world. Its iron ore imports grew sharply from 2016 and reached a 20-year peak in October 2021 at above 16 million USD monthly.[40] With the inflows of natural resources from partner countries to China increasing in value, the linkage between China strengthens, which turns China into an in-degree node.

Considering the aforementioned information, we can infer that China and its FTA partners have a certain degree of interdependence, thanks to the outflows of investment and inflows of resources. However, a huge trade deficit with China prevents the possibility of other nodes staying close to China in a same network. A piece of unequivocal evidence is the China–India relation under RCEP. As we have pointed out in the previous section, India decided to opt out of RCEP for the sake of its domestic factors. In 2017, India's trade deficit with the RCEP nations was $105 billion, of which China accounted for $54 billion, more than 50% of the entire amount of deficit from India–RCEP trade. It was the fear of excessive trade liberalization leading to more severe trade deficits with China and other countries that forced India to walk away from RCEP and maintain a safe distance (by trade barriers) with China.

The communication pattern of China's FTA network can be regarded as *relational* and not *affiliational*, as FTAs are often defined by rules driven by the presence, direction, and immensity of the relationship between the two parties. Even though the standard of this network is characterized by China's willingness to accommodate requests from its FTA partners, it is undeniable that the factors mentioned earlier play a part in defining the rules of the network. For example, Pakistan is known to be one of China's closest allies. Based on the report by China Briefing, the trade volume between the two countries, which amounted to $13.2 billion or 16.4% of Pakistan's trade volume in 2018 (China Briefing, 2020),[41] shows the magnitude of the China-Pakistan relationship and how it affects the CPFTA. In fact, the original CPFTA, which was signed in 2006, underwent the second phase of negotiations from 2011 and was concluded in April 2019. The upgraded agreement introduces a new tariff elimination schedule and widens access to each other's markets. In addition, it includes new safeguard measures to protect the domestic industry. The relational communication pattern can be clearly seen in this regard.

The relational structure – except for the China-ASEAN FTA, which includes all ten ASEAN member states – of the rest of the FTAs under China's network can be regarded as bilateral, as the agreements were discussed and concluded between two parties in the context of economic interests. China is regarded as a newcomer as it only created its first agreements in the early 2000s, but since then, it obviously played a more active role in expanding its network through these bilateral FTAs.

More than that, China mixes financial assistance with relational communication patterns in bilateral FTAs to build a close and tight hub-and-spoke network with its partners. China has positively participated in foreign aid campaigns to different countries and regions around the world. Especially, the establishment of the BRI is a flagship under which China conducted financial assistance in the form of grants, interest-free, or concessional (low-interest rate) loans to developing or least developed countries.[42] China's financial assistance is used to promote poverty alleviation, infrastructure, and industry development, which then helps China to gain an extremely important role in the economic development progress of those countries. Taking the Sino-Africa relationship as an example, China is not only the largest trading partner but also an important source of investment and financial assistance for Africa. China had helped African countries to build more than 6,000 km of railways, a similar amount of roads, nearly 20 ports, more than 80 large-scale power plants, 130-plus medical facilities, 45 stadiums, about 170 schools, and also, the new headquarters of the Africa Centers for Disease Control and Prevention. Recently, the country also promised to offer cash assistance and capacity-building training to the secretariat of the newly founded African Continental Free Trade Area. Apparent is the fact that China's great support for Africa has provided the country with an integral role in the development path of each African country and the process of regionalism among them. However, behind those commitments is the desire of China to make African countries more dependent on the Chinese economy, to tie them and the AfCFTA as spokes around the hub – China – and bolster the growth of China's FTA network.

4.2.8 Characteristics of China's FTA Network

China's FTA network has two distinct characteristics. The first one was mentioned earlier, *gradualist*. In comparison, US FTAs are wider and more comprehensive. As opposed to the US, China often starts with a narrower scope of products and gradually expands it as the FTA progresses. One example is the China–Swiss FTA, wherein 40% of the total Swiss machine tools volume did not benefit from tariff exemptions. This made Swiss exporters upset, and although China committed to lower textile tariffs by 99%, only 1.3% of all Swiss products that entered the Chinese market benefited. It was also mentioned in the first section how the China–South Korea FTA was the most comprehensive one among the other FTAs by China when it was signed, yet it was still considered shallow compared to other global agreements.

Second, China's FTAs can be regarded as *shallow*. According to Sampson (2019),[43] Beijing has pushed for agreements that involved limited liberalization that was subsequently expanded over many years in numerous negotiation rounds. The cooperation, through time, will make China and its partners become more economically interdependent. China is among the most important export destinations to them, especially for agriculture and natural resources;

meanwhile, China is the main exporter of machinery and electronic components for the partner countries. As a consequence of the interdependence, China improves its bargaining position over time in trade deals and pushes for a higher liberalization rate. For example, the liberalization rate of CPFTA was raised from 35% (Phase-I, 2007) to 75% (Phase-II, 2019) after 13 years of FTA implementation.[44] Furthermore, based on the USCC report, China usually sticks with the same agreements it had during the time it joined the WTO and does not try to pursue more advanced provisions. In other cases, it tends to completely remove advanced provisions or restrict them by not including detailed legal language or utilizing other documents such as a memorandum of understanding. After establishing some sort of economic interdependence, China takes advantage of it by negotiating for higher but still shallow commitments.

These characteristics can be attributed to China's FTA strategy, which is unorthodox. In the next section, we will talk about the overall assessment of China's FTA network and pinpoint the issues it must resolve to ensure a more stable future regarding trade.

4.2.9 Assessment and Prospects

Without a doubt, China's FTA network is a force to be reckoned with considering its sheer size and economic value. Its FTA network has grown, and in just a short amount of time, China managed to expand it exponentially. This alone increases the insecurity being felt by the US. With the ongoing trade war between China and the US, it is not surprising to see China further expand its FTA networks, alongside its already extensive BRI. Given China's huge market and production/investment capacity, we can expect more countries to join China's bandwagon, especially now that the COVID pandemic is currently wreaking havoc on the global economy. Smaller nodes will be needing investment support from China more than ever. Those countries will surely be in need of foreign investments to save their economies and keep them from falling apart.

Despite its popularity, China should be keen on addressing the issues that we have identified earlier when we talked about the viability of its FTA network. First, China should be more cooperative in working with the leaders of Asian countries to be able to consolidate the overlapping FTAs, or in other words, the spaghetti bowl effect. Creating one regional agreement that streamlines the redundant FTAs will greatly increase the effectiveness and efficiency of these agreements, and it can also increase the utilization rate by the firms within those countries. RCEP, which is the last FTA signed by China, is a great network that can be utilized to mitigate the effects of these overlapping FTAs. But then again, the withdrawal of India exposed the challenges faced by this multilateral network, and it is a reminder that all parties must be willing to compromise, especially regarding politically driven agendas, in order to make RCEP stronger and more substantial. Moreover, without India, the communication patterns tend to be more unilateral and asymmetric, centering upon a few leading nodes. For instance, Japan and China alone represent 61% of RCEP's GDP, and around 68% if India is excluded (Wardani and Cooray, 2019).[45] As we already mentioned in previous chapters, we can conclude that RCEP is necessary but insufficient to accelerate the trade and investment liberalization in the region.

The consequent economic interdependence that could spark from the regional trade arrangement might translate into a better political and economic relationship between these economic giants.[46] However, many problems need to be addressed. One of those would be the ongoing trade relationship between Japan and the US. Specifically, the USMCA contains a clause that limits Canada and Mexico from making trade ties with 'non-market economies.'[47] Such a limitation encapsulates the US strategy toward the formation of an 'anti-China' bloc and could define how much Japan–China integration will be achieved through RCEP. Although there are no similar clauses in the recent US-Japan trade negotiations except the negotiation objectives of USTR,[48] it is certainly a matter that has to be considered while making predictions toward future trade relationships in the Pacific area. Generally, we can say that in RCEP some low-hanging fruits will be tackled by cuttings tariffs, but many non-tariff barrier issues are still not addressed, making the trade agreement not as effective as it could be.

The second issue that we mentioned is something that only China can fix internally. The domestic actors' lack of knowledge about the said FTAs prevents China's FTA network from being maximized. The Chinese government also needs to identify the domestic consulting agencies that intentionally deprive the investment companies of such information because of their own self-interests. This is harder to address, as collusion motivates the agencies to hide the information from the trading corporations in order to focus on the domestic market only. Until these issues are properly taken care of, China's FTA network will remain huge, only by size but not by its real utilization and effectiveness.

To wrap up this section and tie it back with our analysis using the network theory, I would like to remind the readers of what Grewal (2008) mentioned in his book on how a network, with an already sizable membership, can maximize its power.[49] First, the network should have maximal availability, which pertains to the ease of joining the network for new entrants and adopting its standards. Second, the network should have maximal incompatibility, which means that someone can use either Standard A or Standard B, but not both simultaneously. Lastly, the network should have a low degree of malleability, which means the network's standard should not be easily revised by other players. If we think about these criteria, it can be said that China, through its FTAs and other mediums such as the BRI, is aiming to check all the boxes for maximizing its overall network power. China is clearly configuring these network properties for its network to become the most dominant in the world.

Notes

1 The Office of the United States Trade Representative (USTR), Free Trade Agreements. https://ustr.gov/trade-agreements/free-trade-agreements.
2 Lighthizer, R. (2020), USMCA, Replacing NAFTA Today, Is the Model for All Future Trade Agreements, *Triblive* (July 1, 2020).

3 It is not far-fetched to think that Canada and Mexico had more interest in keeping terms previously agreed to in NAFTA than to shift their trade terms toward China. See USMCA trade pact: for Canada and Mexico, throwing China under bus was a no-brainer, *South China Morning Post* (October 6, 2018).

4 More details can be found in the article written by the CATO Institute. See Lester, S., Manak, I. and Kim, K. (2019), *Trump's First Trade Deal: The Slightly Revised Korea-U.S. Free Trade Agreement,* Free Trade Bulletin No. 73, Washington, DC: CATO Institute.

5 Cha, V. (2018), *KORUS Revision: Not the Worst Outcome,* Washington, DC: Center for Strategic & International Studies (CSIS).

6 The Office of the United States Trade Representative (USTR) (2019), U.S.-Japan Trade Agreement Text. https://ustr.gov/countries-regions/japan-korea-apec/japan/us-japan-trade-agreement-negotiations/us-japan-trade-agreement-text.

7 Cimino-Isaacs, C. and Williams, B. (2020), U.S.-Japan Trade Agreement Negotiations, Informing the Legislative Debate since 1914, *Congressional Research Service (CRS)* IF11120.

8 Destler, I. (2016), America's Uneasy History with Free Trade, *Harvard Business Review* (April 28, 2016).

9 World Bank Data, Exports of Goods and Services (% of GDP) - United States, https://data.worldbank.org/indicator/NE.EXP.GNFS.ZS?end=2018&locations=US&start=2001.

10 Council of Economic Advisors (2015), Economic Report of the President, February 2015, p. 390.

11 U.S. Government Accountability Office (GAO) (2004), International Trade: Intensifying Free Trade Negotiating Agenda Calls for Better Allocation of Staff and Resources, GAO-04-233.

12 Freud, C. and McDaniel, C. (2016), *How Long Does It Take to Conclude a Trade Agreement With the US?,* Trade and Investment Policy Watch, Washington, DC: Peterson Institute for International Economics (PIIE).

13 Jackson, J. (2018), U.S. Trade with Free Trade Agreement (FTA) Partners, *Congressional Research Service (CRS),* R44044.

14 The US also vetoed over the election of the new WTO Director-General, rejecting the nomination of Nigeria's Ngozi Okonjo-Iweala.

15 Citizens Trade Campaign (2016), Over 1,500 Organizations Urge Opposition to the TPP. http://tradeforpeopleandplanet.org/wp-content/uploads/2016/01/.

16 Nienaber, M. (2016), Tens of Thousands Protest in Europe against Atlantic Free Trade Deals, *Reuters* (September 17, 2016).

17 George, E. (2013), *Trading in Peace and Conflict: Colombian Farmers and the U.S. Free Trade Agreement,* Center for Global Justice, Quinney College of Law, Retrieved from https://law.utah.edu/trading-in-peace-and-conflict-colombian-farmers-and-the-u-s-free-trade-agreement/

18 Office of the United States Trade Representative (USTR) (2019), FACT SHEET on U.S.-Japan Digital Trade Agreement.

19 Castells, M. (2011), A Network Theory of Power, *International Journal of Communication,* 5, pp. 773–787.

20 Schott, J. (2004), *Assessing US FTA Policy, Free Trade Agreements: US Strategies and Priorities,* Washington, DC: Peterson Institute for International Economics (PIIE).

21 The hub-and-spoke nature of some FTA systems appears to be 'creating trade' and involves a set of countries connected by a network of FTAs passing through the 'hub,' or the country that shares some overlapping FTAs. For more details, see, Hur, J., Alba, J. D. and Park, D. (2010), Effects of Hub-and-Spoke Free Trade Agreements on Trade: A Panel Data Analysis, *World Development,* 38(8), pp. 1105–1113.

22 Schott, J. (2004), Ibid.

23 As previously mentioned, the four types of power are networking power, network power, networked power, and network-making power. For more details, see Castells, M. (2011), Ibid.

24 Biden, J. (2020), Why America Must Lead Again: Rescuing U.S. Foreign Policy after Trump, *Foreign Affairs*, 99(2), 64–76.

25 Ministry of Commerce, PRC, China FTA Network, http://fta.mofcom.gov.cn/english/index.shtml.

26 Wang, H. (2016), The Features of China's Recent FTA and Their Implications: An Anatomy of the China-Korea FTA, *Asian Journal of WTO & International Health Law and Policy*, 11, p. 115.

27 Müller, M. and Seabra, F. (2019), Partner Country Choices in China's Free Trade Agreements, *The Chinese Economy*, 52(3), 263–278.

28 Heritage.org. (2020), 2020 Index of Economic Freedom, https://www.heritage.org/index/.

29 Societe Generale (2020), Country risk of Mauritius: International Trade.

30 Nyabiage, J. (2020), China-Africa Relations: Beijing Says It Will Help Pay for World's Largest Free-Trade Zone, *South China Morning Post* (November 13, 2020).

31 Baldwin, R. (1997), The Causes of Regionalism. *The World Economy*, 20(7), pp. 865–888.

32 Zhang, Y. and Shen, M. (2013), FTAs in the Asia-Pacific: A Chinese Perspective, *Kokusai Mondai (International Affairs)*, No.622.

33 Ball, J. (2020), The Chinese Communist Party's Biggest Fears Are Separatism and an Economic Crisis, *Global Security Review*. Retrieved from https://globalsecurityreview.com/threats-legitimacy-power-chinese-communist-party/

34 Yonhap News Agency (2014), Farmers protest China FTA in Seoul, *YNA* (July 10, 2014).

35 Heo, Y. (2013), The Tiger Meets the Dragon: The Political Economy of Korea-China FTA, *International Studies Review*, 14(1), pp. 125–154.

36 USCC (2020), Annual Report to Congress, US-China Economic and Security Review Commission.

37 Castells, M. (2011), A Network Theory of Power, *International Journal of Communication*, 5, pp. 773–787.

38 OCED (2018), The Belt and Road Initiative in the Global Trade, Investment and Finance Landscape, *OECD Business and Finance Outlook 2018*.

39 Nedopil, C. (2021), Countries of the Belt and Road Initiative, IIGF Green BRI Center, Central University of Finance and Economics.

40 Trading Economics, China Imports of Iron Ores & Concentrate. 2000–2020 Data. https://tradingeconomics.com/china/imports-of-iron-ores-concentrate.

41 Wong, D. (2020), China-Pakistan FTA Phase-II: Reduced Tariffs, New Safeguard Measures, *China Briefing*. Retrieved from https://www.china-briefing.com/news/china-pakistan-fta-phase-2-reduced-tariffs-safeguard-measures-introduced/

42 Lynch, L., Andersen, S. and Zhu, T. (2020), China's Foreign Aid: A Primer for Recipient Countries, Donors, and Aid Providers, Center for Global Development, CGD Note, Washington, DC: Center for Global Development.

43 Sampson, M. (2019), The Evolution of China's Regional Trade Agreements: Power Dynamics and the Future of the Asia-Pacific, *The Pacific Review*.

44 Pakistan Department of Commerce (2020), China-Pakistan FTA (CPFTA) Phase II.

45 Wardani, R. and Cooray, N. (2019), Saving Potential of Regional Comprehensive Economic Partnership (RCEP): Implication for China and Japan. *Journal of Economic Info*, 6(1), p. 41.

46 Ibid., pp. 35–37.

47 The clause can be found in Chapter 32, article 10. Full text available at: https://ustr.gov/trade-agreements/free-trade-agreements/united-states-mexico-canada-agreement/agreement-between.

48 Tran, H. (2019), US-Japan Trade Negotiations: A Narrow Scope Is Key to Success, Washington, DC: Atlantic Council. Retrieved from https://www.atlanticcouncil.org/blogs/new-atlanticist/us-japan-trade-negotiations-a-narrow-scope-is-key-to-success/

49 Grewal, D. (2008), *Network Power: The Social Dynamics of Globalization*, New Haven: Yale University Press, pp. 172–179.

5 The Ultimate Winner?

The US-Led vs. the China-Led Network

In this chapter, we examine the US-led network (represented by the series of linkages with US allies under the Trump administration and possible projects that the Biden administration would be likely to pursue) and the Belt and Road Initiative (BRI) led by China. Even though the BRI results look to be more extensive and successful than any potential plan led by the US, we will take a look at how network theory can be applied to better understand the development and scope of networks tailor-made by leading nodes like the US and China. Moreover, while introducing both the aforementioned networks, we will examine the connections between them and other related agreements and regional trade agreements (RTAs) of the US and China. The implications derived from the successful introduction of enormous trade agreements like the Regional Comprehensive Economic Partnership (RCEP) have indeed a big influence on these plurilateral alliances and the intra-trade relationships ensuing among member countries. Using network theory, we can individuate such connections and trade mechanisms used in the upcoming bipolar equilibrium.

5.1 The US-Led Network: Options and Development

5.1.1 The US-Led Network in the Pre-Biden Era

We now consider the position of the most powerful economy in the world at present, focusing on the network based on *like-minded* countries and nodes. To better understand the possible directions that the Democratic administration will be taking, it is important to trace back the recent US foreign policy and its strategy in countering the rise of China as a possible hegemonic competitor. This network can be well summarized by the Economic Prosperity Network (EPN), which could have represented a possible base on which further foreign policies could be built on.

Specifically, EPN was initiated by the US Department of State in November 2019. According to Keith Krach,[1] the undersecretary of state for economic growth, EPN is depicted as an alliance of *trusted partners* in which like-minded countries, companies, and civil society groups are involved. Network members operate under a set of trusted principles governing integrity, accountability,

DOI: 10.4324/9781003305705-5

respect for rule of law, respect for the sovereignty of nations, and respect for the property of all kinds, for the planet, for human rights, and transparency. Almost all aspects of economic collaboration are taken into consideration under EPN, namely, commerce, trade, supply chain, investment, energy, digital, infrastructure, health care, education, and research.

In accordance with the initiative, the US embarked on the establishment of EPN with Britain, Canada, and Japan as key members and then added France, Germany, and Italy of the Group of 7. Besides, the role of Latin American countries was expected in supporting US companies to move their production out of China and relocate it closer to home. One salient point of the membership condition was that network members need to agree not to allow their economies to become excessively entangled with the adversaries of America and the West, in particular, China, Russia, the Islamic Republic of Iran, and North Korea.

The network marks an attempt by the Trump administration to reduce the reliance of US strategic supply chains on China for pharmaceuticals, sensitive technology, weapons systems, public health products, and national security. Along with threatening new tariffs of up to 25% on $370 billion in Chinese goods, the turbocharging of EPN was among actions taken by the US to punish China for being the origin of the COVID-19 outbreak, damaging maritime security in the South China Sea and violating human rights in Hong Kong and Xinjiang Uygur Autonomous Region.

5.1.2 *The EPN under Trump Administration*

As clarified in this study, the power of a network is defined by two parameters: the number of network members and the effects of coordination. The exact number of EPN participants remained obscure, but as stated by Mike Pompeo, the former secretary of state, the US government tried to work with Australia, India, Japan, New Zealand, Korea, and Vietnam to "move the global economy forward."[2] Most of the potential nation-states involved in EPN, specified in the previous section, are strategic partners of the US in political, military, and economic areas and have an intense diplomatic relationship with the country. In light of what the US had done with Mexico and Canada during negotiations for the US–Mexico–Canada Agreement (USMCA) trilateral agreement, it is likely that Trump's government wanted to continue to exert its sphere of influence on other countries' decisions to go for or against EPN.

Some countries already set up their own plans to promote reshoring and mitigate the over-concentration on the China market, which is called the *China plus One* strategy. For instance, the Japanese government prepared a budget of 220 billion yen to support firms that shift their production back home and 23.5 billion yen for those that relocate it to countries other than China.[3] As a consequence of the COVID-19 pandemic, Japanese firms realized that the over-reliance on a specific market would be extremely risky in the case of lockdown and started to reconsider the supply chains' optimal location. The case of Japan reflects the harmonization of the inner network with the government's outer network policies. Taiwan shares a similar sentiment with Japan when offering rent assistance, cheap finance, tax breaks, and simplified administration for investments in order to encourage a *non-red supply chain* outside of China.[4] The escalation of political and military tensions makes Taiwan's actions against China to be even stronger as Xi Jinping's government is threatening to invade Taiwan aiming at 'reunification' of all Chinese territories. Besides, Australia stands on the opposite side of China in the confrontation over COVID-19. Despite the dependence of one-third of the country's merchandise and services exports on China, the Australian Prime Minister wrote to leaders of G20, about two weeks after a phone call with the US president, to push for the investigation on the contagion's origin and China's responsibility.[5] Those pieces of evidence prove that there is an intrinsic reason, the compatibility in the direction of networks and members, that makes them ready to join America's anti-China initiative.

Meanwhile, the network forces some other partners to face the dilemma of choosing between Washington and Beijing. For instance, Korea is now standing between its strongest military or economic partner – the US, who maintains troops and military officials in Korean territory to defend against North Korea's aggression – and its biggest trade partner – China, who accounted for 25.9% of total exports and 21% of the total imports of Korea in 2018.[6] While China called for Korea's *proper adjustment* on the potentials of EPN, the US emphasized the importance of the US-Republic of Korea economic cooperation and promised to protect the country from any threats and retaliatory actions from China, which would result from Korea's decision to join the EPN.[7] Encountering a nettlesome diplomatic challenge, Korea and other countries should be deliberate in choosing which side to stand on.

On the other hand, the strength of linkages among vertices within a network is defined by the standard. A scrutiny of the trusted principles of EPN, which is called *American values* (in the US) and *democratic values* (in Europe), shows the expected behaviors of network members, namely, integrity, accountability, transparency, and respect for other nations' values. Yet, the answer to the question about what the shared values of the network are remains obscure, as *against China* or *supply chain without China* cannot be the answer. The connection between EPN's standards and the goal of trade liberalization is tenuous, because EPN is designed as an alliance rather than an FTA or a plan for regional integration. The US, leader of the network, had been applying the *America First* strategy as part of Trump's economic policies, including trade protectionism and immigration restrictions. And the EPN foundation is believed to be a part of the strategy, which will help break China's global dominance and promote the reshoring of American companies back to their home country. Given the current trade policies and intentions of the EPN initiator, it is only logical that the term *free trade* was not mentioned anywhere in the network's standard.

While shared values and gains from EPN were vague, losses suffered by countries and multinational companies are quite visible. The significance of China in the global market is undeniable, as it overtook the world's top manufacturing country from the US in 2010, accounting for a hefty 35% of global manufacturing output and 30% of worldwide consumption in 2019 (CNBC, 2020).[8] Cutting supply chains with China requires an enormous amount of capital and time to relocate production facilities (back to home or to another country), source raw materials and human resources, and apply new strategies to adjust to new business environments. Enterprises will also face losses from diseconomies of scale, a shrink in market size, and certainly, retaliation from the Chinese government, especially in the context of the COVID-19 outbreak, where lockdown policy results in the postponement and interruption of production and disruption of supply chains throughout the world and eventually to a low level of cash flow in almost all economic fields. Hence, *shifting* or *decoupling* supply chains out of China is definitely not a simple movement for any parties and might cause considerable losses. Availability of a rich pool of skilled labor, increasing brand value of *Made in USA* (instead of *Made in China*), and government's incentives for reshoring companies are well recognized by the global firms. However, China still offers an efficient manufacturing base and an attractive (potential) market.

The future direction of EPN has not been declared clearly by the new Biden government. Strong participation in this *anti-China* network would surely bolster the legacy of the Trump administration, but changes by President Biden might halt the effectiveness and scope of such a bloc. It is more than likely that this Democratic presidency will have to review this project carefully, deciding whether to keep the project going as it is, make some changes to better fit its agenda, or push for a different approach altogether with major allies.

The coming into force of EPN would cause a strong impact on the global trading system. The world would be separated into different groups: pro-China, anti-China, and neutral. As a result, existing free trade areas no longer are mutually exclusive since over-dependence on China's economy is not permitted in the EPN. Existing trade pacts where both China and anti-China countries are members might be pushed to the verge of a breakdown or even collapse. The advent of trade barriers, trade wars, and retaliations is also expected among two opposing groups of nations.

5.1.3 Network Structure

In consonance with the types of orders presented by Mearsheimer (2019),[9] EPN could be defined as a bounded liberal order. EPN aimed to include most of the world's great powers, to name only a few, the US, the UK, Japan, Germany, France, etc. Among them, the US is the unipole leading the network. EPN's goal was to foster cooperation among countries sharing common interests and help them to reach agreements. Moreover, the unipole in EPN – the US – professed an anti-China ideology and tried to propagate its ideology widely among its allies and partners in EPN and eventually aimed to make the world in its own image.

The phenomenon of issue linkage, or intertwining of trade and non-trade issues, appeared in EPN. Besides moving the global supply chain out of China, EPN covered other non-trade issues, including cybersecurity, especially in the fifth-generation (5G) technology era. In a teleconference conducted by the US Department of State's Asia-Pacific Media Hub, US undersecretary Keith Krach declared Huawei and ZTE, both Chinese telecommunications equipment companies, as 'untrusted vendors.'[10] Since 5G data plays an integral part in both national and global economic security, he called all of the US allies and partners to join the 5G Clean Path, which "does not use any 5G transmission control, computing or storage equipment from an untrusted vendor and block their ability to siphon sensitive information into the hands of the People's Republic of China." From this point, the American-led EPN does not only aim to block China's growing power in the trading realm but also in a wide variety of non-trade spheres.

Going beyond EPN and the network boundaries set by its framework, we can look at the development of a democratic-led presidency from 2021. According to both defensive and offensive realism, and as mentioned by Zhang (2020),[11] the anarchic order will put constraints on a single leader's behavior and decisions and "force states, especially the great powers, to put a premium on their relative power and influences over rival great powers," making it difficult to significantly change the foreign policy of a country in a limited amount of time. Indeed, the rivalry between the US and China will most likely persist, not only because of the US role as the leader of an anti-China Network (not only represented by the values embedded in the EPN but also by the linkages that the US has made with all its allies) but also because of Biden's positions itself, focusing on his *Buy America and Hire America* and *Build Back Better* plan and his idea about "uniting the economic might of democracies around the world to counter abusive economic practices."[12]

Independently from Biden's specific approach and whether he will push for more alliances in the Asia-Pacific or whether he will seek advantageous partnerships over the Atlantic, the US will keep trying to preserve its position as the leading node and central point of an anti-China network, defining the rules and capitalizing on its position to rearrange its allies' positions and demonstrating its full capabilities when it comes to networking power, network power, networked power, and network-making power.

5.1.4 Strategic Options and Future Directions

Trump's foreign policy toward China was developed around the strategy that brought EPN to light: his efforts were focused on limiting the opposition's available moves, damaging their maneuverability while trying to create a network of like-minded parties that could align their efforts and create an anti-China barrier. The effectiveness of this project, as we mentioned, could be debatable but could be possible now that a new president is set to lead the White House with a new set of rules and topics.

First, we cannot dismiss the possibility of President Biden retrieving EPN, and transforming it into his own version of a like-minded network created ad hoc to counterbalance China's progress. We already analyzed the EPN in its previous form, but the future prospect will surely include a new, EPN-like, set of alliances that are most likely to be extended all over the Atlantic and the Pacific alike. Indeed, during the 2021 G7 meeting, Biden ended up proposing and backing up a new plan to fight China's BRI (Wintour, 2021).[13]

Second, what are the relations of the past network-based foreign policy with other external extensive networks? Are there implications among common parties involved in deals such as the Comprehensive and Progressive Agreement for Trans-Pacific Partnership (CPTPP)? As mentioned above, it is clear that, in general, the US strategy cannot be taken as a stand-alone approach toward the China–America hegemonic competition. The American involvement in the Quad, Japan's leadership of the CPTPP, and a possible move of the US toward the original Trans-Pacific Partnership (TPP) are all events that have to be mentioned and addressed in order to better understand what the options for the Biden administration would be.

The two *external networks* we just presented, FOIPI (as exemplified by IPEF) and CPTPP, together with the Atlantic alliance could represent the starting points of Joe Biden's new policy and approach to the hegemonic competition with China. As we mentioned, his stance toward America's main rival will most likely be aligned with Donald Trump's, meaning that even though the details may vary, the aggressive general stance, at the core, will be maintained. Gift (2020)[14] does underline the key difference – Biden will not adopt a *go-to-alone* approach but will opt for a more inclusive one, seeking more global partners to gather enough strength to accomplish what Trump was not able to do using only the America's limited resources: block China's hegemonic rise on its own. Of course, depending on which countries the US would prefer to include as favored partners, a different strategy might be used, but following our previous analysis of the EPN and some of the related external networks, we can identify three possible main courses of actions: an extended and strengthened Indo-Pacific Initiative, a newly organized *anti-BRI* network, and a more inclusive CPTPP.

5.1.4.1 Indo-Pacific Initiative

The Quadrilateral Security Dialogue (as known as the Quad) consisting of the US, Japan, India, and Australia was founded in 2007.[15] The group was originally called *Tsunami Core Group*, an informal group sharing the common interest of disaster relief. Later, it was considered an enlarged version of the US-India Malabar naval exercise series and was projected to become a security alliance among four nations. However, at the point of formalizing the dialogue, Australia preferred Quad to cover only trade and culture issues; Japanese Prime Minister Abe resigned from the office, and India faced protests against Malabar 07-02 (naval exercise of the Quad and Singapore). All those differences in the outlook distanced the dialogue. A decade later, Quad was resumed with a new name of Quad 2.0, alongside the development of the FOIPI. The initiative was presented for the first time by President Trump during his visit to five Asian countries (Japan, Korea, China, Vietnam, and the Philippines) in November 2017.

FOIPI, a rule-based order, is proposed as a focal point of the US Asian policy as the Trump administration regards Indo-Pacific as a key diplomatic and economic area to deal with China. In the term *free and open*, free stands for the 'freedom to exercise sovereignty without interference by other states,' while open refers to 'the free access to international water, airspace, and digital space, as well as open access to markets and fair, reciprocal trade.' The strategy adopted is based on four points: (1) respect for sovereignty and independence of all nations; (2) peaceful resolution of disputes; (3) free, fair, and reciprocal trade based on open investment, transparent agreements, and connectivity; and (4) adherence to international law, including freedom of navigation and overflight.[16] The US strategic initiative enhances economic prosperity and supports reform toward citizen-responsive governance, which ensures peace and security, and facilitates investment in human capital. Particularly, in enhancing economic prosperity under the FOIPI, improving the market access and level of playing field for US businesses, strengthening business ties in the region, and promoting free, fair, and reciprocal trade are the three main purposes of the USA. A standard has been established to govern *fair* and *reciprocal* trade relations, including respect for intellectual property rights, free trade and protection of private property, fair competition, and open markets.[17] Besides, following the announcement of then-US secretary of state Mike Pompeo, the US promised to make a contribution of 113 million US dollars to support the foundational areas for the future: digital economy, energy, and infrastructure in small countries. Regarding the security and military realms, $300 million in new security funding were pledged to Indo-Pacific countries to counter transnational threats arising in relation to the Chinese militarization of the South China Sea.[18] All in all, FOIPI can be viewed as a rival of China's BRI. It preceded sub-networks like Five Eyes and AUKUS. The two main differences between FOIPI and BRI are (1) investment value in the former is still much smaller than that of the latter (1 trillion US dollars) and (2) the communication mode and goal of the former is relatively *affiliational* for seeking *partnerships*, while in the latter case, the mode is *relational* for pursuing *domination*.

It might seem like a contradiction has arisen between the ideas of trade policy under the FOIPI and the *America First* strategy. Yet, the contradiction fails to materialize when we scrutinize US actions with bilateral partners. From the perspective of the US, the renegotiation of KORUS FTA (2018), the signing of the US–Japan Trade Agreement and Digital Trade Agreement (2019), and the granting of Strategic Trade Authorization Tier 1 status to India aim to eliminate or reduce tariff barriers on US products, protect jobs in American industries, increase US export volume, and boost the trade between two countries. And as mentioned in the previous paragraph, promoting the investment of American private companies in the emerging markets is one of the priorities of the US in its Indo-Pacific strategy. Considering all that evidence, a conclusion can be drawn that promoting free, fair, and reciprocal trade under the FOIPI mainly aims to create preferential opportunities for American enterprises and to amplify the importance of the American economy in the strategic region; thus, FOIPI does not digress from the basic direction of the *America First* strategy. It reflects the consistency in the multilayered decision-making process of the US at the international–regional–national level.

Other Quad nations are making great contributions to the FOIPI, the alternative to China's BRI, as a means of confronting China's militarization in the South China Sea. Besides the US, Japan is another active factor in the network. Together, the two countries play the important role of programmers (who generate standards to share among factors), players (who set goals), and switchers (who link the nodes) in the FOIPI. It should be noted that there are several similarities between Japan and the US strategies in the Indo-Pacific region. Japan's strategy focuses on three connectivities, namely, physical (quality infrastructure), people-to-people (education, training, and friendship), and institutional (harmonization and common rules including through EPA/FTA). The country earmarked $200 billion for Quality Infrastructure projects of roads, railways, ports, and terminals construction in Mozambique, Madagascar, Mumbai, Bangladesh, Myanmar, Vietnam, Laos, Cambodia, etc. They also donated coast guard patrol boats to Sri Lanka, Vietnam, and the Philippines.[19]

Australia is also taking part in infrastructure initiatives with the US and Japan (Blue Dot Initiative). In contrast to China's BRI, the trilateral infrastructure cooperation emphasizes the standard of quality, transparency, sustainability, private-sector involvement, and debt avoidance. In addition, the *New Colombo Plan* has been carried out by Australia since 2014, which commits Australian human resources to study and work in 40 countries in the Indo-Pacific region.

India's strategy is biased toward security cooperation. Though the country claims to seek a free trade agreement in the Indo-Pacific, it opted out of RCEP to protect the domestic market. And they are not participating in the Blue Dot Initiative with three other Quad nations. On the other hand, ministerial-level 2+2 meetings between India and Japan concern possible joint maneuvers and facilitate the mutual use of military bases for logistical purposes. Furthermore, Quad nations have conducted a series of joint naval exercises in the South China Sea, sometimes with the participation of some Association of Southeast Asian Nations (ASEAN) states.[20]

A glance at the FOIPI and original EPN shows us the similarities and differences between them. The two networks share the same purpose and consistency, in maintaining the course of amplifying the USA's sphere of influence in the Indo-Pacific region and countering China's multifaceted dominance. It shares the same concerns in a wide diversity of global issues, from business cooperation, infrastructure development, human capital investment, 5G security, etc. However, EPN showed less concern about military realms. And EPN did not limit its scale in terms of participants. It opened to welcome more and more like-minded countries, companies, and civil society groups.

According to Koga (2020),[21] there is still strategic divergence between the American and the Japanese approaches regarding FOIPI – their vision and posture toward China are not perfectly aligned. Nevertheless, one of the main concerns of Japan itself would be to bring order into the region by ensuring that the rule-based framework of the FOIPI can build its way toward an Indo-Pacific regional order. In order to do so, Japan could gather political support from other parties (not specifically located in the target area) in order to create a strong diplomatic collation of like-minded states and regional institutions (e.g., Australia, India, ASEAN, the UK, and France). The involvement of such strong external partners would surely be an important tool at the disposal of the main players in the FOIPI group. Japan would find an essential partnership in countries that would share its vision of the region, while the US could rely on a major set of alliances in order to strengthen its hegemonic position against the Chinese-led bloc. This very statement denotes how an expansion of the FOIPI and the strengthening of an inclusive institution in the Indo-Pacific region could prove to be a viable strategy in order to get an edge in this US–China competition.

5.1.4.2 Biden's New Initiative

The EPN under the Trump administration was an alliance of like-minded countries set to curb China's trade with the aforementioned parties and bring home some of the businesses that offshored in the mainland in the past two decades. On paper, such an agreement would not clash with Biden's vision toward foreign & China policy. The problem relies on Trump's main strategy, used to push its *America First* agenda and, at the same time, gain an edge in the China-US hegemonic competitions. The US never committed extensively to pursuing a full-on developed EPN agreement, meaning that the basis for a solid deal that could create a bloc capable of challenging China's economic uprise was never settled. Indeed, the trade war did arise during Trump's term and his challenging approach toward multilateralism and WTO, and its troubled relations with institutions like NATO played an important role in the underdevelopment of a strong alternative to the BRI.

Biden, in his article (Foreign Affairs, 2020), criticized Trump's bilateral policy, which involved breaking plurilateral treaties and pulling the US out from several negotiations.[22] He says that

> we need to fortify our collective capabilities with democratic friends beyond North America and Europe by reinvesting in our treaty alliances with Australia, Japan and South Korea; and deepening partnerships from India to Indonesia to advance shared values in a region that will determine the United States' future.

The Asia-Pacific front appears to be of primary importance, and his willingness to act with like-minded countries suggests that a possible 'anti-China' alliance would be possible.

The USA's willingness to once again act as a leader for a *summit for democracy* could well lay down the base for a value-oriented deal as soon as the most urgent disputes for the White House are settled. The democratic values and the European values could be aligned, and existing institutions such as the G7 can be expanded to be D10 (Democracy 10) composed of G7 and India, Australia, and South Korea.

More specifically, Biden could look to unify said values in order to build a better environment of like-minded countries. This can be underlined by the similarities we can find between the values considered by the European Union (EU) and by the president himself regarding not only labor laws and policies but also the focus on Green Deals, clean energy laws, investments, and assessments toward a 'carbon-free economy' and human rights in general.

The plan to create a 'more resilient, sustainable economy' is depicted in Biden's plan regarding clean energy.[23] The focal points revolve around the objective of achieving net-zero emissions for the whole economy by 2050 (also underlined by Biden's will to be part – again – of the Paris Accord on climate change) (Newburger, 2020).[24] It is also specified how creating 'good-paying jobs that provide workers with the choice to join a union' will also be possible while pushing for the creation of modern, sustainable infrastructure that will deliver an equitable clean energy future. According to his plan, investments will be made in infrastructure, the auto industry, transit and public transportation, the power sector, upgrading buildings, housing, innovation, agriculture and conservation, and environmental justice. All of these plans will move along with his original climate plan, focusing on Green Deals while also expanding the American telecommunication system through an expansion of 5G technology.

A series of ad hoc investments will be made to strengthen the car industry, always considering the aforementioned points regarding an emission-free focus. Federal procurements will be used to strengthen the domestic network, and extra funds will be allocated in order to accelerate research on battery technology and support the development of domestic production capabilities.

Climate will be one of the most important topics, and the US could team up with the EU, a forerunner in the field of climate change activism. Secure environmental justice is also a valuable point, but so is the creation of equitable economic opportunity and the matters related to actual human development. Because of this, additional attention will be paid to inclusion policies for the disadvantaged members of society.

Biden's willingness to act in order to push this agenda is reflected in his swiftness in issuing several executive orders to tackle the COVID-19 crisis, reversing many of the changes implemented by the Trump administration, and further focusing on topics related to climate change, resource management, and local business competitiveness. Indeed, the Democratic president ended up signing 52 executive orders and memoranda up to April 30 of his first year in office, more than any of his three predecessors (Hickey et al., 2021).[25] Most notably, Mr. Biden launched a review of American supply chains for several key businesses (rare minerals, semiconductors, and electronic vehicle batteries, among others) with frameworks that intertwine directly with America's national security. The interested sectors are, not by chance, areas in which the Chinese market holds substantial power on the global market, signaling how the US could be seeking to further enhance not only its competitiveness in these very businesses but also enhanced autonomy and a weaker dependency on global value chains (GVCs) that are infamously spread across Southeast Asia, China, and North America.

From a networking point of view, all things considered, the US could try to recover its role as the leading node by establishing itself as the new rule-maker in a plurilateral environment, finding allies both on the Atlantic and Pacific sides and expanding its network in order to confront a China that does not fear to invest in its own set of allies, as we can see with BRI and RCEP. Pivoting on the common ground that the US could find between itself and other like-minded countries or institutions (including supranational organizations) like the EU, Biden could manage to build a stronger network that is able to engage the opposing hegemonic competitor while establishing a totally different environment compared to the one developed by his predecessor.

5.1.4.3 CPTPP

Though CPTPP already includes Japan, Australia, Canada, Mexico, and New Zealand, President Trump preferred to withdraw from the CPTPP and bilaterally negotiate RTAs because the free trade commitment covered in the CPTPP was not compatible with Trump's trade regime.

In Biden's campaign, he expressed strong opposition to Trump's tariff policies and trade war, which was blamed for forcing American farmers into miserable situations. He also emphasized the importance of trade to American producers since '95 percent of the customers'[26] are outside the United States. Noticeable is the fact that he also voted for 'permanent normal trade relations' with China in 2000. Thus, the EPN initiated by Trump's government is seemingly opposed to Biden's economic policies.

Furthermore, in the medium and long run, it is projected that rejoining and renegotiation of CPTPP will be included in Biden's economic policies (although heavy focus would be put on shifting the current trade terms and on renegotiating the deal) since he prefers a fair and open trading system and he was the prime player to promote TPP. It is possible that the US will rejoin and take back the leading position of the network, which was given to Japan after Trump withdrew from TPP. Biden stated that the US would be a fair trader and advocated "treating other countries the way in which they treat us, which is, particularly as it relates to China: If they want to trade here, they're going to be under the same rules." His idea is to "build a united front of allies to challenge China's abusive behavior."[27] In CPTPP, together with Canada, Mexico, Chile, and Peru – all current North and South American member states of the free trade pact – the US aims to hold China accountable for rules of trade set by the US via renegotiations, including a higher standard for environment and labor, as he promised. What can be implied from Biden's campaign trade policy is that the US will continue to contain the development of China in the global trade system but in a less aggressive way. Biden's view toward the CPTPP is one of the few possible options for the US for setting its foreign policy with the hope to gain a marginal advantage over China and settle to a favorable position.

The possibility of developing a *CPTPP-plus* would surely strengthen the position of a bloc that could act as a buffer zone for China's expansionism. The US joining the deal would probably mean a stronger alliance on the Pacific front, with South Korea ready to jump the bandwagon and establish itself as a possible candidate for a *CPTPP-13*. Given the possibility to seek strong allies to counterbalance the fact that China managed to successfully get involved in an Asia-Pacific regional agreement (RCEP), the US could attain even stronger influence by bringing in possible allies like the UK and Thailand. The first one, despite being located far from the core of the Asia-Pacific area, could bring in a solid trade partner for other members of the bloc while bolstering its position as a global player after the escalating events following Brexit; the second would be a natural addendum after, similar to Korea, it missed the chance to join the CPTPP in the past. It would certainly jump at the chance to expand its external market, thanks to this expanded FTA, while also strengthening ASEAN's position in the region.

More recently, on September 16, 2021, China formally applied to join the CPTPP, submitting an application to New Zealand, the repository state of the CPTPP. China's membership bid has symbolic value, as an attempt to become another leading node of the mega-trade network. However, it is highly unlikely that Beijing will get the unanimous approval of the founding members, especially those already ratified the CPTPP, including Canada, Mexico, and Japan. Moreover, China can hardly meet the CPTPP's high standards. Several sticking points for a new entrant like China into the CPTPP include the issues of digital trade, state subsidies for SOEs (state-owned enterprises), and IPRs (intellectual property rights). Nevertheless, China's swift move showing its intention to replace the US and to resume the leading role of the free trade system will influence Washington to move up its schedule to join or rejoin the CPTPP, although the Biden administration seems to be more inclined to Indo-Pacific Economic Framework (IPEF) rather than CPTPP.[28]

The actual networks we just presented above do not appear to be mutually exclusive, and the Biden presidency could have the chance to move in multiple directions in order to create a new, more expansive network of allies and trade partners. As reported by *South China Morning Post* (2021),[29] joint drills between the US and India have been carried out at the beginning of 2021 to show how Quad continues to be of major importance for both the partner countries in their struggle against China. It is also likely to see the Quad expand to become the *Quad-plus* including new members of New Zealand, South Korea, and Vietnam. This signal could show how Biden's strategy will see him move in multiple directions, possibly developing a *multilayered network* inclusive of different nodes (connected through unique linkages that piece through different layers) and different networks that would be partially exclusive and partially overlapping. The US will develop a *network of networks*, where networks that the US creates, for example, Quad-plus, AUKUS, IPEF, and more, are interacting with each other but are formed by various types of nodes on a selective basis. Seeking allies in both the Pacific and the Atlantic would be an extensive yet ambitious plan for the US, which could seek to become (once again) the undisputed leading node of alliance-based sectoral and plurilateral networks.

5.2 The China-Led Network and the BRI

5.2.1 Brief Introduction of the BRI

The BRI, formerly known as the One Belt One Road Strategy (OBOR), is a formidable global strategy of China that aims to connect Asia with Africa and Europe through the revival of historical trading routes such as the Silk Road in order to improve regional integration, which would lead to trade expansion and economic growth. This can also alleviate overcapacity and excess foreign exchange reserves. During his visit to Kazakhstan and Indonesia in 2013, Chinese Leader Xi Jinping revealed the BRI, known to be the primary focus of his foreign policies.

5.2.2 Current Status and Future Direction

The BRI has reached nearly all parts of the world, and a total of 138 countries have joined the BRI by signing a memorandum of understanding under the said initiative (Green Belt and Road Initiative Center, 2020).[30] According to the 2019 database, there were 2,631 projects with a total value of $3.7 trillion. Aside from these projects, trade between China and BRI member countries has seen an average annual growth rate of 4% with a total value of $6 trillion.[31]

However, with the current COVID-19 pandemic and its effects on the global supply chain due to lockdowns and travel restrictions, projects under the BRI are either suspended or slowing down. Although China's economy had started to function normally again after lifting the initial lockdowns in most of its regions, it was the Omicron wave in 2022 that broke the defense line of Shanghai. New lockdowns have hurt local consumption and coerced millions of small businesses to shut down. As long as zero COVID-19 measures strongly remain in place in China, it can potentially shatter China's economic growth. The countries wherein the BRI has the greatest number of projects are also experiencing a high number of COVID-19 and its variants cases. These countries include India, Russia, Pakistan, Saudi Arabia, Bangladesh, Qatar, Egypt, the United Arab Emirates, and Kazakhstan. The number of projects in these ten countries accounts for 34% of all the BRI projects in 2019, and these projects are greatly affected by the uneven application of COVID-19 lockdown and restrictions across different jurisdictions.

Due to these challenges, there are financial viability issues that banks, such as the Chinese development banks, the Silk Road Fund, the New Development Bank, and the Asian Infrastructure Investment Bank, are scrutinizing to find out whether further funding of certain BRI projects will still provide feasibility and profitability as originally expected. The possible contractual termination might cause a collision between inner and outer networks. The BRI projects are known to have generated around 300,000 local jobs, and the initiative has led to the creation of over 80 overseas economic and trade cooperation zones. Totally terminating some of the projects will result in unemployment, and that can create problems within the network through possible objections and participation of social groups, labor unions, and local organizations that will be negatively affected by the abandonment of the projects.

On the other hand, some experts believe that the effects of the COVID-19 pandemic will be relatively short term and that China was able to showcase its success in using artificial intelligence and other technologies in managing the virus. This might potentially expand the BRI projects and create new linkages to the digital sector, which can pave the way for new projects revolving around information and communications technology, e-commerce, and big data (Backer & McKenzie, 2020).[32] We have yet to see the BRI's future direction and whether the projects will be continued and expanded or terminated. Also, comparing the nature of the complementarity and competitiveness of the networks, the complementarity of agri-trade among countries along the BRI exceeded the competitiveness effects of the networks, highlighting the greater potential for agri-trade cooperation among countries in the region (Liu et al., 2019).[33]

5.2.3 Network Structure

The BRI capitalizes on the fact that a large infrastructure gap restricts trade and development in the world. Based on the report of OECD in 2018, Asia would experience a shortfall of USD 26 trillion in infrastructure investment by 2030, and China's BRI can minimize this gap as the initiative focuses on infrastructure and investment funding (OECD, 2018).[34] This situation makes China's network-making power, or to use another term, *interest-driven power,* stronger. With the BRI serving as an instrument to carry out that authority, China definitely has the upper hand in determining the sail of this initiative. If we were to identify China's role in this network, we can say that it holds both the first power position as the programmer and the second power position as the switcher. Programmers and switchers hold network-making power, which is the most important form of power in the network society.

Unlike other trade agreements, the BRI was conceptualized and materialized by one single country. This gives China the ability to reconfigure the network's structure and nodes in order to achieve its goals. In addition, China has the right to control the connecting points between nodes and linkages within the BRI, as the projects mainly involve Chinese leaders, media networks, technological firms, and other state-owned banks and companies (Lowy Institute, 2019).[35] Dominant states can leverage their network centrality to drive greater network interconnection through processes and configurations targeted at state integration or federation (Wellman and Stephen, 1988).[36] This makes the BRI a network that China can freely modify and maximize depending on the interest that it wants to pursue. Through this centrality, China is able to create bilateral and multilateral conditions for Central Asian states' Silk Road Economic Belt (SREB) engagement, thereby endowing itself with the ability to choose network *insiders* and *outsiders* (Reeves, 2018).[37] China binding its Central Asian partners to a regional structure, based on its interests and using its power, is essential for its continued 'win-win' viability. The Xi administration has leveraged its increased SREB prestige to increase network centrality in Central Asia (Reeves, 2018). The three main groups could be identified in the trade network among the BRI countries including the Asia–Europe Group with China as the core and Russia as the second node; the South Asia-West Asia Group with India, United Arab Emirates, and Saudi Arabia as cores; and the Central-Eastern Europe Group with a multi-core structure (Song et al., 2018).[38] Both Turkey and Russia have the largest scope in terms of trade competitive advantages, and China has the strongest intermediation ability in BR-TCANs from three communities, including the West, the North, and the South (Feng et al., 2020).[39]

But even though China is a popular country in the foreign direct investment network, when initially joining the investment network, small nodes tend to choose nearby small nodes for investment (He and Cao, 2019).[40] Countries with small node degrees are generally inclined to establish mutual investment relations with neighboring countries and are less likely to invest with non-neighboring countries across geographical distances. Countries with large node degrees usually not only invest in neighboring countries that are geographically close but also choose to establish investment relationships with many non-neighboring countries. The countries with large node degrees are generally regional powers within the BRI areas, such as China, Singapore, Turkey, India, Russia, Poland, and other countries. The broad purpose of the initiative, which is to ensure a greater level of economic integration between and among countries on the Belt-Road corridor, is gradually being achieved although at a slower pace than may have been expected by the framers of the initiative, with less influence being exerted by China. Beneficial economic integration will be very much enhanced with China in the core position. In the global trade network, most BRI countries are attracted by the core nodes of the BRI regions, such as China, Russia, India, and the United Arab Emirates.

Based on the weight allocation that encompasses geographical distance, factor endowment, culture, and institutional distance, the improved comprehensive distance index is used to divide China and 62 countries along the *One Belt and One Road* into four trading circles. During the initial stage, China is an 'axis power,' and the first-circle countries, such as Russia, Kazakhstan, Indonesia, India, Poland, and Turkey, are the nodes of the network, radiating to the six major regions of Mongolia–Russia, Central Asia, Southeast Asia, South Asia, Central and Eastern Europe, and West Asia. During the development stage, the second-circle countries, such as the Philippines, Qatar, Kuwait, Pakistan, and Israel, become expansion lines. During the formation stage, the first- and second-circle countries can attract the third-circle countries, such as Lebanon, Myanmar, East Timor, Jordan, and Yemen. During the improvement stage, the fourth-circle countries, such as Maldives, Macedonia, Bhutan, Tajikistan, and Armenia, are attracted to form a 'seamless network.' From 2007 to 2016, the proportion of China's exports to the Belt and Road countries of the first, second, third, and fourth circle accounted for 67%, 24%, 6%, and 3%, respectively (Fu et.al., 2018).[41]

5.2.4 Impacts on the Future Global Trading System

Economists regard multilateral trade agreements as the ideal form of international cooperation, as it yields the largest potential gains. Then again, different factors play an important role as to why some countries or networks do not utilize this favorable trade mechanism. As for China, its trade multilateralism faces challenges that slow its progress. One clear example is the RCEP. This trade agreement was watered down when India, one of the biggest members, decided to opt out of RCEP due to concerns about being inundated by imports under the agreement's lower tariff rates. Given concerns regarding such cases, it is not surprising as to why China relies on bilateral trade agreements to further advance its networked power with the aid of the BRI instead. This does not mean that multilateralism is disregarded altogether as there is still a possibility that China can consolidate these bilateral trade agreements and upgrade them to a huge multilateral framework (Casas et al., 2018).[42] If that happens, it can simultaneously further strengthen the networking power of China by increasing the cost of exclusion against the countries outside the increasing size of the BRI.

The global trading system is heavily affected by trading time, and that is why countries focus on developing the means of transportation to improve trade facilitation around the world. Longer trading time acts like a tax on exports, and this is important in relation to the GVCs. This is one of the key points of the BRI as it targets to revive the ancient Silk Road by building economic corridors with two main components: the economic belt that traverses the land and the maritime road that crosses the water. Once these projects intended to link Europe and Asia are completed, it would reduce trade time by 38% on average. The improvement in trading time will eventually increase the total trade volume in Eurasia and will also benefit both consumers and producers, directly and indirectly (Baniya et al., 2019).[43]

However, trade facilitation has two dimensions: physical infrastructure, which includes roads, railways, airports, and ports, and soft infrastructure, which includes regulatory, institutional, and other management-related policies. The BRI focuses on the physical dimension of trade facilitation, and its full potential will not be unlocked unless soft infrastructure receives its due emphasis (Hui et al., 2018).[44] China, aside from leading the BRI, is also a key member of the RCEP. It is one of the nodes that is seeking to take the leading role within the network. This is why the RCEP is seen as a supporting network to the BRI, and in fact, most members of the RCEP are also part of the BRI. This great influence of China in the RCEP made former Australian Prime Minister Tony Abbott classify the mega free trade agreement as "the trading arm of the Belt and Road Initiative."[45] But in reality, China cannot totally push its trade agendas in the RCEP because of the presence of other powerful members such as Japan and, previously, India. Although China's economic size is way beyond the economies of RCEP members, they all have equal bargaining positions in the negotiation, which ensures equal advancement of interests of the respective members.

Both the BRI and RCEP can be seen as networks that China would surely utilize to counter the influence of the US in the world trading system. It is known that RCEP was conceived in 2012 as China's defensive answer to the TPP, which was then backed up by the US. Even though the US had withdrawn from the TPP, the change from the North American Free Trade Agreement to USMCA and its recent ratification increases the need for China to grasp on the BRI and RCEP in order to counter-balance the possible, increased retaliation from the US.

For some countries, their relationship with China's BRI can be regarded as beneficial. The investments provided through the initiative are seen to help stimulate the economies of member countries, especially those that are regarded as low-middle-income economies. One example is the $4.5 billion Chinese-built and financed standard gauge railway (SGR), which connects Ethiopia's capital, Addis Ababa, to Djibouti, which is technically Ethiopia's gateway to maritime transportation. This railway greatly reduces the travel time from Addis Ababa to Djibouti from 2 days to 12 hours, and this can further mobilize Ethiopia's export-led industrialization strategy.[46]

But the BRI projects have invited much suspicion and criticism not only from the skeptic non-member countries but also from the countries that completed the BRI projects. Some accusations referred to the BRI as a debt trap. Aside from the huge investments unleashed by China, it is alarming to note that these big deals were made with countries that had very poor credit ratings. This opens up the possibility of these countries defaulting from paying their dues to the Chinese government, and it is doubtful that China will just let it pass without any consequences (Forbes, 2020).[47] Sri Lanka failed to repay its debt to China and was forced to sign over its strategic Hambantota Port to China Merchants Port Holdings Company on a 99-year lease to mitigate the unpaid debts. This development has been viewed as a critical threat to Sri Lanka's sovereignty.[48] On April 12th of 2022, Sri Lanka suspended payments on the $35bn its government owes foreign creditors. Soaring food and fuel prices, the result of Russia-Ukraine wartime disruption to supply chains, have hit the economy that was already mishandled by President Gotabaya Rajapaksa and his powerful family. Sri Lanka has turned to China and India for emergency loans to purchase food and fuel. Experts believe that China's debt-trap diplomacy is behind this crisis. Malaysia has canceled a multibillion-dollar high-speed rail project linking Singapore to "avoid being declared bankrupt" (Bloomberg, 2018).[49] Some countries such as Japan, Australia, and India have even expanded their regional development plans to counter the BRI.

5.3 Who Will Get the Upper Hand?

The US-led network could be represented by its values and concepts opposing the BRI and China's authoritarian influence, encompassing a strategy that aims at containing China's growing power and dominance. It was described as an alliance of *trusted partners* operating under a set of trust principles and a bounded ideological order where the US is the unipolar leading power. The standard of the FOIPI and the former EPN covers not only trade but also non-trade issues. However, its network power remains questionable due to the ambiguity in the number of nodes, shared values, and gains from the network. It is projected that a newly created 'anti-China' alliance, based on shared values of partners that will make efforts to halt China's economic and technological rise, will have a profound effect on the global trading system. One such effect would be, for instance, a break in existing FTAs, followed by trade wars and retaliations among pro-China and pro-US groups of nations. From the viewpoint of the US, the G7 network that, as we mentioned, will strive to oppose China's BRI, is an expanded part of the Indo-Pacific Initiative serving the same ultimate goal of countering Chinese technological and commercial advancements. Indeed, depending on the number of parties involved, the US could direct its efforts in different directions, including a strengthened FOIPI, US participation in the CPTPP with ally members, and ultimately a renewed G7 plus its allies.

However, the BRI can be considered an ambitious plan, and its influence has been spreading between countries like a wildfire. The BRI amplifies China's network and network-making power, enabling it to program and switch networks depending on the goals it wants to achieve. The BRI offers huge investments to many countries, even to countries that have poor credit ratings, and these relatively weaker nodes might pose a threat to the BRI network's future stability and growth. We have yet to see sincere intentions on the part of China and whether it will continue funding these projects to keep the network intact. But with the ongoing COVID-19 pandemic, the development of these projects has slowed down, and the growth of the network has been threatened by possible contractual termination. In the end, it will depend on the Chinese government – whether it continues taking risks or if the pandemic forces China to play it safe and protect its economy from incurring possible, bigger losses.

When looking at the old EPN, and the possible approaches that a Biden-led US administration and China's network revolving around the BRI and RCEP can take, we can say that both Chinese and the American projects appear to be extensive and ambitious in terms of scale and scope. On the one hand, we have two ambitious leaders of G2 seeking more alliances and plurilateral/sectoral cooperation; on the other hand, we are witnessing the collisions of the networks all over the world.

The increased lending of money by China could translate into a crisis though following the increasingly frequent renegotiations with host countries when it comes to the BRI-based projects (Kratz et al., 2020).[50] Outbound investments are being cut and China's strategy is evolving, turning its attention toward the domestic market that it wants to nurture, in order to become an independent force that could withstand the continuous fire from the American side (Kynge et al., 2020).[51]

Indeed, debt distress and debt sustainability are of primary importance for a project that relies so much on many different parties (He, 2020),[52] and the worries that have been lingering for the past few months did not help this project that is losing much of the traction it had for the past several years. The Digital Silk Road (DSR), a project introduced in 2015, can also be considered part of the BRI. Much of the Chinese investments were indeed directed at this substratum of the initiative, but even here have been concerns, especially considering all the cybersecurity-related discussions that were dragged with the Huawei 5G dilemma.

Looking at the future prospect and at what is going to come next, though, it is clear how much of the weight will be placed on the Biden administration and the path it is going to choose. The US approach could extend, as we mentioned, toward many different directions. Apart from China, though, the macroeconomic instability and supply chain disruptions seem to be of much more importance to the American economy. Biden will have to address his short-term problems before he will have the chance to take the hegemonic rise of China head-on. After the urgent economic matters in the US and its shortcomings are solved, the US-led network will develop in a different format, finding its own like-minded allies to together oppose and counter China-led networks in the global community. The emerging network war between the US and China will reshape the world economy and politics for decades.

From a network perspective, the viability for American and Chinese hegemony will ultimately depend on the structure and power factors of the networks that each generates for the world. The networks that can offer the world a better set of public goods will prevail in the end.

Notes

1 U.S. Department of State (2020), Under Secretary Keith Krach Briefs the Press on Huawei and Clean Telcos, Asia Pacific Media Hub: Special Briefing. Retrieved from https://2017-2021.state.gov/telephonic-briefing-with-keith-krach-under-secretary-for-economic-growth-energy-and-the-environment/index.html
2 Clifford, D. (2020), An American-led 'Economic Prosperity Network' Could Be a Good Start to Not Relying on China, *Washington Times* (May 12, 2020).
3 Bloomberg News (2020), Can the U.S. End China's Control of the Global Supply Chain?, *Bloomberg* (June 08, 2020). Retrieved from https://www.bloomberg.com/news/articles/2020-06-08/why-the-u-s-can-t-easily-break-china-s-grip-on-supply-chains
4 Ibid.
5 Galloway, A. (2020), Morrison Writes to G20 Leaders Calling for Coronavirus Review, *The Sydney Morning Herald* (May 5, 2020).
6 OEC (2020), Data on South Korea's Trade. https://oec.world/en/profile/country/kor/.
7 The Dong-A Ilbo (2020), U.S. Promises to Protect S. Korea against any Chinese Retaliatory Action (June 15, 2020).
8 CNBC (2020), China May Become One of Many Hubs as Companies Diversify Manufacturing after Coronavirus Shock, *CNBC* (May 25, 2020).
9 Mearsheimer, J. (2019), Bound to Fail. *International Security*, 43(4), pp. 7–51.
10 U.S. Department of State (2020), Ibid.
11 Zhang, B. (2020), The Biden Presidency: A Different China Policy? *RSIS Commentaries*, No.195, Singapore: Nanyang Technological University. p. 3.
12 Wasserman, E. (2020), New York Post Tells Trump to "Give It Up" Over Election Claim, *Bloomberg* (December 28, 2020).

13 Wintour, P. (2021), G7 Backs Biden Infrastructure Plan to Rival China's Belt and Road Initiative, *The Guardian* (June 12, 2021).

14 Gift, T. (2020), *Joe Biden's Approach to China Will Not Differ Greatly from Donald Trump's*, London: USApp – United States Politics and Policy Blog.

15 Buchan, P. and Rimland, B. (2020), *Defining the Diamond: The Past, Present, and Future of the Quadrilateral Security Dialogue*, Washington, DC: Center for Strategic and International Studies (CSIS).

16 U.S. Department of State (2019), A Free and Open Indo-Pacific, Advancing a Shared Vision, Bureau of East Asian and Pacific Affairs Report, Retrieved from https://www.state.gov/wp-content/uploads/2019/11/Free-and-Open-Indo-Pacific-4Nov2019.pdf

17 Ibid., pp. 20–28.

18 Reuters (2018), U.S. Pledges Nearly $300 Million Security Funding for Indo-Pacific Region, *Reuters* (August 3, 2021).

19 The Government of Japan (2019), Towards Free and Open Indo-Pacific, Retrieved from https://www.mofa.go.jp/files/000407643.pdf

20 Buchan, P. and Rimland, B. (2020), Ibid.

21 Koga, K. (2020), Japan's 'Indo-Pacific' Question: Countering China or Shaping a New Regional Order? *International Affairs*, 96(1), pp. 49–73.

22 Biden, J. (2020), Why America Must Lead Again: Rescuing U.S. Foreign Policy After Trump, *Foreign Affairs*, 99(2), p. 64.

23 Biden, J. (2020), The Biden Plan to Build a Modern, Sustainable Infrastructure and an Equitable Clean Energy Future. https://joebiden.com/clean-energy/ (last access: 19 January 2021).

24 Newburger, E. (2020), Biden Will Rejoin the Paris Climate Accord. Here's What Happens Next, *CNBC* (November 20, 2020).

25 Hickey, C., Merrill, C., Chang, R., Sullivan, K., Boschma, J. and O'Key, S. (2021), Here Are the Executive Actions Biden Signed in His First 100 Days, *CNN Politics* (April 30, 2021 updated).

26 Lester, S. (2020), *What Would Trade Policy Look Like Under a President Joe Biden?*. Washington, DC: CATO Institute.

27 Ibid.

28 The IPEF under Biden is the EPN under a new label. So far, no details about the IPEF are specified and suggested in concrete terms.

29 Chan M. (2021), US and Indian Troops Start Joint Exercise as Joe Biden Seeks to Build Up Quad as Counterweight to China, *South China Morning Post* (February 13, 2021).

30 Green Belt and Road Initiative Center (2020), Countries of the Belt and Road Initiative (BRI) http://green-bri.org.

31 Refinitive (2019), *BRI Connect: An Initiative in Numbers, China Belt and Road Initiative Report*. Retrieved from https://www.refinitiv.com/content/dam/marketing/en_us/documents/reports/refinitiv-zawya-belt-and-road-initiative-report-2019.pdf

32 Backer and McKenzie (2020), Understanding How COVID-19 alters BRI, *Backer & McKenzie Report*, Retrieved from https://www.bakermckenzie.com/-/media/files/insight/publications/2020/03/covid19-bri-short-report.pdf

33 Liu, C., Xu, J. and Zhang, H. (2019), Competitiveness or Complementarity? A Dynamic Network Analysis of International Agri-Trade along the Belt and Road. *Applied Spatial Analysis and Policy*, 13, pp. 349–374.

34 OECD (2018), The Belt and Road Initiative in the Global Trade, Investment and Finance Landscape, OECD Business and Finance Outlook 2018, pp. 61–101

35 Zhang, D. and Yin J. (2019), *China's Belt and Road Initiative, From the Inside Looking Out*, Sydney: Lowy Institute.

36 Wellman, B. and Berkowitz, S. (1988), *Social Structures: A Network Approach* (Vol. 2), Cambridge: Cambridge Universiry Press, pp. 1512–1514.

37 Reeves, J. (2018), China's Silk Road Economic Belt Initiative: Network and Influence Formation in Central Asia, *Journal of Contemporary China*, 27(12), pp. 502–518.

38 Song, Z., Che, S. and Yu, Y. (2018), The Trade Network of the Belt and Road Initiative and its Topological Relationship to the Global Trade Network, *Journal of Geographical Sciences*, 28(9), pp. 1249–1262.

39 Feng, L., Xu, H., Wu, G., Zhao, Y. and Xu, J. (2020), Exploring the Structure and Influence Factors of Trade Competitive Advantage Network along the Belt and Road, *Physica A: Statistical Mechanics and Its Applications*, 559, 125057.

40 He, Q. and Cao, X. (2019), Pattern and Influencing Factors of Foreign Direct Investment Networks between Countries along the "Belt and Road" Regions. *Sustainability*, 11(17), p. 4724.

41 Fu, X., Chen H. and Xue, Z. (2018), Construction of the Belt and Road Trade Cooperation Network from the Multi-Distances Perspective. *Sustainability*, 10(5), p. 1439.

42 Casas, T. and Klett, O. (2018), Ch.5 Free Trade Agreements as BRI's Stepping-Stone to Multilateralism: Is the Sino–Swiss FTA the Gold Standard? in *China's Belt and Road Initiative*, Springer Int'l Publishing.

43 Baniya, S., Rocha, N. and Ruta, M. (2019), Trade Effects of the New Silk Road: A Gravity Analysis, World Bank *Policy Research Working Paper* 8694.

44 Hui, L., Rohr, C., Hafner, M. and Knack, A. (2018), China Belt and Road Initiative: Measuring the Impact of Improving Transportation Connectivity on Trade in the Region, RAND Europe, pp. 57–60.

45 Press Trust of India (2019), RCEP 'Looks Like Trade Arm' of China's Belt and Road Initiative, says Former Australian Prime Minister, *Business Standard* (November 20, 2019).

46 Chen, Y. (2019), *Ethiopia and Kenya Are Struggling to Manage Debt for Their Chinese-built Railways*, Quartz Africa.

47 Shepard, W. (2020), How China's Belt and Road Became A "Global Trail Of Trouble", *Forbes* (January 29, 2020).

48 Schultz, K. (2017), Sri Lanka, Struggling with Debt, Hands a Major Port to China, *New York Times* (December 12, 2017).

49 Shukry, A. and Park, K. (2018), Malaysia Scraps Multibillion-Dollar High-Speed Rail Project to Singapore, *Bloomberg* (May 28, 2018).

50 Kratz, A., Rosen, D. and Mingey, M. (2020), *Booster or Brake? COVID and the Belt and Road Initiative*, Rhodiu Group Research Note, New York: Rhodium Group.

51 Kynge, J. and Wheatley, J. (2020), China Pulls Back from the World: Rethinking Xi's 'Project of the Century', *Financial Times* (December 11, 2020).

52 He, A. (2020), The Belt and Road Initiative: Motivations, Financing, Expansion and Challenges of Xi's Ever-Expanding Strategy, *Journal of Infrastructure, Policy and Development*, 4(1), pp. 139–169.

6 The Four Waves of Challenges

We revisit the four waves of challenges to free trade and conduct a more detailed analysis of their impacts on the world's three biggest economic blocs: the US, China, and the European Union (EU). Based on the in-depth analysis, this chapter portrays what is to come in the future. The high level of uncertainty brought by these four waves will remain in the limelight for a while. The enemies of globalization already jumped on the wagon to the city of *deglobalization*.

6.1 COVID-19 Pandemic

A group of scientists doing research for the World Health Organization (WHO) argue that 'the window is rapidly closing' to gather crucial evidence on the origins of the coronavirus epidemic. One of the major impediments regarding the task is China's intentional evasion to cooperate with the investigations. So far, scientists have failed to reach any firm conclusions about whether the disease was the result of an accidental leak from a lab in Wuhan city, Hubei province, of China or not. Instead, Beijing has been forwarding conspiracy theories blaming the US, insinuating that the virus had escaped from a US military lab in Maryland. Like in the case of the 1918 Spanish flu, the Chinese government seems to be well aware that the origins of pandemics can never be scientifically identified throughout the history.

Undeniable is the fact that the COVID-19 pandemic has had a significant influence on the global trading system. Breakdown in global supply chains, increase in costs of international trade, reduction in the workforce, rise in government spending, and a decrease in private consumption are the expected and inevitable consequences of the pandemic (PwC, 2020).[1] The WTO Statistical Review released in 2021 offers a comprehensive yet detailed summary of the global trade environment following the disruption caused by the COVID-19 pandemic (WTO, 2021).[2] Not surprisingly, the value of exported merchandise in 2020 diminished by 8% worldwide, while trade in services dropped by 21%. The limitations on transportation (which affected both the movement of people and merchandise) were acutely felt in the second half of 2020, when services trade went down by 30% and trade in goods by 23%. Asian countries were the least affected, thanks to their swift answers in tackling the crisis early on and their natural focus on

DOI: 10.4324/9781003305705-6

supplying key pharmaceutical and protective products. All in all, the effects of the pandemic with new variants of COVID-19 are still far-reaching even at the beginning of 2022, when the trends started in 2020 continued to linger into the new year, with severely limited movement of people and goods. On the other hand, sectors like the ones related to information and communication technology (ICT) and computer services thrive as more and more people are forced to quickly adapt to the new situation of remote working. Digital transformation is put under the spotlight, and we can safely say that a new trading world is being molded under our very eyes.

6.1.1 Impacts of the COVID-19 Pandemic on the USA's Strategies

Before the start of the COVID-19 pandemic, the US experienced its record-long economic expansion, which was obviously halted by the said virus. From June 2009 to February 2020, or a total of 128 months, the US economy has expanded by 2.3% in annualized percentage change in the gross domestic product (GDP). Not only that, the US also experienced a collapse in employment because of the pandemic. Alongside its GDP expansion, the US also experienced the longest period of job creation in its history, wherein jobs were continuously created for 133 consecutive months. Unfortunately, this came to a hard stop in March 2020, and the US lost 870,000 jobs, and by April, it hit a record-high of 21 million lost jobs, twice as high as those lost during the 2008–2009 global financial crisis. The US also experienced a slump in industrial production and retail sales, wherein the output from factories, mines, and utilities steeply dropped by a seasonally adjusted 12.7% in April 2020. Retail sales, a measure of purchases at stores, gas stations, restaurants, bars, and online shops, also fell by 14.7% in April 2020. US financial markets also experienced a severe and sudden shock. Equity markets also recorded the worst quarter since the financial crisis, while bond markets saw a decline in short-term treasury yields, reflective of a situation where economic doubts and aggressive monetary stimulus were holding down long-term interest rates. Although these indicators eventually began to improve, we cannot deny that the pandemic indeed disrupted the normalcy of domestic and international affairs (UNECLAC, 2020).[3]

Taking a broader view, the negative impacts of the pandemic on the US also showed up in its trade flows and supply chains. In the US, exports of goods and services decreased by $141.5 billion (13.6%) and imports by $173.1 billion (13.3%) in the first five months of 2020. In both exports and imports, the automotive industry was the most affected by the pandemic. The decrease in trade could also be clearly seen in the North American region, which also contracted by 26% in the first five months of 2020. The figure is bigger in South America, where trade with the US dropped by 20.4%. As mentioned earlier, the trade related to the automotive industry was hit the hardest. Given that the automotive industry is actually highly integrated through the North American value chain, this affected both Canada and Mexico negatively. Trade in services was also badly hit due to the lockdown and containment measures to control the spread of COVID-19. Border closures, travel bans, and quarantine measures continue to pose challenges to the tourism industry, which is vital to several countries in the Caribbean (UNECLAC, 2020).[4]

The US has taken economic measures to protect its domestic market. First, the Federal Reserve rolled out monetary policies involving interest rate cuts, unlimited quantitative easing, and both old and new tools to keep the financial markets running. At the same time, three-phase fiscal policies were also put into action – Phase One: Coronavirus Preparedness and Response Supplemental Appropriations Act (March 06, 2020); Phase Two: Families First Coronavirus Response Act (March 18, 2020); and Phase Three: Coronavirus Aid, Relief, and Economic Security (CARES) Act (March 27, 2020) (UNECLAC, 2020).[5].

In the second quarter of 2020, the pandemic hit the US economy with the worst recession since the Great Depression. The GDP plunged at a 32.9% annualized rate. The US central bank set interest rates near zero and promised to pump money continuously into the economy. Meanwhile, the US dollar devalued against a basket of currencies. Almost 30.2 million Americans were dependent on unemployment checks provided by the government by the end of July in 2020.[6] At present, the recovery of the US economy is still under the looming threat of the resurgence of COVID-19 cases.

The severity of the pandemic is considered a catalyst for the USA's *decoupling* strategy as well as rising tensions with China. The decoupling strategy was initiated by the former US President Trump to promote reshoring and onshoring and to move the global value chains (GVCs) out of China. As the pandemic forced many countries to adopt border lockdowns, flight suspensions, and social distancing, global supply chains were interrupted, which then blocked the movement of human resources and capitals among countries. Those American companies bringing their production back to the US would reduce the risk of GVC disruption and ensure the stability of production as well as economic development in the US. Recently, President Joe Biden took even stronger action, to impose a tax rate of 30.8% on corporations that "offshore manufacturing and service jobs to foreign nations in order to sell goods or provide services back to the American market."[7]

The pandemic, like a drop of water that overflows the glass, pushes the US government toward *distrusting* and *verifying* the status quo with China.[8] The opacity in the Chinese internal governance model is blamed for covering up the pandemic's information at the early stage and slow reaction to stop it from spreading rapidly and causing devastation. Chinese leader Xi Jinping's playbook challenged American ideas and values with aggressive propaganda and false narratives, clearly visible in the robust Chinese propaganda campaign that suggested that the pandemic originated from the US army. However, Trump believed that China did manipulate the operation of the WHO in reaction to the pandemic. The COVID-19 outbreak was regarded as proof that China could pose a threat to the world and, as a result, cannot be trusted in handling the issues with accountability. The US government has experienced cold wars with the Soviet Union and, now, with China. The deal the US adopted for the former was 'trusting but verifying,' whereas what applies to the latter is 'distrusting and verifying.'

The COVID-19 hit both diplomatic relationships and trading relations between the Group of 20 (G20) countries hard. The COVID-19 recession puts a question mark on the implementation of the Phase One deal with China. In accordance with the agreement signed on January 15, 2020, China pledged to purchase from the US an *additional* $32, $52.4, and $78 billion worth of agricultural products, energy, and manufactured goods in 2020–2021, respectively. However, the recession struck the Chinese demand hard, as well as the American supply. The lower price requires China to purchase more units to satisfy the amount they promised. In addition, considering manufactured goods, there is a high tariff for American products (16.0% on average) whose rates are forcibly being maintained by the Chinese government, whereas tariff rates imposed on goods from other countries are merely one-third. The hefty tariff is regarded as a substantial impediment to Chinese firms' additional purchases (Yeon, 2020).[9] On the supply side, labor shortage, trouble in organizing transportation, and dropping prices are three main problems facing US suppliers. The labor problem is an inevitable result of visa restrictions on Mexican seasonal workers, especially in the farming sector, for the sake of limiting the spread of infection. Transportation also got a negative impact from domestic and international border lockdown and flight suspension. Lastly, the price drop is a mutual problem for both sides. The temporary shutdown or even permanent closure of restaurants, factories, etc. shift the demand curve for foods and energy downward, driving down product prices and eventually putting producers out of business.

On the other side of the coin, together with the Phase One deal, the pandemic provided the two countries with opportunities for cooperation. The signing of the Phase One agreement led to announcing of lists for exemption from retaliatory tariffs by both countries. Thirty-seven exclusion lists and six extensions for exclusions have been released by the US Trade Representative (USTR). The US government is giving priority to waiving Section 301 tariffs on critical medicines and other essential medical products to support efforts for COVID-19 epidemic prevention.[10] In 2019, before the COVID-19 outbreak, the US imported 22 billion USD worth of medical products from the world, among which Chinese products accounted for 26%, equal to 5 billion USD. China is the leading supplier of personal protective equipment, protective goggles, thermometers, and medical headwear (Gereffi, 2020).[11] Noticeably, the country produced 50% of the world's surgical masks at the beginning of the corona crisis (OECD, 2020).[12] Hence, the tariff exclusion for medical products from China is a necessary action to confront the shortfall of COVID-19 products in the US. By the same token, the action of the US is a good signal that the two great powers will join hands for a 'selective and result-oriented cooperation,' as mentioned in the US strategic approach, for the sake of global peace.

But the problem with the US strategy was, up to mid-March of 2020, outgoing President Trump kept on denying the gravity and scope of COVID-19, often shrugging off the threat posed by the virus. The sluggish implementation of these policies, plus the policies being mainly directed toward the domestic economy of the US, can be regarded as a clear indication of Trump's policy priority, which revolves around his *America First* rhetoric. This also resulted in fragmented international engagement, as seen when Trump decided to suspend funding for the WHO over its coronavirus response, thus further jeopardizing the multilateral order (Norrlöf, 2020).[13] With new President Joe Biden in his office, some are hopeful that he will restore the USA's position on top of these international institutions. For starters, President Biden's series of the executive orders were mostly directed toward having the US recover from the crisis as fast as possible while trying to care for people who were struggling the most with the job and healthcare crises. Most of the implemented bills dealt directly with the coronavirus (15 out of 52 in his first 100 days in office) (Hickey et al., 2021),[14] following with measures that reversed Trump's immigration policies and then adding additional 'equity' executive actions. The president also hit his target goal of 200 million vaccinations in his first 100 days (Murphy, 2021),[15] signaling how much of his strategy was centered around swift and effective recovery from a crisis that ended up being much more serious than initially anticipated. As we previously mentioned, Biden's sentiment toward what is needed to be done can also be seen during the 2021 Group of 7 (G7) meeting and the possible Atlantic Alliance, likely to move away from the global dependence on China regarding trade, value chains, and the use of rare materials and resources. Indeed, some of his executive orders focused on investing new strategies into the use and discovery of new materials. Considering the increase in the price of commodities throughout 2021 (WTO, 2021)[16] due to heavy use, the difficulty of access, and disruption of logistical corridors, the US government must step up its strategic game to make its businesses as competitive as ever and hence maintain its position as the most important economy in the world.

6.1.2 Impacts of the COVID-19 Pandemic on China's Strategies

China experienced a 6.8% drop in its year-on-year national GDP during the first quarter of 2020. In the same period, the GDP of Hubei, where Wuhan is located, dropped precipitously by 39.2%. China's industrial production and trade in services were also negatively affected by the pandemic. In terms of industrial production, automobiles and petroleum industries suffered the most, with a drop of 37% in production during the first two months of 2020. Labor-intensive enterprises and export-oriented enterprises were also hit hard, with operating revenue falling by about 24%–30% during the same period. As for the service industry, the revenue went down by 43.1% due to the initial lockdown measures that were imposed across the country, especially in the province of Hubei (Zhang et al., 2020).[17]

Wuhan, where the first COVID-19 case was recorded, is strategically located in the center of China surrounded by key cities and has been an important hub for the country. With the continuous spread of the virus in the first quarter of

2020, China experienced an economic slowdown that impacted its trade patterns significantly. There were serious disruptions in the global supply chain as manufacturing companies in China were forced to close and the service sector was put under limited operations. On the demand side, there was a huge decline in business and leisure travel. Tourism and entertainment services were badly affected. According to a report by PwC China (2020),[18] China's consumption dropped steeply because of the pandemic. The spread of the virus started before the Spring Festival, which is a season with the highest consumption in China, though the virus did cause a drastic drop in the consumption level during the 2020 Spring Festival. It is also worth noting that consumption has been a vital part of China's economy, as it accounted for around 60% of its GDP in 2019, therefore making the impact of the pandemic on the Chinese economy more severe. Investments also dropped as businesses were not able to continue their production on time. These factors eventually contributed to the decrease in China's import and export trade, which is directly connected to the Phase One trade deal with the US.

China's international trade also suffered. Exports of primary products and manufactured goods fell by 3.4% and 16.5%, respectively, making the total exports go down by 15.9% in the first two months of 2020. The country's most important export sectors, textiles and machinery and transport equipment, also fell by 18.7% and 14.4%, respectively. China was able to start its recovery in March, quicker than other countries in the world, and it was made possible through its strict COVID-19 policies and measures that were implemented vigorously across the country (Zhang et al., 2020).[19]

To mitigate the effects of the virus, aside from the lockdown and border control measures that China implemented initially, the country introduced a wide variety of policies to alleviate the impact of the pandemic. A combination of monetary and fiscal policies was created, which encouraged the resumption of business activities in the first quarter of 2020. On March 13, 2020, the Chinese central bank reduced the banks' mandatory reserve ratio, freeing up 550 billion yuan (US $84 billion) to provide a boost to the economy. Supportive policies toward SMEs were also launched, which included deferred tax payments, reduction in rent, waiving administrative fees, and other forms of subsidies. Tax exemption policies were made, which give value-added tax exemption on a wide range of customer services and tax incentives for companies producing medical equipment used for COVID-19. China, tagged as the world's manufacturer, also implemented customs measures to control import and export transactions. This includes regulations on medical products export, easing of custom measures, providing duty relief, and others (KPMG, 2020).[20]

Although China is on its way to recovery from the slump it experienced in early 2020, countries around the world have come to realize their economic over-dependence on China. It should be remembered that many supply chains of personal protective equipment (PPE) involved production in China. Around the world, some countries sourced more than half of their PPE production to China. When production in the world's leading manufacturer decreased, there were significant shortages that arose, and it exposed the configuration of the pre-pandemic supply chains. Some policymakers even went as far as claiming that the globalization of the supply chains had gone too far (Irwin, 2020).[21] Therefore, many global firms started to take steps in adding *stability* to GVCs by reshoring production lines or picking up the *China-plus One* strategy as a contingency plan.

Even before the pandemic, it was apparent that some countries already started reshoring and restructuring their supply chains away from China, partly due to the escalation of the US–China trade war. Of course, we cannot expect companies to totally abandon China. It is very costly to relocate the chain, and also China still remains an attractive market. According to the survey of more than 3,000 companies conducted by Bank of America in February 2020, 10 out of 12 global companies mentioned that they do plan to shift some portion of their supply chains out of China (Yang, 2020).[22] However, major shifts will be limited in terms of size and value. Japan also provided financial assistance to 87 companies to shift production back to their home country or to Southeast Asia. Former US President Trump was quite vocal about his intentions to end the USA's reliance on China.

The initial impact of the pandemic was worse than the current situation that China is experiencing. For example, the ICT sector, wherein China produces 45% of global exports, once sustained a strong network, and China was a major partner of big countries in the global market. But due to the COVID-19 pandemic plus the trade war, China's share in the ICT GVC decreased by 4%. Global trade is negatively affected by the decrease in China's trade volume, and it is expected that the GVC trade will decline continuously because of the strong anti-globalization attitude in different countries.

The COVID-19 pandemic can be regarded as a short-run wave whose impacts might linger for the next three years. In China's case, the country was even able to somehow bounce back after its economy experienced a sharp decline in the first three months of the year because of COVID-19 lockdowns. The Chinese economy showed a –6.8% growth rate in the first quarter of the year 2020, but it was able to turn the tides and grew by 3.2% in the second quarter of the year. In Beijing, residents are now allowed to go out without wearing face masks. This signals China's economy slowly going back to normal, and with this, we can expect consumption, investment, and trading volume of the country to increase again. But it is worth noting that not all industries can recover quickly such as the tourism and hospitality sectors. But these numbers show that more or less, we should expect the effects of the COVID-19 pandemic to be mitigated within the next three years or so.

In the pre-COVID period, the growth rate of global trade decelerated from 5.25% in 2017 to 4% in 2018. Both the US and China have been trying to establish their own networks with their free trade agreements (FTAs) and other multilateral agreements. Therefore, it is only rational for both superpowers to mitigate the negative impacts of COVID-19 by not burdening the global economy already reeling from their trade war. But then again, both the US and China also have different agendas, and that explains why the US decided to start the trade war, to slow China's economic and non-economic growth. For China, backing out is not an option, as it also needs to actualize its plan to become the world's greatest superpower.

The impacts of COVID-19 on the GVC might serve as a challenge for China, as it is eager to continuously expand its global influence through its external circulation. As the world tries to rely on reshoring due to the weaknesses of the GVCs exposed by the COVID-19 pandemic, it seems obvious that changes in the network structure of the GVCs are inevitable. Also, as mentioned in previous chapters, Biden is firm at setting and holding anti-China 'councils' with allies as he also sees China *robbing* the US companies' technology and intellectual property (IP).

6.1.3 Impacts of the COVID-19 Pandemic on the EU's Strategies

The conflagration that is the COVID-19 pandemic heavily influenced most aspects of everyone's lives in the world. The global trading system has been shaken, and the economic implications are already very visible worldwide. In a COVID-19 pandemic timeline developed by Barua (2020),[23] the economic impact will stretch in five different waves based on the length in which they will be developing. The first is based on the initial production and demand shock, which will distort the supply chain and interrupt the flow of people. The second one will translate into a distortion of trade flows and the interruption of capital flows. The third one will have macroeconomic impacts in the short to medium term, with an aggregate supply and demand shock, followed by a loss of employment and income. In the long run, the fourth and fifth waves will consist of reduced economic growth, a recession and depression scenario, and a shift in international cooperation.

As countries tried to isolate themselves trying to contain the spread of the virus, debates ensued about the future of multilateralism, the primary concern for the EU. In contrast with the 2008 financial crisis, a coordinated global response has not been made yet. Each country was on its own while a propaganda war between the US and China started to wreak havoc. The US disputes with international organizations like the WHO assured even less focus on multilateralism and cooperation. As a result, world leaders have done little together to tackle the crisis (Cameron, 2020).[24]

The EU region experienced huge outbreaks of COVID-19 cases in 2020, especially in countries like France, Germany, Italy, and Spain. That is why it is not surprising to know that the region suffered severely from the negative impacts of the pandemic. However, the effect of COVID-19 is uneven among EU regions. A territorial analysis by scientists at the European Commission's Joint Research Center (JRC)[25] shows that the economic consequences of the crisis do not exactly reflect the epidemiological damage caused by the COVID-19 pandemic; rather the impact depends on the economic attributes of the region. The impact is also greater on regions that depend on tourism, hence also correlated with a decline in employment rates (EU Science Hub, 2020).[26] But as a whole, the GDP impact on EU regions is estimated to be negative 6.44% on average.

The region's industrial production was also badly hit by the pandemic. This can be seen in the growth rates of both the EU's imports and exports. During the first six months of 2020, the EU's imports and exports recorded a negative growth rate, with some product groups suffering more than the others. The shrinkage peaked in May 2020 for both imports and exports. The energy sector was hit the hardest, with a negative growth rate of 62.7% and 66.2%, respectively. This was followed by machinery and vehicles, other manufactured products, and raw materials (Eurostat, 2020).[27]

In an attempt to mitigate the pandemic's repercussions, the EU imposed lockdowns and social distancing measures in early/mid-March 2020, and the European Central Bank (ECB) in the same month instituted an aggressive monetary policy with a focus on the expansion of asset purchases to stabilize the euro area sovereign debt and other financial markets. This quick response showed that the ECB has learned important lessons after the 2008 global financial crisis. Fiscal packages were also rolled out in different forms such as direct government wage subsidization of 80%–90% of companies' labor expenses during the lockdown measures. This was done to avoid layoffs and a surge in unemployment during the lockdown period. In addition, the finance ministers negotiated a common fiscal package in April 2020. This focuses on giving member states access to unconditional loans from the European Stability Mechanism (ESM) to be used on pandemic-related expenditures. Additional capital for the European Investment Bank (EIM) was also negotiated to be able to support EU SMEs as well (Kirkegaard, 2020).[28] The EU, Chancellor Merkel and President Macron leading the way, also agreed on the 750 billion euros coronavirus recovery fund (RF) back in July 2020, hence dubbed as the *Merkel-Macron Agreement*. The deal was finally struck last December 2020, together with the EU's seven-year budget worth 1.1 trillion euros. The RF was made possible due to the fact that it can be used for investment grants to boost Europe's movement in fighting climate change and its 5G investments. The EU's goal is to reach carbon neutrality by 2050, and this can be seen as an important part of the EU's pandemic policymaking. Leaders in the EU are utilizing the crisis to implement common fiscal policies in the region (Kirkegaard, 2020).[29]

However, due to the differences in initial endowments and economic characteristics of EU countries, the responses were varied and asymmetrical. The differences between EU member countries were accentuated by the pandemic, as the region noticed the varying capacities of the members in coping with the pandemic. Even before the pandemic, the EU, as a network, has been fragile and divided, and the virus poses a threat that might make this issue worse. One example of the network's instability was the Brexit. Since the UK's joining in 1973, it never fully accepted full control of the EU over British institutions. It even refused to join the Schengen Area, which removed border controls among the members. The UK became more skeptical of the EU after the 2008 financial crisis, and since then, more advocates have argued that the UK would be better outside the EU. Some people argue as well that the EU network is very much unfair and imbalanced. Even powerful countries in the EU felt the strains from continuous efforts to supporting the network and extending help to the smaller members. As Grewal (2008) describes the two broad classes of concern in a network, the one occurring in the EU is an example of a distributional concern.[30] He describes it as a concern resulting from "unequal imposition of costs on some parties, which affects their interests." This type of concern in the EU's network might become bigger as the region tries to keep everything together for it to survive the ongoing crisis.

These distributional concerns have obviously affected the EU network as talks have been slow and were initially focused on a national level. An ESM was developed and is in place though not without internal fights among the constituent members. One such instance of instability and internal clashes is Poland and Hungary's decision to veto the progress on the €1.8 trillion budget for EU's recovery plan in November 2020.[31] Orban has proven to be hostile toward the Rule of Law mechanism, and Mateusz Morawiecki said that he opposes any discretionary mechanisms that are based on arbitrary, politically motivated criteria. As Farrel and Newman (2020)[32] explain, European countries did not behave much better than countries like Russia or Turkey when it came to formulating a common approach to tackling the spread of the virus. Germany prohibited the export of medical masks despite the fact that it is a member of the EU's single market, while France simply seized all available masks. Overall, these beggarthy-neighbor dynamics threatened to escalate as the crisis deepened, severing the global supply chain for several products like medical supplies. Talks, lockdowns, a shift in the allocation of resources, and a shift in the EU's priorities led to inevitable, negative effects on the EU's policies: political agendas, meetings, and plans involving cooperation between the European network and possible other players slowed down and in some cases were put on hold.

Regarding the EU's approach in dealing with each country's demands and necessities to define a proper COVID vaccine distribution strategy, the flaws deriving from the complexity of the Union ended up coming to the surface. The European Commission president acknowledged her mistakes while defining a common strategy that would maximize the distribution of the various vaccines. The problems that arose at the beginning of 2021 in Europe are partially explained by the complexity of the network itself, where many of the singular nodes, despite being connected through different linkages, have to consider both internal and external pressures – more specifically, countries that are part of the European community but at the same time would think of their own interest first and foremost. Going deeper into this network and following additional internal linkages, we can see conflicts arose even between counties and regions inside individual countries, proving how difficulties and complexity are innate characteristics of a multiplex network[33] like the EU.

For these very reasons, Cameron (2020) argued that it was the right time for the EU to take a definitive direction with its strategy and invest its efforts toward multilateralism and create ties with Asia. According to him, despite the

American critics of WHO, the EU and Asia should have pressed for the international organization to monitor governments' health policies and ensured better exchange of information. Moreover, he suggested that Taiwan's observer status should be restored. Economically, the G20 is the right entity to coordinate fiscal and monetary stimulus measures to avoid beggar-my-neighbor approaches. From a trade policy perspective, emphasis should be put on pressing China to reform instead of isolating it with the USA's aggressive approach.

Although the EU did not discuss multilateralism in detail, the EU's High Representative for Foreign Affairs and Security Policy Josep Borrell did manage to voice his views on the matter, saying that Europe

> *needs a new kind of globalization capable of striking a balance between the advantages of open markets and interdependence, and between the sovereignty and security of countries. Europe should work to prevent the US-China rivalry from having repercussions in certain regions of the world – particularly Africa.*
>
> (Lazarou, 2020)[34]

The EU's standards and propensity toward a multilateral approach will probably prevail. The EU–Japan summit held in May 2020 is an example of this, and Europe's foreign policy in general.

We have yet to see how the EU will stand against the crisis. Although its fragility is being tested by the virus, EU leaders still have hopes of keeping the club together. If that happens, companies from the region might also resort to reshoring and simplifying value chains, hence relying on more EU region-centered value chains (Celi et al., 2020).[35] This can be achieved through a coordinated industrial policy at an EU level to integrate the European production networks. With the approval of the RF, we can see that the EU leaders are trying their best to turn this crisis into an opportunity for stronger regional cooperation.

6.2 The US–China Trade War

6.2.1 *Current Development from the USA's Perspective*

While observing the linkages, nodes, and networks intertwining the modern global landscape of international trade, one cannot overlook a series of events as important as the ones tied to what we can call *hegemonic competition* between the two largest economies in the world, the US and China. This phenomenon implies a rivalry between the established, first-place economy (the US, which led much of the economic, technological, and cultural development in the Western world after World War II [WWII]) and a country that is trying to challenge it from different areas of the world (China).

Globalization, technological competition, and attempts to achieve regional supremacy in various parts of the globe all converged to set up a scenario in which these two countries started to press each other with increasingly aggressive policies, colliding on security issues, wrestling each other with different stances on multilateralism, and ultimately, a trade war starting in 2018.

Indeed, we can say that the trade war has led to a continuous series of repercussions that will affect all countries involved with any of the two countries. This means essentially the whole world will be affected, as much of the global economy is ultimately interdependent with the economies of its most influential states. Li and Zhang (2018)[36] explore the term *interdependent hegemony* and how it explains the role of multiple emerging powers when it confronts a strong hegemon. In this specific case, we can consider the US as the hegemon (leading note of its network and its surrounding allies) and China as the main contender.

The situation the current world is in sees a hegemon that, to hold and maintain power, has to seek interconnection with different players in order to stay afloat. This is especially true in the domain of space and time where distances are made shorter and the costs of international trade and communication are becoming much cheaper.

With the gradual erosion of US hegemonic power especially since the 2008 global financial crisis, it is true that the ascendance of China has successfully penetrated into various global domains in terms of economic competition, global mergers and acquisitions, capital accumulation, military influence, territorial disputes, as well as technical and material capacities. The current status of the world can be described by a strong hegemon that will no longer allow *free usage* of global public goods that it has provided hitherto using its own resources, yet still has to rely on connections with emerging powers when it comes to various key issues including global production sharing, system of standards, global governance of finance and credit, material capacity and availability, cultural and ideological leadership, and global climate change.

What this situation means is that networks are most likely playing a role that is as important as ever, showcasing how networking power, network power, networked power, and network-making power have an ever-increasing influence over the present multilateral stability.

China, as the other contender in this *hegemonic competition*, is seen as a potential threat for the post–WWII hegemony due to the fact that it is shifting its position from *rule-taker* to *rule-maker*. Being the new focus of an anti-US network, the competition will naturally occur, and this phenomenon will ultimately lead to the development of a *hegemonic war*. Nevertheless, even in the current world system, China (and, of course, the US too) is both beneficiary and contributor to the capitalist world system, showing how the root of integration managed to dig deep into the global trading environment.

Although it could be argued that culture and ideology aspects would also be an important part of this clash, it is the economic struggle between the US and China that is certainly seen as the most important aspect as a whole. This challenge goes beyond the mere imposition of tariffs, though, and will most likely drag on for several years into the future, posing a real concern for the global trading system.

One of the most important players in the whole situation was Former US President Donald Trump, who dictated the foreign policy of the US toward China from 2016 to 2020. His protectionist and bilateral approach sparked a series of events and tit-for-tat trade fights that eventually escalated into the aforementioned trade war.

Donald Trump maintained an aggressive stance toward China, even before running for president. His tweet in 2011 stated that "China is neither an ally nor a friend – they want to beat us and own our country," and during his campaign in 2016, China was blamed for "raping the US" and committing "the greatest theft in the history of the world." And the trade war in the form of tariff retaliation is regarded as a tough response of the US to China's aggressive trade policies, unfair trade practices, and IP theft.

At the start of the trade war, the US applied the US Section 301 tariffs consecutively on \$34 billion, \$16 billion, and \$200 billion worth of China exports in the second half of 2018. In 2019, despite tariff reductions on solar panels and washing machines, the US continued to apply Section 301 with an increase of 10% to 25% tariffs on \$200 billion and a 15% tariff on a subset of \$300 billion worth of China export value.

On the surface, we noticed a phenomenon similar to the one presented in Chapter 2, an *issue linkage* defined as *enforcement linkage*. Following the definition used by Maggi (2016)[37]: "there is enforcement linkage if a violation of an agreement in area A is punished with sanctions (also) in area B." Indeed, the US started to apply the initial tariffs as retaliation due to the 'unfair trade practices' of China and its aggressive policy, at least on paper. The scale of this economic conflict, though, is better represented by the hegemonic competition between the two biggest economies on the planet. The US decided to adopt coercive trade sanctions, a move that could lead to successful results if the country starting the quarrel could commit to a trade war in which the target country would not be able to counter the economic attack and not commit with equal force. Quoting Maggi's work, the countries will find themselves in a *coercive linkage*, which would be positive only if "the sender country has a superior commitment ability relative to the target country" (Maggi, 2016).[38] If the target country could retaliate with equal strength, the quarrel would prove ineffective; if the target country could apply more leverage, the home country could actually find itself worse off compared to the pre-conflict situation.

As for how the trade war developed, so far the US has levied tariffs on \$550 billion worth of Chinese products, and the average rate of tariffs recorded in March 2020 remained elevated at 19.3%, six times higher than the rate before the trade war in 2018 (Bown, 2020).[39]

The trade war that started in July 2018 escalated quickly. On August 23, 2018, the tariff collection of 25% tariff on List 2, including 279 goods (worth US \$16 billion), took effect. The targeted goods involve semiconductors, chemicals, plastics, motorbikes, and electric scooters. The final revision of this list was released 16 days before the effective date. According to the revised version, the levied tariff was raised from the previously announced level of 10% to 25%. And 5 items (out of 284), of which collective value was $400 million in 2017, were removed.

A month later, on September 24, the US implemented tariffs on $200 billion worth of Chinese products. List 3 comprises a wide diversity of good categories, namely, consumer products, chemical and construction materials, textiles, tools, food and agriculture products, commercial electronic equipment, and vehicle/automotive parts. The initial rate applied on this list was 10% and would be increased to 25% on January 1, 2019. The tariff raising deadline was then delayed to March 1 and then May 10, 2019, thanks to progress in trade talks between the two countries during the temporary truce period. The discussion is divided into two areas – trade and structural issues. The latter covers forced technology transfers, IP protection, and non-tariff barriers. During three-day trade talks in Beijing in January 2019, China pledged to purchase a 'substantial amount' of US products and services, which was considered a preliminary for the Phase One deal signed one year later.

In the middle of 2019, the US placed Huawei and other five Chinese companies on the *entity list*, namely, Sugon, the Wuxi Jiangnan Institute of Computing Technology, Higon, Chengdu Haiguang Integrated Circuit, and Chengdu Haiguang Microelectronics Technology. Through this measure, the US prevented these entities from buying American parts and components without prior government approval. The ban on Huawei was eased as the trade talks restarted by the end of June 2019.

To discuss more about Huawei, China's largest telecom giant and the world's second-biggest smartphone company has been blocked or investigated by the world's big powers, including the US, EU, Germany, the UK, Australia, Canada, and New Zealand. Those countries have banned Huawei or carried out a security review of its products relating to the 5G mobile network development. Additionally, Huawei was prosecuted for trade secrets theft in the US according to the charges made by the US Department of Justice (2020).[40] The misappropriation of IP was conducted with methods of entering into confidentiality agreements with IP owners or recruiting employees of other companies and directing them to steal their former employers' IP. Noticeably, a substantial financial bonus and reward program was offered for those providing valuable information for Huawei. The Chinese conglomerate was also entangled to the allegation of involvement in business and technology projects and concealing the full scope of that involvement in Iran and North Korea, which are countries subjected to the US, EU, and/or UN sanctions. From the vantage point of the US, Huawei is regarded as an espier for the Chinese Communist Party (CCP), and its threat to US national security is obvious and considerable. Thus, taking advantage of the USA's network, its allies and partners are called for cooperation in blocking this 'untrusted vendor.' Disrupting the made-in-the-US semiconductor supply chain and confining the development of Huawei on a global scale comprise a tough confrontation of the US toward China in the technology realm.

Another important aspect to consider is the fact that the US Treasury Department labeled China as a *currency manipulator*,[41] further showcasing how the US foreign policy was ready to have a full-on fight against its new hegemonic competitor from many different angles. As Ajibo et al. (2019)[42] pinpointed, this operation has various consequences not only for China but also for its neighboring countries, in case it allows China to "reroute trade to their territories to escape tariffs or for onward export to the US." Additionally, being considered a 'currency manipulator' means that, as a result, China would be excluded from different US procurement contracts and agreements and further sanctions would be carried out.

Returning to the development of trade war, on September 1, 2019, List 4A tariffs came into force as scheduled, which was an inevitable outcome of various factors: little progress made in the Shanghai meeting, the USA's calling out China for the latter's supposed currency manipulation to boost exports, the suspension of agriculture products purchase of Chinese companies, and China's plan of imposing 5% and 10% of tariffs on 5,078 US goods. List 4A, valued at $125 billion, covers goods ranging from footwear, diapers, and food to smartwatches, dishwashers, and flat-panel televisions.

A concession in the trade war was attributed to a plan for a high-level trade talk in October 2019. The US released a new list to exempt 437 Chinese goods from US tariffs. Furthermore, in the high-level meeting on October 10–11, 2019, between the two countries, the Phase One deal agreement was reached. According to the agreement, China should purchase approximately $200 billion in US agricultural, energy, and manufacturing products additionally over the next two years (2020–2021), reinforce IP provisions, and issue new guidelines on currency management. In exchange, the US agreed to delay the tariff increase from 25% to 30% on $250 billion of Chinese goods. The negotiation process in the last months of 2019 witnessed more efforts on making concessions. Eventually, the Phase One deal was signed on January 15, 2020.

On July 22, 2020, the USTR announced 37 batches of exemptions to specific Chinese products from US tariffs. The review process of exclusion requests from USA's interested groups was impacted considerably by the COVID-19 pandemic. The USTR is now giving priority to requests on medical products and pursuing public comments on the removal of Section 301 tariffs on products that are vital for the US response to the outbreak.

6.2.1.1 The Phase One Deal from the USA's Point of View

The Economic Trade Agreement, as known as the Phase One deal, between the governments of the US and China was signed on January 15, 2020. The USA's perspective on the trade war, in the form of tariffs levied on Chinese goods, was that it was implemented for the purpose of confronting market-distorting practices of China. The tariffs would be maintained until a fair Phase Two deal could be reached between the two countries.

The Agreement covers eight chapters on (1) IP, (2) technology transfer, (3) trade in good and agricultural products, (4) financial services, (5) macroeconomic policies and exchange rate matters and transparency, (6) expanding trade, (7) bilateral evaluation and dispute resolution, and (8) final provisions. A general look at the trade agreement reveals that the US is trying to make China comply with 'existing US measures.' In every article, the commitments of China are defined specifically and clearly, while those of the US are to "affirm that existing U.S. measures afford treatment equivalent to that provided for in this Article."

IP protection, technology transfer, and currency manipulation constituted the most prominent issues causing the US–China tension; therefore, said issues were carefully regulated in this agreement. In accordance with the deal, China commits to strengthen IP protection, combat against online infringement, eliminate pressure for foreign firms to transfer technology, and protect trade secrets and confidential business information. In the currency issue, China pledged to refrain from competitive devaluation.

Regarding the trade issue, the US consented to not proceed with new tariff imposition on $160 billion worth of consumer goods scheduled to take effect on December 25 and to reduce by half the tariff rate on List 4A, from 15% to 7.5%; however, 25% tariff on $250 billion Chinese goods maintains. Meanwhile, China agreed to buy an additional $200 billion worth of US goods and services over the next two years. The two-year total increases are divided into four product categories, namely, manufactured goods ($77.7 billion), agriculture ($32 billion), energy ($52.4 billion), and services ($37.9 billion).

Reviewing the prospect of the Phase One deal after seven months, both US and China showed an optimistic view as China is trying to purchase more from the US and taking action to fulfill other obligations. However, none of the countries could guarantee the trade deal's completion, owing to several factors.

The relations between the two countries have been deteriorating, heading toward a possible collapse. On July 23, 2020, Mike Pompeo,[43] the US secretary of state, announced to end the engagement era with the CCP, owing to its unfair trade practices, IP theft, human rights abuse in Xinjiang and Hong Kong, as well as aggressive moves in the East and South China Seas. The accusation leveled on China for being the origin of worldwide COVID-19 pandemic is another reason for the surge of tensions between the two countries. Moreover, both China and America each took action to expel and limit the number of journalists from media outlets from the other country. And as China's National Security Law entered into force, the US revoked the special status of Hong Kong. This was followed by requirements for Hong Kong–origin products to be labeled 'made in China,' and the US-Hong Kong bilateral agreement of reciprocal tax exemption for Hong Kong shipping companies is suspended. In addition, there was a drastic escalation of diplomatic friction, with the Chinese Consulate in Houston and US Consulate in Chengdu being ordered to close. There are those who criticize that if Trump truly respects the cooperative spirit of the Phase One deal, he should not treat China that way.

As mentioned in the previous section of this chapter, the situation between G2 countries got worse not only by the fact that the Chinese demand got negative impacts but also in that American supply capacity faced hardship presented by the pandemic, which left the implementation of commitments in Phase One deal uncertain. Trade data from January 2020 through November 2021 shows that China's imports of all covered amounted to 62% (Chinese imports) or 60% (US exports) of the Phase One target (Bown, 2021).[44] Malkawi (2021) assesses the result of the Phase One deal arguing that "managing trade to improve the economic relationship is the wrong approach" but "despite its flaws, the deal has had some success. ... China was willing to import from the US in increased quantities, making the sentiments behind the deal valid."[45]

The multifaceted escalation between the two countries and the outbreak of COVID-19 cast a long shadow on the prospect of the Phase One deal. The decoupling of the GVC from China continues at a rapid pace. The US and China continue to counter and retaliate against each other with tit-for-tat measures in various areas. More and more global firms based in the US, EU, and Japan are moving their production process out of China as a result of government policies, COVID-19, and especially the CCP risk. Additionally, the diplomatic tensions forced some Chinese private firms to change their attitude to wait and see and voluntarily delay imports from the US and seek alternative solutions.

6.2.1.2 Prospects of USA's Policy Shifts in the Future

Analyzing the situation from a network-theory perspective, the US proposes policies to empower the inner strength in order to exert its sphere of influence over the outer network. The US is now facing domestic instability owing to a variety of social issues, for instance, the slowdown in economic recovery, high trade deficit, high unemployment rate (caused by free trade and, more recently, COVID-19), inflation, racial injustice with mass protests and violence, etc. On the global scale, the rise of China is considered the biggest challenge to the US, as the former has voiced threatening rhetoric to the latter in many aspects, including politics, diplomacy, economy, technological development, and even the leading position in the world. The policies proposed by the Republican administration from 2016 to 2020 were based on the ideology of economic nationalism, which means protecting the American interests and future growth from the *unfair behavior* including *theft* of China. The reasons for adopting such an approach lie in two main keywords that drove the infamous Trumpian policies: money and containment (Sun, 2020).[46]

While money is of course a focus for all countries, having a positive balance (or, at least, a 'less negative' one) appeared to be one of the main concerns driving USA's foreign economic policies. Containment underlines China's position as a possible competitor in multiple fields, reflected in the USA's ultimate goal of slowing down *Made in China 2025* (MIC 2025); the US-centered distribution and development of new technologies, the threat of *decoupling* and *damaging*

China's outward export-based economy and ultimately the decision to take extremely aggressive stances in the roaring trade war.

Meanwhile, plans proposed by the Democratic Party focus on the improvement of national competitiveness in tandem with the increase in international commitments. All in all, it is believed by both sides of the House that the US cannot compete with China without a vibrant domestic economy. The policies of both parties aim to improve the domestic situation by strengthening the links of the inner network via investments in cutting-edge industries, including semiconductors, batteries, pharmaceuticals, and rare earth elements.

The US government and bipartisan congressional announcements pushed US–China relations toward a point of no return. As commented by Ryan Hass, a China director on Obama's National Security Council, Trump's administration members were pursuing a goal of reorientation of the US–China relationship toward an all-encompassing systemic rivalry, which is upheld no matter who will take office. The Republicans' policy direction is well captured by the US Strategic Approach to the People's Republic of China (2020),[47] while the strategies of Democrats are clearly revealed in the LEADS Act (2020),[48] which, although ultimately did not end up being enacted, clearly expressed their main points.

On behalf of the Republican administration, Pompeo, former Secretary of State, declared in his speech that the only way to deal with China is to 'distrust and verify'; in other words, to "respond to China's actions rather than its stated commitments." Confrontation and coercion, aggression, and antagonism should be the status quo with the CCP, which would support the US intentions to ensure "a free 21st century, not the Chinese century of Xi Jinping dreams."[49]

The current US policy on China has undergone a sea change, in comparison to what was set up by Former President Nixon. Nearly half a century ago, Nixon's policy was aimed at inducing a change in the internal governance model of China in order to build a freer and safer world. However, the new strategies presented in the US Strategic Approach to the People's Republic of China (2020)[50] do not attempt to change China's domestic model but focus on the response to the challenges posed by China in economic, diplomatic, and security realms.

The competitive approach is designed with two purposes: first, to improve the resiliency of American institutional alliances and partnerships so that the US would prevail against the challenges presented by China; second, to compel Beijing to cease or reduce actions harmful to the vital national interest of the US and those of their allies and partners. The US also announced that it will treat China under the same standards and principles applied to other nations, including the rules of the Free and Open Indo-Pacific Initiative (FOIPI). However, the agreements with Beijing must involve stringent verification and enforcement mechanisms. Despite the competition, the US welcomes selective and result-oriented cooperation between two countries toward shared objectives that benefit world peace, stability, and prosperity. They are also committed to maintaining open channels of communication with China to reduce risks and manage crises.

The implementation of strategies by the US against China is a multifaceted plan, which is divided according to four main goals. The first group of actions is to protect the American people, the US homeland, and the American way of life. The US will bolster the investigation on theft of trade secrets, hacking and industrial espionage, the protection against malign foreign direct investment (FDI) in US infrastructure, supply chain threats, and foreign agents seeking to manipulate American policy. They also work with universities to protect Chinese students on American campuses against coercion from their own government and provide them with information to counter the CCP's propaganda and disinformation. In addition, two Executive Orders were issued to prevent malign foreign actors from gaining access to the US information network, including sensitive military and intelligence data. Advanced technologies such as hypersonics, quantum computing, artificial intelligence (AI), biotechnology, and other emerging and foundational technologies are also protected from the access and exploitation of Chinese companies. The US government also takes action to protect consumers from counterfeit and substandard products, of which the China-origin shipments accounted for more than $2.1 billion in 2017–2018.

Promoting American property, both physical and intellectual, is the second purpose of the implementation. The trade war with China is an important element of these measures aimed at protecting American businesses, workers, and farmers against the unjust market-distorting subsidies and overcapacity of China. After the signing of the Phase One deal, the tension between the world's two great powers seemed to decline; however, the US expects to maintain high tariffs on Chinese products until an agreement is reached on the Phase Two deal. Furthermore, in the domestic market, the US strengthens the economy and economic sectors of the future via tax reforms and a robust deregulatory agenda. Internationally, cooperation with like-minded nations is facilitated to promote an economic vision based on the standard of sovereignty, free markets, and sustainable development. Particularly several global projects like Prosper Africa, America Crece (in Latin America and the Caribbean), Enhancing Development, and Growth through Energy (in the Indo-Pacific region) are being carried out in pursuit of economic goals.

The third purpose of the strategy implementation is to preserve peace through the US strength. The US is prioritizing military and military technology power to deter China from using its weapons of mass destruction and strategic attacks. It is also meant to build partner capacity and deepen interoperability with allies and partners, to deter and deny China's aggression.

These measures to advance American influence have a fourth purpose – the US exerting its leadership on a global scale to resist and counter the spread of authoritarianism, self-censorship, corruption, mercantilist economics, and intolerance of ethnic and religious diversity. The US, together with its allies and partners, criticizes the human rights violation and repressive policies of China in Xinjiang and Hong Kong that are harmful to global peace and security. The actions such as visa bans and blocking imports are taken as a determination of the US to force China to obey international human rights commitments. Moreover, the establishment of the Blue Dot Network under the FOIPI is intended to bolster transparently financed, high-quality infrastructure around the world and, at the same time, enhance the US sphere of influence in more and more countries.

On the other hand, the Senate Democrat's LEADS Act was announced in mid-September 2020, in which LEADS stands for Labor, Economic Competitiveness, Alliances, Democracy, and Security. The Democratic bill shared similarities in vision and direction of implementation with that of the Republican measures explained earlier. This plan was expected to be combined with the Republican proposals for a bipartisan plan since the relationship with China is "an American issue, not a partisan issue," said Senator Jim Risch, chairman of the Senate Foreign Relations Committee.

First, the Democratic plan focused on the improvement of national competitiveness with $350 billion worth of investments in American workers and entrepreneurs, the education system, scientific research and technology, and manufacturing. This funding and support from the government sought to promote domestic research and development (R&D) and manufacturing network toward greater prominence of 'Made in America' and to gain leadership in cutting-edge technologies like 5G, quantum, and AI and semiconductor industry. Additionally, the investment would provide new resources for building a diverse and inclusive innovation and manufacturing workforce.

Second, the LEADS Act underpinned the renewal and reorientation of the USA's diplomatic, military, and human rights strategy toward China. The US wanted to reaffirm its commitment to its allies around the globe and in the Indo-Pacific region. The reestablishment of its leadership in international organizations, for instance, WHO and G7, was also proposed, which marked the biggest difference between Republican and Democratic strategies. Based on the Act, the US would take action for the sake of international security and peace by providing assistance and training to countries under the Indo-Pacific Maritime Security Initiative. Furthermore, the human rights protection strategy of the US directly focused on Tibet, Hong Kong, and Xinjiang.

Third, the US President was mandated to use a full range of sanctions authority to combat the malign behavior of the Chinese government, entities, and individuals. The plan also countered and confronted China's predatory economic behavior relating to IP theft, currency manipulation, counterfeit goods, subsidies and dumping, foreign corrupt practices, etc.

The main motivation for the drafting of such a bill was the possibility of bolstering local businesses and research in order to compete with China. Ranking Member Menendez argued that China challenges the US across every dimension of power, and Trump's policies are not strong enough to prevent China from exerting the power of its authoritarian system to reshape international institutions and establish global rules and norms. The complex bilateral relationship with China indeed does impose threats to American economic prosperity and national security. "The Trump administration's *America Alone* approach is failing," said Senator Shaheen; hence, the LEADS Act was considered an urgent first step of a comprehensive and long-term strategy on China. Although the bill did not end up coming to fruition as a whole (Govtrack, 2020),[51] this doesn't mean that several parts of the bill cannot be implemented separately in the future. Indeed, based on President Biden's stance on China and his foreign policy, it is more than likely that a further push to counterbalance China's strength internationally will be made. US Innovation and Competition Act (USICA) of 2021 is part of those efforts.

USICA is a $200 billion proposal composed of several individual acts aimed at securing supply chain resiliency of the US economic network and countering China's influence on the global economy. USICA represents a dramatic expansion in the federal government's role in facilitating technological growth. It has gained bipartisan support and already passed the Senate and is expected to pass the House. A significant part of the USICA focuses on diminishing the global influence of China. It proposes multiple strategies.[52] First, it directs the US government to increase public investment, lending, and trade abroad, focusing mainly on Latin America, the Caribbean, Taiwan, Africa, and Southeast Asia. Second, it established IP protections from China, exclusion of China from federal funding programs, and diminishing purchases of goods and services from China. Additionally, it highlights the importance of regaining the position as leading node in international standard-setting boards in order to make sure international trade standards benefit the US.

Overall, the rivalry between the world's two great powers has been set up to be a long-term relationship. The approach of the US to China has been modified from inducing an internal governance model change to confrontation, coercion, aggression, and antagonism. Both parties developed specific strategies for long-term competition between the two countries, which involves the US response to the challenges that are derived from the actions of China. Despite the differences in foreign strategy regarding international institutions and organizations, the bipartisan goals definitely lie in national interest protection, exertion of pressure on China, and the reestablishment of US leadership in the world.

6.2.2 Current Development from China's Perspective

The trade war poses a visceral threat to the global trading system and free trade. China, being a large trading partner of many countries in the world, holds an important position, especially in the GVC. The negative impacts of the trade war are reflected in China's GDP growth. China's annual GDP growth rate decreased slightly since the trade war started in March 2018. The annual GDP growth rate was 6.95% in 2017 but slowed down to 6.75% in 2018 and 6.11% in 2019 and plummeted to 1.85% in 2020. It is forecast that China's economy and GDP growth will bounce back and grow by 8.50% in 2021 but will again experience a growth rate slowdown from 2022 onward.[53]

The Ministry of Commerce in China mentioned that even though China does not intend to fight against the US, China is not afraid to engage in a trade war. The ministry also emphasized that "China must implement a new comprehensive reaction plan and resolutely defend the interests of the nation and its citizens."[54]

This explains China's initial responses to the additional tariffs and other sanctions imposed by the US at the onset of the trade war where it also increased tariffs on US imports from 6.2% to 16.4%. But the negative impacts of the trade war must have forced both countries to at least try meeting in the middle.

The escalation of the US–China trade war seemed to be tapering and was headed in a somewhat different direction as both parties started to conduct high-level economic and trade negotiations. This sounded like good news for the smaller countries that are caught in the crossfire. In October 2019, Former US President Donald Trump and Chinese Vice-Premier Liu He met after the conclusion of the said talks. Liu expressed that properly addressing the bilateral relationship is in the interests of both the US and China, as well as the world.

Chinese leader Xi Jinping believes that China holds a stronger position on the negotiation table. He admitted that although China's economy was negatively affected by the additional tariffs imposed by the US, it was not impacted as badly as Washington had expected to (Nathan, 2019).[55] Despite the relatively positive indicators of China's endurance in the face of additional tariffs, it was reported that the Chinese do not see any benefits from severing its relationship with the US. There are strong disadvantages such as the Chinese tech giants' dependency on US semiconductor manufacturers. Some sources in China quote Xi claiming that because of its global rise, China must expect 30 years of 'containment and provocation' from the US until 2049. China expects itself to surpass the US in both economic and military prowess by that time. Until then, it should continue to diversify its markets and maintain sound foreign policies.

The World Trade Organization (WTO) ruled that the tariffs imposed by the US on Chinese imports are illegal under the global trade rules. Although the US can file an appeal against this ruling, it is an interesting development in the trade war between the two giants, as even US allies Australia and the EU stated that the US arguments on multilateral trade rules were wrong. The US insisted that the ruling was unnecessary as both parties had reached a resolution as China imposed retaliatory tariffs and have also signed the US-China Phase One trade deal, which will be discussed in the next section from China's point of view.

We can say that although efforts are being made to mend the worsening relationship between the US and China, it is far from over. But the new ruling of the WTO might also put pressure on Biden whether to keep the tariffs in place or remove them in the name of the rule-based international order. There are also new incidents under the Fourth Industrial Revolution section that will bring this trade war back to square one. For now, let us discuss the main deal serving as the bridge to better the relationship between these two countries.

6.2.2.1 The Phase One Trade Deal from China's Point of View

As both sides tried to catch up with the trade war with a sense of reciprocity, the US-China Phase One trade deal was signed by both then US President Donald Trump and Chinese Vice-Premier Liu in January 2020. Beijing promised to purchase an additional $200 billion worth of US goods and services (compared to 2017 levels) over the following two years. As part of this agreement, China also agreed to make structural reforms, strengthening IP rights (such as patents, trademarks, and copyrights) and opening up its financial services that would benefit American companies. The deal also addressed the initial concerns raised by the US regarding China's pressuring of foreign companies for technology transfer and currency agreements. What has been the result of the Phase One deal?

Data from January 2020 to November 2021 show that China imported 62% of manufacturing products, 76% of the agricultural products, and only 47% of the energy products it committed to under the Phase One deal. Overall, China has reached 62% of the original target (Bown, 2001),[56] raising the question of enforcement and compliance under the Phase One deal. China's purchases declined 16% for items not covered by the agreement yet which accounted for nearly 30% of the US–China trade. As explained already in this book, China has committed to the following additional purchases from the US: $77.7 billion in manufacturing goods, at least $52.4 billion in energy, $37.6 billion in services, and $32 billion in agriculture products.

From China's viewpoint, the $200 billion in additional commitments by China meant it should increase its imports from the US by more than 40% per year. This would require some kind of serious government intervention into the market. China might have to utilize trade diversion and move away from other countries' exports in order to fulfill this Phase One trade deal agreement (Bekkers and Schroeter, 2020).[57] Moreover, some critics argue that, even at the time of signing, Beijing already knew that the deal would never be realized. Beijing wanted the deal in return for a truce in the trade war with America since it could buy them the time they need and also the core issues, for example, state subsidies and preferential treatment for state-owned enterprises, were left anyway for a subsequent Phase Two deal that would never come. Beijing understood that Trump needed this *historic* deal for serving a single purpose – to fulfill his desire to have a deal.

Clear is the fact that China failed to live up to its commitments. This development can send both countries back to the starting line. Will Washington give China more time to keep to its promise? Or will Biden opt for a hard-line policy toward China? Malkawi (2021) suggests that Washington should open the Phase One deal to re-adjustment and re-attempt to establish diplomacy and negotiations.[58]

6.2.2.2 Prospects for Shifts in Chinese Policy in the Future

As analyzed by Sun (2020),[59] China held different possible positions when it came to decide which foreign policy stance to hold toward the US and their protectionist approach.

These three theoretical options were (1) China takes no or few retaliatory measures and completely yields to the pressure of the US, (2) China responds flexibly according to the situation in order to cope with the US pressure and re-shape Sino–US relations, and (3) China does not make any compromise and ab-solutely fights the US to the end. In general, China could decide how extensive and aggressive their retaliatory measures could be. Different from the approach that a third party could have (as in the case of the EU, as we will analyze shortly), China does not have any kind of say on who to rely on in terms of alliances, since the mainland appears to be the only target of the US attack.

Considering the background of the situation, choices (1) and (3) certainly appear to be the riskiest ones. By taking no retaliatory measures, China would not only be subject to the USA's *predatory move*, damaging the Chinese market and its competitiveness worldwide, but this situation would also set a precedent and allow other potential competitors to pull out similar cards against China. Moreover, China still holds considerable economic power even against the most powerful economy in the world, meaning that China would indeed have some effective means to oppose, to an extent, the USA's actions. The third option would still prove to be risky due to the power difference between what is (on pa-per) still a developing country and the most advanced among developed nations. The difference in GDP (not PPP based) is still significant, and in a tariff war of attrition, the US holds the upper hand due to its massive imports from China (as we've seen in the last set of impositions from the US, and the retaliatory measure from China that did not manage to offset the American move).

Because of this, in theory, a balanced approach appears to be the best possible course of action for China. Fighting back while reorganizing the economy in order to focus more on the domestic market will allow China to hold its ground while preparing itself to grow even further in the near future.

China's central bank governor, Yi Gang, said that China will continue to ful-fill its role in the Phase One trade deal with the US, according to an interview with the official Xinhua news agency in 2020.[60] This goes to show that China is exerting efforts to prevent its relationship with the US from totally falling apart. Yi also emphasized that Beijing would open up its financial sector by letting Wall Street trading houses own brokerage and fund-management operations in China exclusively. In June 2020, JP Morgan was allowed by Beijing to operate on the mainland as the first fully foreign-owned business. Taking his words at face value, we can say that China is trying its best to satisfy the US to the extent that it does not threaten the existential ground of the CCP.

To further understand the prospects of China's policies, we need to take a look at one of the probable reasons as to why the implementation of the Phase One deal on the Chinese side was postponed and the slow progress of China in meeting its commitments on the increase of imports from the US.

The interpretation of the US–China trade war in this part of the chapter might look optimistic but remember that we are trying to look at this deal from Chi-na's perspective. In reality, we can say that the Phase One deal is clearly headed toward failure. As shown previously, China is still far from fulfilling its $200 billion worth of commitments indicated in this trade deal. The USA's attitude toward the progress of the trade deal clearly shows its disinterest and its lack of confidence toward the other party. The US will maintain its existing tariffs as its leverage in negotiation until the next opportunity for a big trade deal with China strikes. Of course, we can expect China to insist on the validity of this deal and try to make it look like it is working hard to avoid additional sanctions from its rival.

6.2.3 Current Development from the EU's Perspective

Because we covered some background points about the EU's network in the previous chapter, it will be easier to analyze its foreign policy stance toward what some call 'the new Cold War': the commercial dispute between the US and China.

Since the US, China, and the EU are the three biggest economic blocs in the world, the relationship that ties each of these giants is of major importance when we consider the global economic situation and its status. More specifically, the EU's stance on the matter would be fundamental especially because the US and China represent both the biggest importers and exporters of the Union (Eurostat, 2020).[61]

Given the pro-multilateralism stance of the EU, protectionist policies are viewed as dangerous for a multilateral network that is losing its international momentum in favor of a set of bilateral or regional deals and alignments. Moreover, the complexity of GVCs in which European companies are intertwined could be damaged by these sets of import duties, which are affecting many sectors and manufactured products. However, the EU's favorable position as a trade partner for both China and the US could allow it to gain a comparative advantage against US exporters in the Chinese market (given that China maintains the EU's accessibility to its market) (Wolff, 2018).[62]

Data from the UNCTAD predicts that EU exports can benefit, gaining $70 billion from the shift in export destinations from both the US and China (UNCTAD, 2019).[63] Garcia (2019)[64] estimates that gains would be even superior, considering sectors like office, accounting and computing, and machinery. Short-term gains would probably be overshadowed by further consequences, though. The US–China conflict hinders markets, creates uncertainty, and damages the integrity of the global system (Plummer, 2019).[65] Real results are oftentimes not easily predicted by models and calculations due to the intrinsic complexity of networks and the involvement of different factors that cannot be initially quantified.

Indeed, the maximum gains predicted by Garcia (2019) could have been obtained only in optimal conditions, and there were even countries that were predicted to gain substantially more than the EU, thanks to this trade war (Vietnam, for example) (Goulard, 2020).[66] Although quantitative research also depicts the EU as a marginal winner in most situations, there are certain instances in which the EU can actually lose market and investment opportunities. We can find some evidence of it in Bolt et al.'s (2019)[67] analysis, or simply by looking at a scenario that was foreshadowed in Garcia's paper: the upcoming China–US deal that could actually strengthen their trade relationship while damaging the EU's trade influxes. The Phase One deal can be seen as the actualization of such an eventuality, with China's pledge to acquire goods valued billions of USD. Gonzalez and Veron (2019) underlined how a settlement involving quotas or acquisition of goods between the involved parties could actually nullify all the benefits that the EU stood to gain from the trade war, further depicting how numerous trading and investment advantages could be wiped out in a short time.[68]

The situation gets even more complicated considering the events that have been wreaking havoc in the past year. The outbreak of the coronavirus raised uncertainty and managed to shake the outcome of the Phase One deal itself. The pledges made by China appear unrealistic, and overall, the deal could actually end up a failure. In this case, the EU would be most likely to remain unscathed under a fully developed Phase One deal, but ultimately, such a positive situation will not last and will be unsustainable.

The GVCs and their involvement with European companies have to be considered as well. Although decoupling does not seem to be a feasible plan for China-based companies from the Union, the effects of the ongoing quarrel between the US and China could indirectly damage producers dealing directly in the mainland (as debated by Goulard). Such damage would be difficult to quantify, but nevertheless, it adds up as we analyze all the pros and cons from a European point of view.

6.2.3.1 EU–China Relations

The EU and China's relationship can be summed up by looking at the Comprehensive Agreement on Investment (CAI) between the two players. The CAI is a set of negotiations agreed upon between China and the EU that was put into effect from February 2012. In brief, the Agreement would improve market access conditions for European companies beyond China's commitments under the WTO. In this regard, it is clear that the EU needs to ensure its investors' access to the Chinese market. The Agreement should also ensure equal footing when operating in China with Chinese competitors. Transparency and legal certainty are also focal points, like reciprocal commitments from the EU and China in bilateral investment relations. Facilitating dispute settlements, providing investment protection, stressing sustainable development, and clarifying the behavior of state-owned enterprises would be additional points to be discussed (European Commission, 2020).[69]

In this regard, steps toward cooperation have been slow and started with the first round of negotiations only in 2014. The exchange of first offers came in 2018 with the first substantial Joint Statement that dealt mainly with market access and discriminatory measures. Further steps have been made in the following summits, highlighting the EU's desire to keep talks open with China during the 21st annual EU–China summit. Later attempts to keep the negotiations going have been hampered by the COVID-19 outbreak, but the following summit has been held via video conference on June 22, 2020 (European Council, 2020)[70] with a follow-up meeting on September 14, 2020, where the signature of the agreement on geographical indications (the first significant bilateral trade agreement signed between the two parties) was welcomed, among other discussions (European Council, 2020).[71]

Overall, the EU–China relationship seems to be progressing slowly. The lack of reciprocity in market access between the two blocks, diverging views on principles to be applied to building physical and digital connectivity, and the different views on human rights are all points on which the EU and China are finding it difficult to find common solutions (Grieger, 2020).[72] The situation further escalated with China's imposition of sanctions on several EU-based think tanks and scholars as a consequence of EU's sanctions of their own on Chinese officials due to the Union's concerns about the abuse of human rights in the Xinjiang region. The European Parliament ended up freezing the CAI, confirming the existence of mutual tension between the two blocs and ultimately putting a temporary stop to the (although slow) advancement of China–EU trade and financial relations (Koty, 2021).[73]

The EU's view of the Belt and Road Initiative (BRI) has also to be considered. Different from the US, the Union does not have an exclusively critical view of the Initiative. We can say that from its perspective, the BRI might generate not only challenges but also potential benefits. Generally, Eastern European countries tend to support the project, while Germany, France, and other Northern European countries are still skeptical about the potential benefits versus the risks it could bring (Sarsenbayev and Veron, 2020).[74] Italy could be seen as an exception due to being the only country among the major powers of Europe to fully support the Chinese project.

Smith and Taussig (2019)[75] highlight the changes in Germany's stance toward China, once deemed a *comprehensive strategic partner*. Indeed, after the Chinese government's announcement regarding a new technological plan modeled on Germany's Industry 4.0 initiative, European countries have started to limit Chinese investment in crucial industries. China's repressive political turn alerted Germany too, increasing the level of anxiety that was already high due to many scandals involving the theft of industrial and technological assets by Chinese corporations from foreign countries. Angela Merkel already stated that China became a *systemic competitor* rather than a partner, starting to push for a united EU stance on matters that undermine the EU unity against China's position (even though, as we mentioned, such unity will not be seen in the foreseeable future).

6.2.3.2 EU–US Relations

The US and EU have undoubtedly been close partners while trying to build a liberal global system in the past several decades. Because of this, it is not hard to see why their perspectives remained mostly aligned over the years. That is why former President Trump's *America First* Policies have raised much skepticism among European countries (Plummer, 2019).[76] This anti-multilateralist sentiment and its aggressive policy will hurt WTO and rule-based organizations, which share part of EU's standards concerning integration and global cooperation. Such unilateral measures also opened the door for additional trade barriers, with the EU being one of the targets due to its trade surplus with the US.

The long-running legal battle over subsidies to Airbus began with duties being levied on $7.5 billion worth of EU goods from October 2019. The Trump administration announced additional tariffs on $3.1 billion in exports from France, Germany, Spain, and the UK in June 2020. The move coincided with a review of the Trump administration's tariffs on European goods as a retaliatory measure for illegal subsidies (Baschuk, 2020).[77] Airbus later announced that it had moved to eliminate subsidies deemed illegal by the WTO to end the dispute over state aid to aircraft manufactures (Brunsden, 2020).[78] The move was not deemed sufficient, and the US held off on the threatened tariff hike.

Issues like this are just a part of the bigger picture. Obviously, we can't evaluate the health of current US–EU relations following just a single dispute, but it certainly sets a precedent and shows how the USA's strategy might influence the EU. Meanwhile, we have also to consider that regardless of the ongoing 'mini-trade war' between the EU and the US, it is clear that the former will prefer a reserved approach due to the fear of losing the US market, which is currently greater than losing the Chinese one (Garcia, 2019).[79]

Overall, what can be seen is a cautious approach by the EU, which has tried to come to terms with China while not fully committing to it, probably not to damage its ties with a historically strong partner like the US. This is especially true in a time of power transition from a Republican to a Democratic administration in the US. The uncertainty derived from a presidency by Joe Biden, which is stated to have a much more liberal approach compared to Mr. Trump, is definitely a good reason for the EU to act with circumspection (Anderson, 2020).[80]

6.2.3.3 Prospects of EU's Policy Shifts in the Future

In the analyzed context, it is clear that the EU will have to take a decision regarding the direction of its foreign policies. So far, as we have seen, the impact of the US–China trade war has had a relatively little impact on the European economy. The gains were offset by the multilateral instability that shook the global system. Since the US and China will arguably be the most influential blocs in the 21st century, their clash is probably going to be a long-lasting one. Garcia (2019)[81] suggests that China could contribute to the global economy around three times more than the US in the next ten years, implying that although the US might be a more important market for the EU in the short term, soon it would not be the case anymore.

Under these circumstances, the EU's policy could shift in many directions. The one direction based on its strong standards would surely be for safeguarding multilateralism and enhancing the links of cooperation among the global nodes of the network. In her analysis, Garcia (2019) suggests that it is the EU that could lead the reforms of institutions like the WTO to bolster fair trade and impose common practices on the member countries.

Problems like the large role of state-owned enterprises in China, and generally many of the problems that the EU is trying to address in its CAI, should be dealt with. The USA's concerns over China's unfair practices dovetail with similar concerns of the EU, which would surely bring together the two Western blocs. Finding common ground with China would be extremely difficult. The fact that, despite several EU–China summits, many points remain unresolved to this day tells us that so far European and Chinese standards do not and cannot be harmonized. Moreover, China would probably expect to enjoy special status in order to keep its authoritarian economic model. The EU would also find it difficult to reform the WTO due to Biden's current policy. The main risk would then be the EU finding itself isolated in the pursuit of multilateralism, which can only become stronger when the involved nodes are connected in a bigger network.[82]

The EU's higher consideration (relative to other countries like the US) toward multilateralism-based international organizations can be seen with the development of the multi-party interim appeal arrangement (MPIA) in the WTO. After the US decided to block new appointments to the Appellate Body (AB), effectively hibernating it in December 2019, the EU and 15 WTO members established a contingency appeal arrangement for trade disputes. This could be seen as a move made to show how the global trade system could move ahead even without the guidance of the US.

According to a study, the prevailing sentiment among WTO members was that although the settlement mechanism had a strong basic design, it was sometimes perceived as if it was going beyond its mandate (Wolfe and Mavroidis, 2020).[83] Hoekman and Mavroidis (2020) also argue that, so far, the dispute resolution mechanism has focused primarily on the AB, neglecting the principle of depoliticized conflict resolution. Further adjustments and reforms would be needed, and the implementation of a roaster composed of 'full-time professional adjudicators' would help with the introduction of a coherent and consistent WTO dispute-resolution body.[84]

Resolving the WTO AB impasse as part of a wider reform of the WTO is stated to be one of the EU's priorities (European Commission, 2020),[85] underlining its will to pursue an international organization-based multilateral system despite the USA's current stance on the matter.

Ullah et al. (2020)[86] finds a strategy based on multilateral efforts, through which the EU should negotiate with WTO members in order to preserve its global rule-based system. The EU could also practice an independent trade policy, strengthening its core trade network by focusing on both the domestic side and its foreign network with aligned countries like Japan and China.

Smith and Taussig (2019)[87] suggest how, in order to withstand pressures from both ends, the EU could achieve an autonomous strategy under the lead of Germany, assessing their own values and creating their own environment to counter external competition. They also list some of the major obstacles for applying this plan, though, like the ongoing Brexit problem and the growing anti-EU sentiment (tied to economic nationalism) in many of the member countries. Plummer (2019)[88] stresses the attention that the EU must devote to updating trade rules, to strengthen the global system by directly dealing with both the Asia-Pacific partners and the US.

6.2.3.4 Stuck between the US and China?

The possibility of strengthening the ties on the transatlantic alliance looks possible but not without risks. The current US policy; the threat of tariffs on EU steel, aluminum, and cars; and its general stance against multilateralism and the EU's trade surplus would probably negate attempts to pursue a deeper collaboration. Moreover, since the EU is not a single entity per se, but a group of countries with different views toward the US and China, it could be a costly approach. It has to be considered that Eastern Europe, Western Balkans, and the Southern European members are getting more and more involved in the BRI project, meaning that moving unitedly to a closer transatlantic alliance would not be a route without costs (Garcia, 2019).[89]

While talking about expanding the EU's ties with China, one has to consider that the US is making it increasingly costly to move away from them. China's market is becoming too large, and it will be unrealistic to ignore it. Maintaining connections with it will be beneficial in case the EU-China talks on full-fledged market opening to foreign competition end up being successful. This would also include assurances of equal treatment in the local market, which is a difficult objective to achieve with the current premises.[90] As we already mentioned, the EU–China bilateral investment talks have not been as successful as many European policymakers hoped. Also, according to the European Union Chamber of Commerce in China (2019),[91] European FDI in China has been reduced due to poor investor protection, limited market access, and unfair competition. Because of this, the possibility of China opening up its market in the near future seems unlikely.

The EU's position toward either US or Chinese side is reflected in its stance on the Huawei dilemma that we presented beforehand. The EU's cautious approach is surely tied to the fear of losing out on being part of the Chinese network. If European countries will go ahead with a ban on Chinese communication technology, China may retaliate against European companies like Nokia and Ericsson (Lin et al., 2020),[92] impairing connections and sabotaging the pursuit of multilateral cooperation.

Another aspect worth considering would be China's vision toward a future world, relative to the one that the US seems to have. As pointed out by Westad (2019) in his paper where he analyzes the premises for the *New Cold War*,[93] in theory, China's commitment and appeal in areas like climate change, the possibility of trade, and inequality (topics discussed in the CAI, and in all the recent meetings between the EU and China) seem to be more in line with the EU's values. Given China's controversies involving human rights, protectionism, and pollution, such a stance could sound contradictory, but Westad argues that "because the United States has failed to take the lead on any of these issues, China's communist government may be able to convince foreigners that authoritarian governments handle such problems better than democracies do."

Ultimately, it is clear that the best-case scenario for the EU would be the strengthening of multilateral ties and international organizations, together with a liberalization of the Chinese market. This way, a new potential source of business would open up for European investors, and the global network would grow stronger. This situation looks very unlikely, though, and considering that any other extreme choices would cause turmoil and damage the relationships of the EU with its other trading partners, a cautious approach looks to be the most probable.

We have to consider that everything could change depending on the development of events that would involve one of the major actors. For instance, a change in the USA's foreign policy direction followed by Biden could make negotiations for a more liberal global environment more likely (Lester, 2020).[94] If such a situation ensues, the EU's future policy will gravitate more toward a push for multilateralism (in the best-case scenario) or for a push toward a strengthened transatlantic partnership. The new president in Washington, although most likely will keep the aggressive stance toward China, could be more sympathetic toward both the EU and a more inclusive plurilateral system. This kind of deal could prove to be positive for the EU, especially in the short term.

During the trade war, while the EU was forecast to be in a slightly advantageous position relative to China and the US, in general, the benefits for its trade and investment fluxes have been rather marginal and relevant only on paper. The face-to-face trade duel between the US and China presented opportunities to some European sectors while destabilizing much of the multilateral global framework, a scenario likely not appreciated by European institutions and businesses alike.

Up until now, the EU did not manage to get any meaningful advantage out of this hegemonic competition, especially considering the global economic slowdown from the COVID-19 outbreak caused havoc in almost every country.

Overall, the two biggest questions going forward would be how the Biden administration will effectively turn the USA's foreign policy around (and hence, how the EU will answer to it) and how much of an impact will the coronavirus outbreak have on the EU's future decisions regarding trade and investments with China and the US. Events like the impasse on the CAI (the investment agreement between China and the EU) and the G7 meeting where Biden proposed an Atlantic Alliance seem to suggest that going forward, the stakes will be changing and that the pace set between 2016 and 2020 will not be followed as a footprint for plans in near-future concerning Western foreign policy.

6.3 Economic Nationalism

Georg Friedrich List in the early 19th century argued that international trade jeopardizes the security of the states who take part in it. His fundamental doctrine was that a nation's true wealth is the full and many-sided development of its productive power rather than its current exchange values. He supported the free exchange of domestic goods only within the nation and believed that tariffs on imported goods would stimulate domestic economic growth. Regarding

List's doctrine, Helleiner (2002)[95] explains that "the ideology as defined by List will retain a powerful place in today's global political economy as long as national identities and nationalism more generally remain powerful," underlining how influential it was even though scholars disregarded it throughout the 20th century. Koffman (1990)[96] defined economic nationalism as "everything that did not fit in with the liberal definition of economy and development, usually conjured up in a doctrinaire manner." List's ideas were often misunderstood and often radicalized in spite of his advocacy for – although limited – free trade. This happened due to a more extreme view from other national economists (Harlen, 1999)[97] that were most likely more aligned, for example, with Germany's protectionist stance between the 19th and 20th centuries.

To a large extent, recent economic nationalism is the product of neo-liberal policies actively pursued in the hyper-globalization period (from the early 1990s to the 2008 global financial crisis). Trade liberalization, privatization, deregulation, and macroeconomic stabilization represented a speeding up of the process of globalization.[98] Increased disparities in income, resource depletion, and rising unemployment due to freer mobility of merchants, labor, and capital promoted an environment for growing concerns over globalization and its unintended consequences. Moreover, the liberal idea could not provide any valid standards on problems such as fair borders between ethnic communities and states. Economic nationalism emerged, therefore, as a major force to fill the void.

6.3.1 The USA's Economic Nationalism

The former US President Trump's economic nationalism, well illustrated in the *America First* strategy, is unprecedented in the post–WWII era. Since the establishment of the General Agreement on Tariffs and Trade (GATT) (1947), the US has been the leading node in building rules of international trade and multilateral trading system (Shoenbaum and Chow, 2019).[99] Trump's trade policies, for the first time after the WWII, disregarded those multilateral rules and sought to promote national interests through four pillars: protectionism, GVC decoupling, US-centric regionalism, and anti-immigration. And as the waves of challenges caused by economic nationalism and US–China trade are intertwined, all protectionist actions taken under Trump's tenure aimed at both obtaining economic welfare for the US and containing the fast growth of China.

If we divide the Trump administration's *America First* Policy into four pillars, we can observe that the USA's actions are not separated but all intertwined. On the one hand, Trump adopted various types of trade remedies, such as anti-dumping, countervailing duty, global safeguard (Section 201), national security restrictions (Section 232), and import tariffs on Chinese products based on unfair trade practices (Section 301). The federal government also promoted reshoring and onshoring by offering the US firms incentives. Trade remediation and onshoring were aimed at reducing trade deficits between the US and its bilateral trading partners, keeping the US market for American producers, and breaking the dominance of China's goods and services in the US market by cutting off the links made by China to the US and its allies. To Trump, tightening immigration policies was a part of his economic reform plan as it reduces the number of non-Americans residing in the US, aimed at saving American jobs. All in all, trade and immigration policies serve the purpose of protecting US national interests and containing the fast growth of China. On the other hand, the USA's blockage of WTO's Dispute Settlement Body (DSB) can be regarded as retribution against the WTO for disregarding the USA's right to impose trade remedy measures in many cases and failing to counter or constrain China's market-distorting practices. More than that, if we link this action to protectionist trade policies, blocking what is essentially the world's supreme court for international trade seemed to pave the way for the USA's unilateral remediation of trade. It undermined the power of the DSB in preventing or allowing other countries to retaliate against the USA's aggressive actions. Hence, from this perspective, it can be said that the four pillars of US policies of economic nationalism are working as a complement for each other. However, the outcomes of the *America First* Policy to make America 'great again' and its impacts on the US economy remain uncertain.

6.3.1.1 Undermining WTO

The most notable aspect of US trade policies of the Trump era is the derogation of current multilateral trading rules and commitments to pursue control over national trade policies (McCorriston and Sheldon, 2020).[100] From the vantage point of the Trump administration, global trade was a zero-sum, win-lose game rather than a win-win game that was analyzed in numerous international trade theories. In other words, with a permanently fixed, single-size economic pie, if one country earns benefits, the other ones face losses from trade as quantified by trade balance. As the stage changes from hyper-globalization to *slobalization* (slow down + globalization) or *deglobalization*, trade agreements become more about redistribution and less about expanding the overall economic pie. Moreover, the multilateral trading system under WTO has not functioned well because of several shortcomings in the WTO's standard, which put the US at a disadvantage. First, multilateralism failed to achieve a consensus in the Doha Round of WTO after almost 20 years of negotiation. Second, the WTO lacks the power to prevent harm, caused by China's unjust practices, from occurring. Third, the WTO fails to cover major agreements governing current prominent issues, for example, FDI, foreign investor protection, IP protections, and harmonization of domestic regulatory standards (e.g., labor and environment standards). To address all aforementioned concerns, the US is now seeking to undermine the multilateral trading system and dictate regional/sectoral trade agreements so that it can win at the expense of its trading partners and build regional trade blocs that better serve its interests.

Therefore, three measures were adopted by the Trump administration to attack the WTO: (1) an offensive against the WTO's AB, (2) a return to unilateral adjudication and remediation of trade disputes, and (3) an interpretation of the WTO's national security exception that would permit economic concerns to qualify (Brewster, 2018).[101] First, the USA's blockage of the WTO AB nominations is regarded as a direct assault on the rules-based dispute settlement mechanism and will push international trade law back to the GATT-era-type system, in which WTO members resolve their disputes by a power-based process. The world trading system run by discriminatory trade blocs will inevitably hurt small countries and push them to align with more powerful ones for self-preservation. Second, the act of unilaterally imposing trade sanctions against China and other countries for their unfair trade practices under Section 301 is deemed unfair and implies a flat rejection of WTO's commitment to the multilateral resolution of disputes through neutral adjudication.[102] As the multilateral network deteriorated, the US is pursuing an alternative trade bloc and dispute settlement in smaller-scale regional trade agreements (RTAs). Yet, unless it serves as stepping stones to a freer trade network, the forming of RTAs can also be a threat to multilateralism since RTAs operate as an exception to the most favored nation principle.[103] In this case, RTAs will raise the costs of commerce, make trade negotiations harder and discriminatory, and encourage retaliation.[104] Third, the US under the Trump administration claimed national security as a rationale for import tariff imposition, which is a broad terminology that could be abused as justification to provide economic protection to industries.[105] Trump used it to defeat WTO challenge to his protectionist tariff policies under Section 232. The invoking of national security rationale on steel and aluminum tariffs imposed on the USA's allies and trade partners is criticized as unreasonable both economically and politically as it not only interrupts economic cooperation but also hurts diplomatic relationships (Bown and Irwin, 2019).[106]

As a result of the three aforementioned policies, WTO's authority as a legitimate constraint on member countries and its influence on transnational relations are seriously undermined. Scholars have different opinions about the power of WTO in China issues. Brewster (2018) stated that the current laws and process norms of the WTO formed an economic order that would constrain China's increasing economic power, which is opposed to the view of Trump mentioned by Chow et al. (2019)[107] that the WTO fails to confront unfair trade practices of China. However, all of them believed that the failure of WTO would be a leverage for China's bargaining power in the future. In the post-WTO era, the Chinese government can simply copy Trump's behavior to disregard the trade rules that are not favorable to them, impose unilateral sanctions, demand bilateral negotiations, and claim national security rationale to reject WTO jurisdiction.

Overall, Trump's acts of flouting international trade rules with his economic nationalism in the last four years have been criticized for having damaged the rule-based trading system.[108] As mentioned by Chow et al. (2019), "the revival of economic nationalism by Trump's government poses a significant threat to the continuing function of the GATT/WTO system."[109] However, in the long term, there is little possibility of any permanent damage to the WTO because the US might be the biggest power but not the sole big power in the WTO. For example, the EU and other WTO members already started to take action to establish the MPIA, which can serve the same function of WTO AB.

Viewing the situation through the prism of network theory, we posit the global trading system as a network of networks where the WTO is the most powerful. Within the network, however, two types of *homophily* are recognized, pro-US and pro-China, which result in the establishment of two corresponding communities. Hogan (2017)[110] believed that the coexistence of many kinds of homophily would lead to the fragmentation or disruption of the global trading system. Nevertheless, it can be observed that the modularity of the two communities is low, which means that the networks have not distinctive but fuzzy faces. Instead of clarifying themselves with its unique features, many nodes are trying to maintain normal trade relations with both powers to prevent the negative consequences, such as trade restriction or retaliation, derived from the US-China tensions. As the network becomes fuzzy, the extreme fragmentation or disruption of the global trading system into two is not likely to happen.

Trump's economic nationalism was, in essence, a hurt-the-other ideology. Since the post–WWII era, the US had been one of the key demanders in building the international trade rules and multilateral trading system under GATT (1947) and then WTO (1995). However, in the Trump era, "the US no longer sees itself as a demander, which explains why it has not tabled any proposals of its own for reforming the WTO Appellate Body (AB) or restoring it to operational status" (Schneider-Petsinger, 2020).[111] And if the EU is successful in reforming the WTO according to their six-point initiative, as mentioned in Chapter 1, the leading position of the US in the multilateral trading system in the past 70 years can be taken over by the EU.

6.3.1.2 *The US-Led RTAs*

Viewing the RTA as an important tactic to redistribute welfares and reinforce power in the global trading system, the Trump administration renegotiated old FTAs with Mexico, Canada, and Korea, in addition to embarking on plans for a trade agreement with the EU, Japan, and the UK. By building RTAs, the US could adopt a uniform standard concerning 'deep integration' in multifaceted cooperation to govern the trade relationship with all partners, like what they are doing with the existing FTAs, which can help protect US welfare and benefits for American domestic factors in all trade agreements. More than that, the new trade agreements between the US and other major economies, once successfully concluded, are expected to serve as the powerful instrument of the US in Sino-American rivalry. The agreements can act as a forum for dealing with extra-WTO topics, which could then be brought out from the plurilateral (or sectoral) to the multilateral level (VanGrasstek, 2019).[112]

In contrast to the expectations of the administration, the RTA tactics of Trump faced criticism. Bown and Irwin (2019)[113] agreed with Noland (2018)[114] in that the revision of the North American Free Trade Agreement (NAFTA) to US–Mexico–Canada Agreement (USMCA) was an unnecessary exercise since its shortcomings (American trade deficits and job loss) could have been remedied by the Trans-Pacific Partnership (TPP). Trump's goal in NAFTA renegotiation was criticized as an exercise of government intervention in the market, not meant to further free up trade but to constrain trade. Moreover, the withdrawal of the US from the TPP was actually damaging to US interests and opened the door to the Chinese leadership.

The USA's renegotiation of NAFTA to USMCA, KORUS 2.0, the establishment of US-Japan trade agreement and FOIPI is unequivocal evidence of the USA's pursuit of bilateralism and regionalism as alternatives to multilateralism under WTO. According to Chow et al. (2019), RTAs are classified into two types: a building bloc (which increases trade volumes for all members of multilateral agreements) and a stumbling bloc (which will block the development of new multilateral agreements).[115] Taking KORUS as an example, after renegotiation, Korea is obliged to impose the voluntary export restraint on steel exports, to raise import quota for US automobiles, to extend the hefty US tariff on Korean light trucks for two more decades, etc.[116] Reviewing major changes in KORUS FTA gives us an insight that the renegotiation does not aim at increasing the trade volume for all members but granting American producers better Korean market access. Moreover, the forming of FOIPI and Economic Prosperity Network (EPN)-type network between the US and like-minded countries supports the idea of establishing a hub-and-spoke, multifaceted co-operation network where the US is the central hub and allies and partners are spokes surrounding the hub. Hence, it can be concluded that the creation of new RTAs or renegotiation of existing RTAs under the Trump administration, which were driven by nationalist political considerations, is more like stumbling blocs that aim at reinforcing the USA's power without the further expansion of the multilateral trading system.

6.3.1.3 Trade Remedies and Decoupling

Concerning the protectionism in trade, Noland (2018) interpreted the Trump administration's three themes in trade policies, namely, bilateral trade deficits, currency manipulation, and *disastrous* trade agreements.[117] Since the inauguration in January 2017, Trump opted the US out of TPP, issued the Executive Order Regarding the Omnibus Report on Significant Trade Deficits (intellectual and policy basement for new protection), issued Executive Order on Buy America and Hire America (domestic preference in public procurement and limiting immigration rules), embarked on the renegotiation of NAFTA and KORUS, and initiated contingent and process protection.

New protections adopted by the Trump administration are in the form of anti-dumping, countervailing duty, global safeguard (Section 201), and national security restrictions (Section 232); nevertheless, these policies are undesirable by both American producers and consumers because of the price increase and potential retaliation. For instance, the US steel and aluminum tariff threats in Section 232 on its allies and China triggered retaliation from Canada, China, Mexico, the EU, and other countries on the USA's agriculture products, posing a threat to the welfare of 3.2 million US farmers.[118]

Moreover, trade remedies adopted by Trump were criticized as government intervention in the market. Summing up the pursuit of RTAs and the adoption of trade remedies, as the US was trying to eliminate efficient producers and save the market for (currently) inefficient neighbors, it is possible that the trade diversion effect would exceed the trade creation effect, which hurts the market and economy.[119] More than that, those remedies aimed at, except for China, the long-standing allies and trade partners of the US, for instance, Canada, Mexico, and Korea. The USA's Section 232 had triggered retaliation from Canada on 2.7 billion worth of US aluminum products. The EU also promised to retaliate if the US imposes tariffs on 6.8 billion euros of EU goods, igniting the transatlantic trade war.[120] When we consider the impacts of both FTA renegotiation and remediation on trading partners, it could be said that the economic nationalism of the US created harsh conditions for trading and soured diplomatic relations between countries.

In general, the USA's imports of goods from the world and from China show a similar upward pattern during the period of 2010–2018. Amount of imports increased gradually from the beginning of the decade, slightly declined in 2016, and then bounced back and reached its peak in 2018, while the amount of goods exports remained stable throughout the years and remained far below the amount of the imports. In bilateral trading with China, the USA's import value is 4–4.5 times higher than the USA's export value in the same year; therefore, the trade deficit between the two countries is remarkably high. The year 2018 witnessed the largest deficit in trade between the US and the world, at $872,040.8 million, and between US and China, at $418,953.9 million. After that, the trading situation between the US and the world has not changed much in 2019, except for a decrease of approximately 15% in US imports from China, with US trade deficits improving. Overall, the data provides us with an insight that there has yet to be a positive change in US trading with the world after the US imposed trade remedies; however, the effects of Section 301 on limiting trade with China were observed in 2019 and the first ten months of 2020.

Economic decoupling from China is another important long-run goal of the US protectionism, even if "the Trump administration did not openly embrace the idea of decoupling, its various policies effectively added up to a decoupling strategy" (Kennedy and Tan, 2020).[121] Moreover, compared to other strategies and stances taken by Trump, the hard position on foreign policy toward China appeared to be widely accepted by Congress and foreign policy institutions alike.

It also has to be understood that decoupling and substituting key components of the modern GVC is a process that cannot be rushed, as they will lead to complications and consequences in many different sectors. After all, China has doubtlessly attained the status of 'hegemonic competitor of the US,' along with the position as an interdependent and fundamental node in numerous value chains around the world. "By the end of the 20th century the world economy was more tightly linked than ever before (Capie et al., 2020),"[122] and as mentioned by Ravenhill (2013),[123] the networks connecting all transnational production sites changed the nature of interdependence between countries, making it very expensive to disrupt these linkages in case of international conflict. Because of this, up until 2016, the US allowed this interdependent network to continue growing, effectively allowing China to maintain its position as the ultimate intermediary in many of the GVCs that connected developing and developed countries.

As previously mentioned, COVID-19 has had a significant impact on China's capacity to honor and actually take care of its Phase One deal commitments. The trade war between China and the US will have a discernible impact on many of the manufactured parts and components exported from the US to China regardless of the signature of the said deal, making the integration process between American companies and supply chains connected to China costlier.[124]

Evaluating the impacts of the USA's decoupling strategy on China, Wyne (2020)[125] emphasized the significance of the support of US allies and partners, since it is less likely that the US can pressure China into cracking down on IP theft, cyberespionage, and other unfair practices. The implementation of the Phase One deal, criticized by VanGrasstek (2019)[126] as the manifestation of governmental dictate in trade, has proved the ability of China to withstand and adapt to unilateral economic threats. Forcing China to resume market-oriented reforms would make the country become more attractive to foreign investors. And selective decoupling from China, in other words, breaking the linkage in trade and technology between the US and China, would bolster China's efforts on indigenous innovation and economic self-sufficiency.

Wyne (2020)[127] predicted that the hegemonic war between the two countries would not end with winner and loser but more probably an *unsettled cohabitation* for two reasons. First, it is unclear whether China pursues to act as the underwriter of a global order, who would establish a web of global alliances, send troops to other countries, lead international institutions, etc. Next, while the US is in relative decline, it maintains significant strengths, and while China has undergone an extraordinary resurgence, it possesses critical liabilities. And due to the interrelation of countries in the global capital markets and supply chains, a comprehensive decoupling seems to be beyond the reach of both the US and China.

The *decoupling strategy* in the GVC is another measure in trade initiated by the Trump government under its ideology of economic nationalism. According to Lighthizer (2020), over the past two decades, offshoring to China, Vietnam, and Indonesia has costed the US 5 million manufacturing jobs, in which China accounted for at least 2 million.[128] Reshoring and nearshoring were promoted with the hope of bringing back production chains to the US and providing more jobs for Americans.

Besides trade remedies and RTA renegotiation, the US has been preparing proposals to offer tax breaks, new rules, and carefully structured subsidies with a $25 billion 'reshoring fund.'[129] In a tougher action, Trump even threatened to block businesses that outsource jobs to China from being granted federal contracts. His policy of moving the supply chain out of China does not stop at the US border but spreads to other countries through both the FOIPI and EPN projects. Mixing both strategies of decoupling and tariff war, Trump believed, would bring back manufacturing jobs and crucial GVCs to the US. According to USTR Lighthizer, as a result of the impacts of import tariffs imposed on products originating from China, "Apple, Whirlpool, and Stanley Black &

Decker have either scrapped offshoring plans or announced decisions to move production to the United States." And thanks to the NAFTA to USMCA re-negotiation, "automotive companies have announced $34 billion in new U.S. investment."[130]

Contrary to the optimistic view of USTR, however, according to the survey of the American Chamber of Commerce in Shanghai of 200 US companies operating in China, more than 70% of the respondents do not have any plans to move their production away from China despite the hefty tariffs from Trump's trade war. They even view China as a promising market in the post-COVID-19 era, thanks to the huge market of 1.4 billion people (Mitchell, 2020).[131] And Foxconn, the pro-China manufacturer of Apple's iPad tablet and MacBook laptop, decided to move out of China as a result of the US–China trade war; however, they will shift their assembly lines to Vietnam and not reshore back to Taiwan or the US.[132]

Moreover, as portrayed by Capie et al. (2020),[133] the overall sentiment of American companies based in China regarded economic decoupling of the US and China as not feasible and, in fact, impossible. It has to be considered, though, that there has been a substantial shift in the general opinion, since more and more businessmen are actually reconsidering, seeing a decoupling plan eventually doable. This is because the *CCP risk* is growing faster than ever in the global business community. Therefore, it can be concluded that the decoupling strategy of Trump has created some but limited impacts on the GVC of global firms.

'Buy America, Hire America' is also supported by President Biden. To pool the critical production chains outside the USA's borders back to the nation, he promised to make new targeted investments and create new incentives, for instance, tax deduction, R&D credits, and even a 30.8% of tax penalty (including 28% corporate tax rate and additional 10% 'offshoring penalty surtax') on US companies that produce goods or launch service centers in foreign countries and then sell it back to the US. The actions of Biden on offshoring firms actually appear to be stronger than what Trump did; therefore, bipartisan promotion of strategic decoupling and utilization of trade remedy measures continues under the Biden administration.

6.3.1.4 Anti-Immigration

Besides undermining of the WTO and protectionism in trade, immigration is another pillar of the USA's economic nationalism. Since the inauguration of President Trump in 2017, major changes to the US immigration system have been made, namely, enhancing immigration enforcement, cutting back on humanitarian programs, and increasing vetting and obstacles for legal immigration, all of which have considerable effects not only on US society but also on the economy and trading system (Pierce et al., 2018).[134] First, the administration strengthened enforcement against non-citizens inside the US. Regarding the removal of non-citizens, from January 20 to September 30, 2017, the US Immigration and

Customs Enforcement arrested more than 110,000 non-citizens and deported 61,000 immigrants from the US. Moreover, since May 2018, the Trump administration implemented a 'zero-tolerance' policy at the US-Mexico border to deter future unauthorized border crossers and make life harder for those who do cross. Second, the number of refugee admissions is limited to the lowest level since 1980, to 45,000 refugees in the fiscal year 2018. The administration also ended a refugee and parole program for vulnerable youngsters in need of protection in Central America, which was created in the Obama era. The Temporary Protected Status (TPS) for hundreds of thousands of migrants who are unable to return to their countries was also terminated. Third, 'extreme' vetting of all visa applicants is carried out for the purpose of preventing the entry of people deemed to be threats to public safety, which means the visa process is slowed and prolonged. The government also made changes to the H-1B visa, which is the temporary visa program that employers use to bring in high-skilled employees, and ended the related H-4 program that allows H-1B visa holders' dependent spouses to work in the US.

Anti-immigration policies not only have a huge impact on the lives of non-Americans who reside in the country but also present both advantages and disadvantages for the US economy. On the one hand, the Trump administration is praised for reducing the USA's unemployment rate to its lowest level since 1970 (3.68%) and maintained it at 3.5% until the COVID-19 pandemic hit.

On the other hand, Trump's immigration policies have had serious effects on the lives of 11 million unauthorized immigrants in the US. Besides, owing to the difficulties in the visa process, huge losses were seen in the tourist industry (a decrease by 2.3 million international arrivals) and the education field (a large drop in international applications).[135] Moreover, anti-immigration policies also caused trouble for the US in terms of labor forces. Stepping up enforcement against non-citizens inside the country and tightening visa vetting for non-citizens outside the country reduced the source of low-skilled labors for US industries and, at the same time, placed financial burdens on American firm owners as they would have to pay higher wages for American laborers. In addition, changes in H-1B and H-4 visa programs narrow the door to the US for high-skilled employees and make the US a less attractive working destination. This especially impacted well-trained Chinese workers, as allegations of IP theft and cyberespionage halved the number of Chinese nationals being granted a working license in the Silicon Valley (from 771 to 350 in 2018), as well as increases in unfair or poor treatment for Chinese employees and greater scrutiny.[136] The harsh working environment in the US would motivate talented Chinese workers, trained in the US and possessed of valuable work experience and know-how from the USA's top companies, to go back to their home country – effectively a brain drain for the US. This represents a huge loss, a disadvantage for the US in their competition with China under the Fourth Industrial Revolution (4IR).

Nevertheless, considering the flurry of executive orders signed by US President Joe Biden concerning immigration and social equity, the widespread economic nationalism driven by anti-immigration sentiments could be tempered, at least in the near future (Hickey et al., 2021).[137] However, seeing the actual effects of the newly established policies could be difficult considering the fact that the COVID-19 pandemic ravaged the employment situation not only in the US but also in many related partner countries.

6.3.2 *China's Economic Nationalism*

Economic nationalism is a dynamic concept. Its goal is to ensure a nation's economic development and sovereignty. Along with other countries, China is a good example of how dynamic its economic nationalism has evolved to be. During the period of Mao Zedong's anti-imperialist nationalism, China was heavily dominated by state-owned enterprises and state planning. Foreign investors and companies were seen as enemies and the People's Republic of China (PRC) strived to be self-sufficient. In the late 1970s, after the death of Mao Zedong, China underwent an economic reform that was dubbed 'Socialism with Chinese characteristics.' Its closed economy made the country lag behind its neighbors in terms of economic growth; therefore the Communist Party started to switch the country's struggling economy into a market-oriented one (Brandt and Rawski, 2008).[138] China had seen growth in terms of FDIs, and many state-owned enterprises were also privatized in an effort to make these entities more efficient and competitive. As mentioned previously, one of the clearest signs that China was opening up its market was when it joined the WTO in 2001. Its private sector grew remarkably, and it accounted for 70% of the country's GDP in 2005 (Engardio, 2005).[139] Comparing it with the level of economic nationalism China had under Mao, we can say that the country was somewhat less nationalistic during this reform period.

However, China's economic nationalism seems to be on the rise again under Chinese leader Xi Jinping, who stoked the ideology via the championing of its industries.[140] Xi made constitutional amendments that reflected his vision that was different compared to those of the leaders who began China's reform after Mao (Ching, 2018).[141] Although Xi's administration still continues to aim for greater participation of China in the global trading system, this does not mean that the country is rigorously adhering to the ideology of reform, especially those of Deng Xiaoping's era. We need to remember that economic nationalism does not always equate to protectionism or closed-border policies, as economic nationalism has two faces. When foreign investments from abroad are perceived to threaten economic security, protectionist nationalism arises. However, when foreign investments benefit the host country's economic development, liberal nationalism can gain the ground. Now, with China's MIC 2025 and BRI in place, we can say that even though China is not going back to Maoist nationalism, it is undeniable that Xi is more aggressive in forging deals that somehow, one-sidedly, benefit China's own economic development. Examples of this were mentioned in China's FTA network and BRI section of this book, such as the jeopardized BRI investment case of Sri Lanka. As Sri Lanka failed to repay its debt to China's investment under BRI, the country was forced to sign over its strategic Hambantota Port to the China Merchants Port Holdings Company on a 99-year lease to mitigate the unpaid debts. BRI, on the one hand, is the infrastructure modernization for developing countries. On the other hand, it can be seen as a debt trap that pushes the host countries into the danger of losing their sovereignty.

MIC 2025 was initiated by Xi administration in 2015 with the aim of making China a global powerhouse in high-tech industries. The plan focuses on electric cars and other new energy vehicles, next-generation information and communication technology, advanced robotics, and AI. After ten years of implementing this policy, China expects to replace its foreign technology imports with indigenous innovations and to raise the domestic content of core components and materials to 40% and 70% in 2020 and 2025, respectively,[142] which is similar to the goal of self-sufficiency and localization of manufacturing process in the *decoupling* strategy concomitant with Trump's economic nationalism. There is the additional purpose of MIC 2025 – building up powerful Chinese corporations possessing high competitiveness in both domestic and international markets.

Nevertheless, MIC 2025 would be regarded as a good strategy that contributes positively to the world's industrial and technological development as well as the world trade, if it was free from unfair government subsidies, unjust state-owned or state-supported enterprises, and forced IP acquisition, for instance, the case of Huawei. According to the US Congressional Research Service (2020),[143] there were 1,800 Chinese government guidance funds with a collective value of $426 billion linked to MIC 2025, as of March 2018. The state funding to Chinese companies is used to support R&D, overseas acquisition, and talent recruitment. The MIC 2025 invited serious criticism from the US and the suspicion of other advanced countries for discriminatory treatment of foreign investment, cyberespionage, IP and trade secret theft, and overall, "distorting global markets by prioritizing political considerations over economic incentives."[144] Therefore, it can be said that China's promotion of the nation's industrial champion is a one-sided tactic, in which China wants to win while other countries are hurt by unfair competition. The allegations of China's unfair practices triggered the USA's retaliation under the Trump administration and are likely to result in a historical fragmentation of the global trading system, dividing the world into anti-China, pro-China, and neutral blocks.

Amid the ongoing US–China trade war, Vice-Premier Han Zheng said that China will continue to open up its economy even though other countries are resorting to protectionism. Han mentioned that "it is wrong to blame economic globalization" for the problems of a country. He also stressed the need to work with different international organizations such as the UN, the G20, and the WTO.[145] But it is important not to take this statement as it is. Remember that economic nationalism goes beyond the dichotomy of liberalism and protectionism. I would like to emphasize again that although China might be keeping its market open, we cannot deny the fact that its agendas now heavily lean toward satisfying its national and political interests.

Indeed, we can pinpoint the policies implemented by China that elicited major pushbacks from the US and how many of them can also be considered policy action performed as part of an economic decoupling strategy, which represents an aggressive action to decrease China's dependence on US tech companies while pushing for entry into new markets (Capie et al., 2020).[146] There have been debates about China's need to implement a diversified export strategy to strengthen its linkages with other possible partners and slow its interdependence with a competitor like the US. The PRC did this by expanding into developing markets in the Middle East, Africa, Asia, the Pacific, and Latin America (Link, 2019),[147] which are the major areas and also important partners present in the BRI project. Here, Chinese companies can offset the increasing labor costs of their home country, and as the focus of their projects is on technology and innovation, they can easily gain domestic support from local governments at the same time.

Such economic nationalism is expected to become stronger due to the COVID-19 pandemic. Not to single out China, the same trend is expected or is being seen in other major trading blocs such as the US and the EU, which are both discussed in other sections of this chapter. The hegemonic struggle between the US and China will intensify economic nationalism, which we can regard as a trend that might continue for the next 30 years. Even before this pandemic, economic nationalism had already negatively affected the rule-based world trade order. The WTO's stagnant condition for almost two decades will definitely not get any better. This will only exacerbate economic nationalism within the nodes of this global trading system. In the case of China, it has already lost its desire for economic reform and has started to reinvest in its *authoritarian state capitalism* model. Countries that suffered comparatively less from this pandemic will certainly see these dark times as an opportunity to dominate the global trading system and become the ultimate leading node. While the US is bogged down by the COVID-19 pandemic and domestic instability after Trump's term in office, the Chinese economy has already bounced back. If the Biden administration and other great powers in the West fail to deter and stop the spread and development of this hybrid system of China where state-hub leads firm-spokes with various unfair trade practices, it is possible that China will fully exploit the MIC 2025, BRI, and the hub-and-spoke inner and outer networks to obtain hegemonic power and rearrange the world order.

6.3.3 The EU's Economic Nationalism

Economic nationalism is not new in Europe, since it had appeared in many countries that are now part of the EU. Berend (2000)[148] explains how Central and Eastern European countries turned to economic nationalism after World War I, carrying an 'anti-West' sentiment that had been expanding for several decades prior. Satellite countries of the Soviet Union like Hungary, Romania, and Poland adopted import-substitution strategies by focusing on their domestic markets and applying an increased level of tariffs in order to thwart foreign competition and reach 'new heights of advancement and industrialization.' This localized episode of economic nationalism failed due to the lack of development of competitive exporting industries, along with other reasons such as the leakage of the Great Depression crisis even in these semi-isolated countries. This autonomy-oriented strategy serves as a precedent.

More recently, it appears that the roots of a newfound economic nationalist sentiment can be traced back to the globalization boom in the 1990s. Indeed, in an outstanding study, Colantone and Stanig (2018)[149] found out that globalization is a key determinant in the rise of economic nationalism (especially in the EU). By imposing uneven costs across regions, massive imports from China provoked a global shock that hit the hardest economic sectors that one paper calls 'the losers of globalization,' represented by the segments most fragile to changes in international trade. A surge in support for nationalist and radical-right parties in the West ensued, endangering the open world that we have known so far. Specifically, confidence in values based on multilateralism took a hit, proving that "globalization is not suitable if the welfare gains are not shared within society." Protectionism, though, is not showing any ability to problems, meaning the world would probably be better off with globalization, albeit a more inclusive one.

At the stage of hyper-globalization, it is likely that a country or an intergovernmental institution, like the EU, will adjust its trade policy toward protectionism to prevent the negative effects of accelerated globalization. While Bolle and Zettlemeyer (2019)[150] stated that economic nationalism in the EU took place in the form of restrictions on inward FDI, Koeth (2018)[151] argued that it started sooner with the pursuit of RTAs. The author explained the institutional change in Europe through the impact of the Chinese shock and the rising economic nationalism in the US. From the best option of Global Europe, i.e. promotion of multilateral trade liberalization under the WTO Doha Round, in 2006, the EU turned to the second-best option of pursuing bilateral and regional FTAs. Via FTAs and RTAs, the Union participated in deep liberalization by addressing issues that lay behind national borders or those not ready to be negotiated at the multilateral level. Trade talks with the US (Transatlantic Trade and Investment Partnership [TTIP]) and 12 countries of the Pacific Rim were a remarkable event at that time; however, the negotiation of TTIP is heading nowhere owing to challenges imposed on EU governance and the opposition of the EU citizens (the collision of the inner and outer network, as explained in the USA's FTA network section). Later, in 2016, the EU announced the change of trade policy to its third-best option – fortification of the EU trade protection mechanism, attributable to the deadline of granting market economy status (MES) to China and the result of the 2016 US election. First, the classification of China as a market economy would make it harder for Chinese trading partners to impose anti-dumping duties on Chinese products that are deemed to be underpriced as an effect of unfair subsidies and national support. As steel is regarded as a 'loser' in globalization, the fear of Chinese MES triggered a vocal protest from the EU Steel Commission, pushing the EU to join with the US in a lawsuit against China over the

MES claim in the WTO. Second, the 2016 US election result presented the EU with the possibility that the prospect of TTIP could reach zero under Trump, a nationalist administration. As a result of the significant increase in US–EU trade uncertainties, the EU decided to upgrade its trade defense instruments.

Looking further at China-related global issues, the Union also responded to the Chinese shock in a way that reinforced data protection regulations and investment screening mechanisms. Coming into effect in May 2018, General Data Protection Regulation (GDPR), as explained in Section 3.1.1 of EU standards, is the legal framework addressing the protection of various types of personal data. GDPR strictly governs the rights and obligations of individual users, data processors and controllers, and independent public supervisory authorities in data handling and protection. A noticeable point is that GDPR does not only influence companies located in the EU but also those located outside and processing the personal data of European residents. As China and Chinese commercial practices have been perceived by many partner countries as lacking data privacy, the implementation of GDPR with strict rules and heavy penalties is definitely an impediment to the operation and expansion of Chinese business in the EU. In addition to GDPR implementation, the very first framework for FDI screening at the EU level also took effect in April 2019. It contains provisions that affect a considerable proportion of Chinese investment in the EU, especially in infrastructure and transportation sectors. The mechanism calls for special scrutiny of inward investments by, both directly and indirectly, state-controlled entities, for potential reviews of investments that form part of state-led outward projects or programs. From this point, we can understand that the EU is now trying to capture Chinese government–driven investments to the EU via the BRI channel (Kirkegaard, 2019).[152]

Though the EU is seeking RTAs, trade defense instruments, and other strict regulations, economic nationalism in the EU is different from the US strategy regarding its responsibility for multilateralism (Koeth, 2018).[153] When the US is no longer regarded as the demander of free multilateral trade and China is unwilling to give up government intervention in trade, the EU has to become an important leading node to lead the WTO reforms, so as to prevent the malfunctioning or the collapse of the institution with the establishment of the MPIA and the initiative of six-point WTO reform plan.

Besides the externalities of Chinese shock and US economic nationalism, the spread of these beliefs has led to the rise of *deglobalization* movements. They are also linked to the structural network of problems that come from the unchecked explosion of interconnectivity among actors of different social, economic, and political backgrounds all around the world. As pointed out in an article by Balsa-Barreiro et al. (2020),[154] what is being highlighted with these anti-globalization movements is how national problems like financial instability, immigration shock, ever-increasing inequality of the *losers of globalization*, and social polarization are all part of a systemic problem coming from poorly designed networks. Overly interdependent systems that are not designed to manage risks properly, which trigger a contagion effect in the financial system, and all in all, establishing too many connections would make collapse even more likely. Networks that are too polarized might be too sensitive to the malfunctioning of the central node, which will spread the malfunction through many of the linkages serving the function of interconnection.

This *crisis of globalization*, which, as we said, is spreading a sentiment and attitudes antithetical to multilateral values, is particularly relevant for the EU since its very institutions are based on multilateralism. As we have seen, a decrease in the belief in a Euro community of shared values with a simultaneous increase in Euroscepticism can very well culminate in events like Brexit. Studies like the one conducted by Biancotti et al. (2017)[155] state that a sense of Euroscepticism is indeed increasing among the EU member countries. This phenomenon looks, unsurprisingly, more prevalent among the 'losers of globalization.' In case this situation continues, there is a chance that cultural convergence, which managed to unify old and new members alike, would be halted altogether.

The Union has been gaining strength over the past 30 years. However, what will be the consequences of trends in the opposite direction, including Brexit, the rise of national and populist movements, and the spread of economic national and anti-immigration sentiments? Indeed, the connection between anti-immigration policies in neighboring countries of the Union and a rise in popularity of populist movements has already been made (Czaika and Di Lillo, 2018).[156]

When the calls for communitarian good go unheard by its national constituents, the EU's internal network would weaken, and more situations like the ones we already presented (i.e. the difference in view between Eastern and Western Europe regarding BRI, different stances toward Huawei, and the internal disputes during the COVID-19 pandemic) expose risks and bring them to the fore.

6.4 The Fourth Industrial Revolution

6.4.1 The US and 4IR

According to Doshi (2020),[157] China is believed to have four main advantages with which it can outcompete the US in the 4IR race, namely, heavy investment in R&D (roughly $2.5 billion annually), superior institutions and industrial policies bolstering the MIC 2025 campaign, manufacturing prowess and centrality in relation to global supply chains, and a robust operation to set global technology standards (known as China Standard 2035 Plan), which could determine the future of key industries.

The more exponential the growth of Chinese technology, the greater the long-term threat to the USA's future owing to China's acts of espionage and theft of trade secrets and technology. "China is engaging in a whole-of-state effort to become the world's only superpower by any means necessary," said Christopher Wray, the director of the Federal Bureau of Investigation (FBI). Thus, the core elements of economic nationalism, including GVC decoupling, onshoring, and anti-immigration policies, were also adopted in the technology development realm, aiming at confronting China's technological growth as well as maintaining the USA's leadership in the world's technology.

First, the US government has been placing restrictions on the US supply chain for China's leading tech corporations. GVC disruption, i.e. decoupling, is executed in two ways: prohibiting American and foreign companies from trading with Chinese enterprises and forcing Chinese firms to sell their operation in the US to an American one. It is a process of *delinking* China from the high-tech networks of Uncle Sam. To present, Huawei, TikTok, WeChat, and Semiconductor Manufacturing International Corporation (SMIC) are among the prominent targets. In the case of Huawei, which was described as "an arm of Chinese Communist Party" by Former Secretary of State Pompeo, the US government banned the supply of American components and software to Huawei, on Huawei's purchase of American microchips and US-designed software. The US also led a campaign to call for their allies and partners around the world to oppose Huawei's installation of 5G systems in their countries, which was successful in Israel and the UK. Trump even promised not to share intelligence with countries that use the Chinese company's telecom gear owing to the fear of Chinese espionage. Recently, the same restriction is imposed on SMIC as the US concluded that the company's chip may be used by the Chinese military and defense industry. In a related measure, TikTok was forced to sell its US operations to a trusted American company. The deal between ByteDance (TikTok's parent), Oracle, and Walmart had been forced by the Trump administration. Following his order, the deal would give the two American firms a combined 20% stake in the new US-based TikTok Global. And Oracle, the cofounder of which possesses a close relationship with Trump, will take over the viral video app's US user data. Additionally, the IPO for TikTok Global is planned to take place within 12 months of its establishment, which means the control right of ByteDance over the new business entity will be reduced considerably. Overall, the actions of China's large tech firms serve three main purposes of preventing the transmission of US sensitive information to the CCP, curtailing the control over the US market, and constraining the dramatic rise of Chinese technology development. However, the US government's restriction orders, which deepen the technology conflict between the two countries, would not be smoothly executed owing to the enforcement and subsequent retaliation from China.

Second, onshoring is one of the strategies of the US to maintain its technological leadership and shore up domestic sources for microelectronics and related technology. In May 2020, the US government held a discussion with Intel, the world's second-largest semiconductor company, to encourage them to increase design, R&D, and manufacturing activities in the US. The country's Department of Commerce also worked with the world's largest semiconductor foundry, Taiwan Semiconductor Manufacturing Company (TSMC), regarding its planned factory in Arizona. However, while TSMC's response was ambiguous, Intel expressed a possibility of outsourcing rather than manufacturing its own chips and suggested that TSMC could be their producer in the back-up plan, which would seriously damage the US industrial base and competitiveness in 4IR. The USA's lack of a comparable ecosystem of specialized engineering capability, tacit knowledge, and professional networks in chip production would be attributable to Intel's plan.

Third, the US adopted a more stringent immigration procedure for Chinese nationals. According to Yang (2020),[158] the number of Chinese-national employees granted export licenses in 2018 (350 people) was half the figures for the previous year. And the approval rates for H-1B visas were only 75.4% in the last quarter of 2018, compared to 94.5% in the same quarter in 2015. The visa granting and visa extending procedures for many Chinese workers were prolonged considerably as a result of working in jobs related to AI or microprocessor chips. In addition, the Chinese, along with Russians and Iranians, are classified as sensitive nationals in the investigation of trade secret theft in Silicon Valley. As stated in the speech of the FBI director, this department is "opening a new China-related counter-intelligence case every 10 hours." And China-related counter-intelligence cases account for almost half of the total 5,000 active cases underway across the country. The more stringent immigration conditions for high-skilled Chinese workers in the technology field intend to lower the risk of US IP extortion; nevertheless, it would reluctantly promote those workers to stay in China and greatly contribute to the US rival as the semiconductor industry in China is expanding bigger and bigger.

Overall, the 4IR is expected to have a noticeable effect on the world's future, in the race for technological advancement, where China and the US are the biggest rivals. The US utilized strategies based on economic nationalism, namely, GVC decoupling, onshoring promotion, and immigration restriction, to confront and undermine the growth of Chinese companies; however, the country is also struggling to keep the global technological value chain within the US territory. Observing the US–China tech war from this vantage point, it can be said that while China is pouring much money and resources into technological R&D, manufacturers, and management improvement, the US is exerting its power to disrupt the GVC essential for China's development. The confrontation is continuing without a compromise. Thus, the answer to the question of whether there would be a winner in the tech war remains uncertain.

6.4.2 *China and the 4IR*

Another challenge to the global trading system that we will be discussing is related to the 4IR, especially the unbelievably quick progress of China in this race. According to a 2018 PwC report,[159] China is the fastest automating country in the world. This can be a direct result of the Chinese government's efforts to push its development in the era of automation of traditional manufacturing and industrial practices through smart technology. In 2015, a ten-year national strategic plan to develop China's manufacturing sector was introduced by Premier Li Keqiang, which is called MIC 2025. This, in essence, is said to be a blueprint for upgrading China's manufacturing sector with total funding exceeding 10 billion Yuan or $1.5 billion. MIC 2025 is also said to be helping China achieve self-sufficiency and push Beijing to the top of the GVC. It was already leading in the manufacturing of electric vehicles and the production of rare-earth metals. It is also expected that with MIC 2025, China can expect many developments in 5G, integrated circuit chips, smart devices, and autonomous vehicles in the next ten years.[160]

But even before this plan, China has been expanding the use of robots in different sectors. In addition, the new strategic plan improved China's average productivity by 38% in its first 109 pilot projects under smart manufacturing.[161] With this greater efficiency, the operating cost decreased by 21% (The State Council of the People's Republic of China, 2017).[162] This manufacturing advancement is evident with China's increasing share in the global export market. But it should also be noted that other countries are also gearing up for the 4IR race, as discussed in Chapter 1. The developments resulting from this revolution will likely encourage other nations to relocate their production lines back to their homelands.

China's main objective is to lessen its reliance on foreign technology providers and develop its own and achieve self-sufficiency in the advanced technology ecosystem. China's demand for semiconductors represents 60% of the world's total demand, but it only produces around 5% of the global supply (45% US, 23% Korea, 9% Japan, 9% EU). As outlined, it aims to reach 70% self-sufficiency in these tech industries by 2025. Ultimately, it aims to be a dominant player globally in high-tech industries by 2049.

China, in the pre-4IR era, also started low-carbon projects, like the Sino-Singapore Tianjin Eco-city and National Low-Carbon Province and Low-Carbon City Experimental Project, to further push its development of low-carbon growth plans in different places in the country (Stern, 2010).[163] China expects that these action plans and other initiatives will result in China reaching its carbon peak earlier than expected, as early as 2023 (China Dialogue, 2017).[164]

China's economic rise and digitalization have been remarkable, coupled with its accelerated growth, and especially the emergence of Chinese IT giants such as Tencent Holdings and Alibaba Group. This garnered China international interest and research and examinations of the Chinese economy. From the 1980s to the 1990s, Huang, who examined China's economy, described the characteristics of this period as economic forces driving to change the balance of power between the private sector and the state (Ito, 2020).[165] As mentioned previously, China experienced considerable growth after the Mao era, and domestic private companies contributed to this progress. The period was also known as *Boluan Fanzheng*, which means eliminating chaos and returning to normal, and this period was led by Deng Xiaoping from 1978 to 1989. This served as the foundation of China's historic reform and opening up its market. But in the 1990s, state intervention became stronger, which also led to the belief that the market reforms and economic changes in China were halted, as seen in its economic development in the late 2010s. Since the 1990s, China has been expanding policies on science and technology. This was done to emphasize the importance of domestic innovations especially in core technologies and vital industries. As mentioned previously, MIC 2025 is a good example of such an industrial policy. In addition, China rolled out several policies such as the Big Data Development Action Plan and the Internet Plus Action Plan (2015), which focus on the collection of data related to trusts, finance, tax, agriculture, and trade, to be used by the government to create a new model of social governance. There were other development plans as well as focus on the development of AI, and the push for global level competence in applied technology by 2020, with the ultimate goal of reaching the highest level in the world in theoretical knowledge, technology, and application by 2030 (Ito, 2020).[166]

China also capitalized on its BRI to further pursue digitalization, dubbing the BRI as the *Digital Belt and Road* or *Digital Silk Road*. As mentioned in Chapter 2, it can be said that China replaced the Soviet Union, as the balance of power is shifting again from a unipolar to a bipolar one. In 2017, President Xi Jinping expressed China's intentions to

> *adhere to innovation-driven development; support cooperation in frontier areas such as the digital economy, AI, nanotechnology, and quantum computers; promote big data, cloud computing, and the construction of smart cities; and connect the digital silk road of the 21st century.[167]*

With the world going in the same direction of digitalization, China's commitment to promote information sharing, such as its plan to lay fiberoptic cables, can prompt countries to join the bandwagon and improve their big data technology. Another example that shows China's move to expand its digital market is Alibaba and Tencent's expansion in Southeast Asia. Alibaba bought a controlling stake of Lazada Group, the largest e-commerce company in Southeast Asia, which represents Alibaba's biggest overseas investment so far.[168] Ironically, although China is expanding its digital services abroad, internet freedom is still limited in its domestic market. This is the total opposite of the USA's belief in the importance of being able to freely use the internet. In this regard, the two countries do have a growing mistrust, accusing each other of spying and mishandling private information that can be acquired through the two countries' ICT and telecom firms. Therefore, China is taking steps to remove most foreign technologies from several of its industries such as banks, the military, and state enterprises and agencies (Tourk and Marsh, 2016).[169] In the reverse, the US took action against several Chinese firms, which will be discussed next.

From a distance, the 4IR comes with tons of benefits as it can greatly increase efficiency in production and integrate smart technology with many sectors such as agriculture, data management, medicine, transportation infrastructure, maritime engineering, etc. But China's approach to developing its industries has been a lightning rod for criticisms from other countries. Its archrival, the US, released a warning and tagged China as a national security threat. Former US president Trump reiterated his call for the US and its allies to refrain from using Huawei's services in developing their 5G networks. Huawei, China's biggest tech company and the torchbearer of its 4IR team, was again hit hard by several bans imposed by the US. From September 15, 2020, all of Huawei's non-American suppliers were made to stop shipping to Huawei parts and components that contain US technology. This restriction puts Huawei, and its suppliers, in a difficult situation as the supplier needs to secure a license from the US Commerce

Department to continue its business with Huawei. This creates a whole new set of challenges for China as Huawei plays an important role in upgrading China's 5G infrastructure.[170] This problem with the supply chain strengthened China's desire to rapidly de-Americanize its supply chain. This will surely take some time as Huawei tries to find its way to develop its technology to produce parts that were previously found only in about one-seventh of Huawei's components. The company also seeks to find new suppliers and establish new linkages in Europe and Japan, which it believes are capable of replacing the US-produced parts.[171]

China's espionage has also been a lingering issue for quite some time. Of course, this is nothing new as the US, Russia, and other countries engage in both espionage and counterespionage, which have been important tools of state-craft for centuries. But there are clear indications that the intelligence war is being raised to a whole new level, especially by China. The case of Kevin Mallory, who was a former member of the military, the Central Intelligence Agency, and the Defense Intelligence Agency and was directly contacted by a recruiter from a think-tank company in China, is one of the many cases that demonstrates China's more aggressive actions to get access to the USA's top-secret files and documents.[172] These issues may have added to the skepticism toward Huawei's products and services, as tools to advance China's spying agendas. Senator Mark Warner, in an interview with tech site The Verge, stated, "There is ample evidence to suggest that no major Chinese company is independent of the Chinese government and Communist Party – and Huawei, which China's government and military tout as a national champion, is no exception."

Many policymakers also claim that China's enthusiasm in rolling out its MIC 2025 policies is resulting in excessive state subsidies, which other countries are concerned about as it might lead to skewed markets, overproduction, and eventually dumping of products in the global market. A report prepared for the USCC by Capitol Trade Incorporated in 2009 contains the list of subsidies provided by the Chinese government to strategic and heavyweight industries. The ICT sector was also included in this report, and companies such as China Electronics Corporation Holdings Company Limited (CEC) and IRICO Group Electronics Company Limited (IGE) benefited greatly from subsidies by government grants, preferential tax rates, and preferential lending rates. Given that this report came out in 2009, it is safe to assume that subsidies by the Chinese government have grown exponentially considering the fact that it has several development plans in place such as the BRI, MIC 2025, *de-Americanization* of its supply chain, and the ultimate goal of the Chinese Dream, the dream of its full modernization and achievement as the number one developed nation on the 100th anniversary of the founding of the PRC in 2049. The report highlighted that China's increasing role in the global economy also expands the role of Chinese firms that are heavily subsidized and controlled by the Chinese government. This might lead to actions geared toward meeting government demands instead of satisfying market demands.

Even the comparative policy analysis among China, Germany, and the US and their respective industrial revitalization via Industry 4.0 reflects the glaring difference of China's priorities in terms of its MIC 2025. Both the USA's

Advanced Manufacturing Partner and Germany's INDUSTRIE 4.0 policies favor demand-side policies mainly under public services, while China focuses on the environmental side with political support making up 50% of MIC 2025. China has a high ratio of both legal and political regulatory policies to aid its ambitious MIC 2025 plan (Kuo et al., 2018).[173]

This technology dilemma, upon further interpretation in a network power framework, becomes easy to understand. As Grewal (2008)[174] mentions: "where a technology embodies a successful standard, economies of scale will drive the adoption of that standard by increasing numbers of users, leading to the establishment of a single, universal standard of coordination, all else being equal." In this era of technology, an upper hand in the ICT field provides huge advantages over other nodes within the network. Grewal also emphasized that the situation mentioned above comes with threats of giving 'too much control' to a single private actor, wherein he used Microsoft's case as an example. This might also be the reason behind the USA's suspicion toward Huawei and other Chinese ICT firms. Although it is a private entity, the US consistently claimed that Huawei receives special funding from the Chinese government and that the company is backed by the Chinese military, which Huawei denies. It is possible that aside from the security issue and the alleged theft of US technology and IP, Washington is also threatened by the rise of Chinese tech firms gaining market competitiveness, as mid-range devices manufactured by Huawei, Xiaomi, Oppo, and Vivo are on the rise and due to the fact that the Chinese government has full control over these companies.

We can look at the 4IR as a long-developing wave that might last for the next 50 to 60 years. This will change the current status of different sectors such as trade in services, capital, and even anti-foreign sentiments. With China continuously gearing up for the CCP's 100th anniversary, we can see more automation in what is considered the world's factory as the country embraces the 4IR. More smart cities and smart factories will be built, thus reducing the need for human labor and also decreasing the marginal cost with automation. Recently, a cement factory in China, Conch Group, has claimed that its 5G Smart Factories reduced the production costs through its successful integration of 5G and Internet of Things (IoT) into its facilities. The said smart factory has automated the whole process including quality sampling, testing, and feedback. Freeman (2020) said, "If only one of the 40 production lines can be equipped with such technologies, we can gain 1 billion RMB a year or around $137 million."[175] This is only one example of how AI and 5G can greatly change the production process. It is true that the Chinese government will not be hesitant to tighten its grip on power and continue to develop its technology in order to achieve these advancements and gain the benefits of such smart systems.

As China accelerates its efforts in the 4IR race, it will marginalize the extent of its comparative advantage in manufacturing. The relocation of the factories in China by multinational corporations and the reduction of inter-industry trade volume between China and the rest of the world are inevitable. Automation and AI will reshape the overall production process through labor saving and labor cost reducing.

6.4.3 The EU and the 4IR

The 4IR is a phenomenon that brought 'Profound and Systemic Change,' which is shaping the way we live our lives and how our world will evolve thanks to the ever-growing harmonization and integration of many disciplines and discoveries (Schwab, 2016).[176] Among these, we can find technologies like blockchain, AI, and 5G, which are considered by many the foundation of said Revolution. It can create "windows of opportunity for developing and emerging economies but also raise red flags in terms of the main challenges that these changes pose to developing and emerging economies firms, industrial systems and policy approaches" (Lee et al., 2020).[177] Specifically, the advent of the 5G technology could potentially bring levels of economic development and technological evolution that would be comparable to the ones brought by the investment in the 2G-GSM network (Lemstra, 2018).[178]

As discussed in Chapter 1, the 4IR concept is brought to the world during the World Economic Forum in 2015. But originally, Germany coined the term *Industry 4.0* in 2011 as a part of its plan to boost digitalization in the manufacturing sector. Industry 4.0 is also expected to change the conventional approaches to manufacturing in order to achieve four paradigm shifts: Factory and Nature, Factory and Local Communities, Factory and Value Chains, and Factory and Humans. In a nutshell, these changes include the sustainability and resource efficiency of the manufacturing sector, as well as increased geographical proximity and more improved work conditions (Santos et al., 2017).[179] This complements the European Green Deal, which is aimed at making Europe carbon neutral by 2050. This deal is set to be financed through InvestEU, which is an investment plan worth 1 trillion euros.

It is not surprising that the EU would address the topic, especially considering its ongoing Digital Single Market (DSM) plan. The 2014–2019 commission indeed had identified the DSM plan as one of its priorities, mainly streamlining a set of investments based on four main pillars to digitize industries: Digital Innovation Hubs, strengthening leadership through partnerships and industrial platforms, a regulatory framework fit for the digital age, and preparing Europeans for the digital future.

Regarding 5G, the EU went ahead and funded studies that forecast the socioeconomic benefits of 5G and its supporting platforms such as the European 5G Observatory. According to one such study, in 2025

> *benefits from the introduction of 5G capabilities could reach €113.1 billion per year in four key sectors which will be the first users of 5G connectivity: automotive, health, transport and energy. Investments of approximately €56.6 billion will be likely to create 2.3 million jobs in Europe.*
>
> (European Commission, 2016)[180]

The issue gains increasing importance when we consider the ongoing fight between the US and many Chinese IT companies, among which we can find Huawei, one of the global leaders when it comes to the 5G network expansion. In

2019, the US banned in practice the use of products and telecommunication systems that could be seen as a national security risk (Federal Register, 2019).[181]

An exhaustive publication by the NATO Cooperative Cyber Defense Centre of Excellence (2019)[182] concludes that although "there is no public evidence of serious technological vulnerabilities in specific Huawei or ZTE equipment," "China's legal and political environment, along with its known practice of 'public-private partnership' in cyber espionage remains a concern." The battle could be seen as an extension of the *US–China cold war*, but many concerns were raised by other countries as well. By 2019, these concerns were translated into concrete action by many sovereign states (like Australia, New Zealand, Japan, and others) that decided to join forces with the US and ban the use of Huawei technology in their 5G networks (Buchholz, 2020).[183] The UK followed suit by banning the use of new Huawei equipment from the end of 2020, saying that existing kits must be stripped from the 5G network by 2027 (Parker et al., 2020).[184] The British response shifted the focus on the EU and its member states, which did not seem to agree on a common plan of action regarding the Huawei issue.

The general EU stance may be defined by their general policy on cybersecurity and their strategic outlook toward relations with China. Both these items are discussed in the Joint Communication and strategic outlook regarding the EU and China (2019).[185] The need to formulate a coordinated EU risk assessment and risk management measures was underlined, and the EU said it would support multilateral efforts to promote free and secure data flows based on privacy protection. Cooperation with China to support effective multilateralism is a key point of communication.

The fact that future 5G networks would be considered a 'backbone of our societies and economies' suggests a cautious approach from the European community, which actually streamlined an additional plan to bolster Union-wide digital development. The basis of this plan can be found in the Commission Recommendation, the *Recommendation on Cybersecurity of 5G Networks* (2019),[186] where it is stated that the member states of the EU should consider relevant cybersecurity-related issues and prepare a plan of action by October 2020.

Risk assessment of 5G structures, national risk, collaboration and exchange of information, security, and privacy concerns are all topics that were touched upon in the Huawei-related events. These talks related to the implementation of a solid 5G network in Europe culminated with the introduction of a *European 5G Toolbox*, a set of measures described in Communication "Secure 5G deployment in the EU: Implementing the EU toolbox" (2020).[187] The objective of these measures focuses on providing the tools to conduct country-wide and European-level risk assessments, help with standardization among country members, maintain a diverse and sustainable 5G supply chain, provide guidance with existing tools, and bring further convergence regarding technical and organizational security.

Considering the upcoming investments that will be made on a scale never seen before, it is only natural that special focus has been put on the matter. This new 'toolbox' and set of risk assessment measures become even more relevant considering the 11 technology and trial projects (European Commission, 2020),[188] which are being funded as part of an intra-European effort to bolster cross-border corridors, infrastructures, and projects consistent with the Green Deal from December 2019 and other 5G-related investment networks.

While the EU still lacks a clear position on the matter, many of the member countries seem to be at least skeptical about the widespread use of Huawei technology. The head of the French cybersecurity agency ANSSI declared that although France would not ban the use of Chinese tech for the deployment of a 5G network, he would push operators to not use Huawei technologies (Reuters, 2020).[189] Nonetheless, a bill that could hamper Huawei's involvement in Germany's 5G network is being discussed and will be able, at least in theory, to set heavy restrictions on 5G hardware coming from China (Chazan and Fildes, 2020).[190] Italy did not include Huawei among the companies that would be supplying new-generation 5G services but decided not to ban it altogether, and the company is still a supplier of Telecom Italia's radio access network. Germany approved tougher security measures but did not side with the UK's decision to ban Huawei altogether (Der Spiegel, 2020).[191]

With none of the major countries of the EU taking a definite side, it is clear that the Huawei dilemma will keep the talks going and that, given the circumstances, the Union's general direction will probably remain uncertain in the near future. What can be said for sure, though, is that Germany's final stance on the matter will probably set a precedent and shift the EU's general consensus at least by a small margin. Being the de facto economical leading node of the Union means that depending on Germany's decision, the cautious approach taken by Europe could move to a slightly bolder direction. As we said earlier, due to the very structure of the EU, Germany does no longer fulfill completely the role of a programmer and a switcher, limiting its position as the most influential member. Nevertheless, as the European country with the largest exports to China (Eurostat, 2020)[192] and as a country with a domestic market that accounted for 28% of the Euro-Zone as of 2017 (IMF, 2017),[193] its *network-making power* and *networked power* cannot be underestimated. Germany will most likely face a challenge where it will have to find a balance between national economic interest and the communitarian interest, which can be better translated into the interest of its network.

The neutrality of the EU's biggest countries can be understood when we look at the EU's agenda. Similar to China, the EU also plans to digitalize its supply chain and further develop its technology sector. Although in contrast, China started its technological advancement later than the west, just as the EU started to work on its technological policies in the early 1980s focusing on funding R&D projects. However, the Union is seen to have failed in maintaining the same growth rates of other regions, and calls for increasing the EU's role in R&D policies were thus made. From there, the Lisbon Agenda in 2000 was adopted, and it gave a new drive for the EU to push its R&D and technological policy. With the advent of the 4IR, the EU should fully reveal its R&D and technological strategies to all member states (Schafer, 2018).[194]

However, as the EU moves forward in the 4IR race, the downside of this advancement becomes apparent. Similar to the US and China, the relocation through reshoring is becoming more commonplace in Europe as well. These reshoring strategies do place free trade at a crossroads. The operational efficiency and productivity brought by the 4IR through IT-enabled and AI-backed manufacturing facilities change the current status of the GVC. It is no secret that offshoring became a trend due to differences in costs, especially in labor costs, between manufacturing something, say in Germany, and building a factory in a labor-abundant country, like Vietnam. Automated and smart factories can cut down labor costs by removing the need for the actual human worker, therefore making the 4IR an equalizer of additional costs that may arise from reshoring. In addition, reshoring presents benefits in product innovation, as the closer proximity of the R&D center and production plant of a certain firm allows better management of complexities, such as the need for joint problem solving, and improvements of non-modular products, involved in the production-development process (Ancarani et al., 2019).[195] It is just a matter of time for the adoption of new technologies for further progress. Then, we can further analyze which companies are utilizing them, as they increasingly rely on reshoring strategies. Whatever the merits of reshoring, one thing is certain – switching to new technologies will strengthen the regional value content and debilitate the current GVC.

6.5 Lingering Uncertainty

New incidents continue to arise in different places around the world, some of which are predictable but some are not. Because of these events happening on top of the four waves of challenges that the world is facing, it makes researchers cautious as to predicting the future landscape of the global trading system. However, based on what we analyzed, we can portray what is to come.

First, the rigid position of different countries due to the COVID-19 pandemic poses threats to global trade and cooperation. With many nations imposing lockdowns and travel restrictions, it is difficult to expect things to go back the way they were. The USA's COVID-19 response has been criticized not only by Americans themselves but also by different countries around the world (Pew Research Center, 2020).[196] Even with Joe Biden taking over the presidency, no drastic changes in how the US is handling the pandemic have been observed. China banned travelers from COVID-19 hotspots such as India, the UK, France, Belgium, and the Philippines (Forbes, 2020).[197] Several European countries are experiencing a group of new COVID-19 variant cases, and this will definitely be a reason for China to continue adding countries to the entry ban list. The tables have really turned, and until a cure is widely released, we should expect more countries to implement protective measures to curb the spread of the virus.

Second, the trade war is an integral part of the USA's economic nationalism, in which the US has taken tough actions to confront and deter the dominance of China in various aspects. Confrontation and coercion, aggression, and antagonism have been the strategic approaches of the US to China in this new Cold

War. The Phase One deal, which China keeps holding as valid, still remains in place despite the non-compliance of China. We can clearly see a tug-of-war happening between China and the US, where one pulls the rope harder whenever it sees the other side engaged in unflattering actions. Should the US backtrack from its attempt to reclaim its role as the leading node of the liberal network? The answer is negative. The EU would probably focus its efforts toward expanding the multilateral network while forming a bloc that could challenge the upcoming rise of China as a global competitor. Petri and Plummer (2020)[198] mentioned that this trade war will change the trading relationship in the world, moving away from the US–China link. Some links will be loosened, and some severed.

Third, economic nationalism still has substantial impacts on the global trading system. The ideology is clearly illustrated in Trump's *America First* Policy. From the perspective of the current Biden administration, free trade still remains a win-lose, and not a win-win, game. This has led to a series of actions that undermine the existing multilateral trading network. As for China, it still continues to practice seemingly liberal nationalism, wherein the country remains open to trade with others but only to serve its national interests. If Biden continues his *Build Back Better* policy, which also has some anti-immigration and protectionist undertones, it is not too far-fetched to think that the Union will seek new alliances in the East while pushing for new reforms in international organizations like the WTO. Then again, the EU and many countries expect Biden to have a more liberal and multilateral approach than Trump. However, we have yet to see economic nationalism in the US decrease under Biden's lead.

Lastly, the new race, in the name of the 4IR, is another way to regain the leading position in the global trading system. As noted by Dorussen and Ward (2010),[199] security, peacekeeping, and trade are remarkably interconnected. Possessing a competitive advantage over international trade through technological means would yield significant positives in other sectors and would hence help the 'winner' of this New Industrial Revolution race to firmly hold the position as the main hegemonic force in the international environment. The newly (or old) established hegemon would gain a significant hedge toward smaller nodes, especially while dealing with issue linkage and the possibility of upholding favorable trades and non-trade deals with their 'target partners' (or simply put, any other node they will be dealing with).

From a strategic standpoint, it seems that China possesses more structural and organizational advantages to outcompete the US. However, when it comes to utilizing its network of allies and partners, the US takes the lead. If China could successfully complete *de-Americanizing* its technological supply chain, it would be easier for the country to pursue its goal of moving ahead in the 4IR race. In reality, the practicability of the plan is in doubt. The EU's position toward the 'Huawei Dilemma' and China's alleged security issues will also prove to be key issues in future progress toward a technology-based trading world.

The high level of uncertainty brought by the COVID-19 pandemic, the US–China trade war, economic nationalism, and the 4IR race will remain in the limelight for a while, as globalization did not keep its promises to the victims and losers of the process. The enemies of globalization already jumped on the wagon to the city of *deglobalization*.[200] We might not know until when these issues will linger, but one thing is for certain – we should prepare for more challenges in the world in the days ahead.

Notes

1 PwC (2020), *The Possible Economic Consequences of a Novel Coronavirus (Covid-19) Pandemic*, London: PricewaterhouseCoopers.
2 WTO (2021), *World Trade Statistical Review 2021*, Geneva: World Trade Organization.
3 UNECLAC (2020), *COVID-19 Response*, pp. 1–12, Santiago: United Nations Economic Commission for Latin America and the Caribbean.
4 Ibid., pp. 12–13.
5 Ibid., pp. 19–25.
6 Mutikani, L. (2020), COVID-19 Crushes U.S. Economy in Second Quarter; Rising Virus Cases Loom Over Recovery, *Reuters* (July 29, 2020).
7 Watson, G., Li, H. and LaJoie, T. (2020), *Details and Analysis of President-Elect Joe Biden's Tax Proposals*, October 2020 Update, Tax Foundation, Fiscal Fact No. 730, p. 3.
8 Gertz, B. (2020), Mike Pompeo Details 'Distrust and Verify' China Policy at Nixon Library, *The Washington Times* (July 23, 2020).
9 Yeon, W. (2020), *The Impact of COVID-19 on the U.S.-China Phase One Agreement*, Korea Institute for International Economic Policy (KIEP). Retrieved from http://hdl.handle.net/11540/11841
10 Zhang, Z. (2020), US Tariff Exclusion for Chinese Imports: What Is the Status? *China Briefing* (March 18, 2020).
11 Gereffi, G. (2020), What Does the COVID-19 Pandemic Teach Us about Global Value Chains? The Case of Medical Supplies, Commentary, *Journal of International Business Policy*, 3, pp. 287–301, p. 290.
12 OECD (2020), *The Face Mask Global Value Chain in the COVID-19 Outbreak: Evidence and Policy Lessons*, OECD. Paris: OECD. Retrieved from https://www.oecd.org/coronavirus/policy-responses/the-face-mask-global-value-chain-in-the-COVID-19-outbreak-evidence-and-policy-lessons-a4df866d/
13 Norrlöfm C. (2020), Is COVID-19 the End of US Hegemony? Public Bads, Leadership Failures and Monetary Hegemony, *International Affairs*, 96(5), pp. 1281–1303.
14 Hickey, C., Merrill, C., Chang, R., Sullivan, K., Boschma, J. and O'Key, S. (2021), Here Are the Executive Actions Biden Signed in His First 100 days, *CNN Politics* (April 30, 2021 updated).
15 Murphy, J. (2021), Biden Pledged 200 Million Covid Vaccinations in 100 Days. The Country Hit That Goal with a Week to Spare, *NBC News* (January 26, 2021).
16 WTO (2021), Ibid.
17 Zhang, Y., Diao X., Chen, K., Robinson, S. and Fan, S. (2020), Impact of COVID-19 on China's Macroeconomy and Agri-food system – an Economy-wide Multiplier Model Analysis, *China Agricultural Economic Review*, 12(3), pp. 388–391.
18 PwC (2020), Macroeconomic Impact of the COVID-19 in China and Policy Suggestions, PricewaterhouseCoopers, pp. 5–10. Retrieved from https://www.pwccn.com/en/covid-19/macroeconomic-impact-covid19-policy-suggestions.pdf
19 Ibid., p. 392.
20 KPMG (2020), *Government and Institution Measures in Response to COVID-19*, Amstelveen: KPMG. Retrieved from https://home.kpmg/bg/en/home/insights/2020/05/government-and-institution-measures-in-response-to-covid-19.html

21 Irwin, D. (2020), *The Pandemic Adds Momentum to the Deglobalisation Trend,*. *Peterson Institute for International Economics.* Washington, DC: PIIE. Retrieved from https://www. piie. com/blogs/realtime-economic-issues-watch/pandemic-adds-momentum-deglobalization-trend.

22 Yang, L. (2020), Covid-19, Global Value Chain and China's Foreign Trade, p. 27, *FMM*, East China Normal University.

23 Barua, S. (2020), Understanding Coronanomics: The Economic Implications of the Coronavirus (COVID-19) Pandemic, *MPRA* Paper 99693, University Library of Munich, Germany.

24 Cameron, F. (2020), EU-Asia Should Defend Multilateralism, *Asia Europe Journal*, 18(2), pp. 217–221.

25 Conte, A., Lecca, P., Salotti, S. and Sakkas, S. (2020), *The Territorial Economic Impact of COVID-19 in the EU*. A Rhomolo Analysis, Territorial Development Insights Series, JRC121261, European Commission.

26 EU Science Hub (2020), *JRC Analyses COVID-19 Impact on Economy and Labour Markets to Help Guide EU Responses*, Brussels: European Commission. Retrieved from https://ec.europa.eu/jrc/communities/en/community/jrc-alumni-network/article/jrc-analyses-covid-19-impact-economy-and-labour-markets-help

27 Eurostat (2020), Eurostat Data Browser. EU27 (from 2020) trade by SITC product group. Retrieved from https://ec.europa.eu/eurostat/databrowser/view/ext_st_eu27_2020sitc/default/table?lang=en

28 Kirkegaard, J. (2020), *The European Policy Response to the COVID-19 Pandemic*, pp. 1–5, Washington, DC: PIIE.

29 Ibid., pp. 5–6.

30 Grewal, D. (2008), *Network Power: The Social Dynamics of Globalization*, p. 142, New Haven: Yale University Press.

31 Fleming S. and Khan, M. (2020), EU's Budget and Recovery Package Stalls Over Rule of Law Spat, *Financial Times* (November 16, 2020).

32 Farrell, H. and Newman, A. (2020), Will the Coronavirus End Globalization as We Know It? *Foreign Affairs* (March 16, 2020).

33 As defined in Chapter 2, a multiplex network is a network formed by the same set of nodes interacting through different types of networks (also called layers) as, for example, a set of people interacting through different means of communication.

34 Lazarou, E. (2020), *Foreign Policy Consequences of Coronavirus*. European Parliament Think Tank. Strasbourg: EPTT.

35 Celi, G., Guarascio, D. and Simonazzi, A. (2020), A Fragile and Divided European Union Meets COVID-19: Further Disintegration or 'Hamiltonian Moment'? *Journal of Industrial and Business Economics*, 47(3), pp. 411–424.

36 Li, X. and Zhang, S. (2018). Interdependent Hegemony: China's Rise Under the Emerging New World Order, *China Quarterly of International Strategic Studies*, 4(2), pp. 159–175.

37 Maggi, G. (2016), Issue linkage in *Handbook of Commercial Policy*, 1, pp. 513–564, North-Holland.

38 Ibid., pp. 556–558.

39 Bown, C. (2020), *Trump's Trade Policy Is Hampering the US Fight against COVID-19*, Washington, DC: PIIE.

40 US Department of Justice (2020), *Chinese Telecommunications Conglomerate Huawei and Subsidiaries Charged in Racketeering Conspiracy and Conspiracy to Steal Trade Secrets*, Washington, DC: USDOJ.

41 US Department of Treasury. (2019). Treasury Designates China as a Currency Manipulator. Washington, DC: USDT. Retrieved from https://home.treasury.gov/news/press-releases/sm751

42 Ajibo, C., Nwatu, S., Ukwueze, F., Adibe, E., Lloyd, C. and Richards, N. (2019), RCEP, CPTPP and the Changing Dynamics in International Trade Standard-Setting, *Manchester Journal of International Economic Law*, 16(3), p. 439.

43 Pompeo, M. (2020), *Communist China and the Free World's Future*, Washington, DC: US Department of State.

44 Bown, C. (2021), *US-China Phase One Tracker; China's Purchases of US Goods*, Washington, DC: PIIE CHARTS.

45 Malkawi, B. (2021), 'Phase One' *US-China Trade Deal Better Than No Deal – Analysis*, East Asia Forum.

46 Sun, X. (2020), Looking Before Leaping: Can We Afford an Unlimited Trade War between the World's Two Largest Economies, *Global Journal of Emerging Market Economies*, 12(1), pp. 24–41.

47 White House (2020), United States Strategic Approach to the People's Republic of China. Washington, DC: White House. Retrieved from https://trumpwhitehouse. archives.gov/wp-content/uploads/2020/05/U.S.-Strategic-Approach-to-The-Peoples-Republic-of-China-Report-5.24v1.pdf

48 Brown, S. (US Senator for Ohio) (2020), Senate Democrats Unveil the America Leads Act to Make Comprehensive Investments in American Workers, Competitiveness, Alliances, and Diplomacy to Confront the Rise of China, Washington, DC: US Senate. Retrieved from https://www.brown.senate.gov/newsroom/press/release/democrats-america-leads-act-investments-american-workers-competitiveness-china

49 Pompeo, M. (2020), Ibid.

50 White House (2020), Ibid.

51 Govtrack, S. (2020), 4629 (116th), 116th Congress, Washington, DC: US Senate.

52 Lee, T. and Londono, J. (2021), The United States Innovation and Competition Act (USICA): A Primer, American Action Forum, *Insight* (June 9, 2021).

53 OECD, Interim Economic Outlook. For a longer forecasts, see Statista (2020), Growth Rate of Real Gross Domestic Product (GDP) in China from 2011 to 2019 with Forecasts until 2025. Retrieved from https://www.oecd.org/economic-outlook/september-2020/

54 Ministry of Commerce (2020), PRC, China FTA Network. Ministry of Commerce, PRC. Retrieved from http://fta.mofcom.gov.cn/english/index.shtml

55 Nathan, A. (2019), How China Really Sees the Trade War, *Foreign Affairs* (June 27, 2019).

56 Bown, C. (2021), Ibid.

57 Bekkers, E. and Schroeter, S. (2020), *An Economic Analysis of US-China Trade Conflict*, WTO Economic Research and Statistics Division. Geneva: WTO. Retrieved from https://www.wto.org/english/res_e/reser_e/ersd202004_e.htm

58 Malkawi, B. (2021), Ibid.

59 Sun, X. (2020), Ibid.

60 Xinhua Net (2020), Factbox: China's Progress in Economic Resumption, *Xinhua* (Sep. 7, 2020).

61 Eurostat (2020), International Trade in Goods – A Statistical Picture. Eurostat, statistics Explained. Retrieved from https://ec.europa.eu/eurostat/statistics-explained/index.php?title=International_trade_in_goods_-_a_statistical_picture

62 Wolff, G. (2018), How Could Europe Benefit from the US-China Trade War? *Bruegel Blog* (October 18, 2018).

63 UNCTAD (2019), Key Statistics and Trends in Trade Policy 2018, New York and Geneva, United Nations Conference on Trade and Development. Geneva: UNCTAD. Retrieved from https://unctad.org/system/files/official-document/ditctab2019d9_en.pdf

64 Garcia, H. (2019), Europe in the Midst of China–US Strategic Economic Competition: What Are the European Union's Options? *Journal of Chinese Economic and Business Studies*, 17(4), pp. 403–423.

65 Plummer, M. (2019), The US-China Trade War and Its Implications for Europe. *Intereconomics*, 54(3), pp. 195–196.

66 Goulard, S. (2020), The Impact of the US–China Trade War on the European Union, *Global Journal of Emerging Market Economies*, 12(1), pp. 56–68.

67 Bolt, W., Mavromatis, K. and Van Wijnbergen, S. (2019), The Global Macroeconomics of a Trade War: The EAGLE Model on the US-China Trade Conflict, *Tinbergen Institute Discussion Paper*, 2019-015.

68 González, A. and Veron, N. (2019), EU Trade Policy amid the China-US Clash: Caught in the Cross-Fire? *PIIE Working Paper* (19-13). Washington D.C.: PIIE.

69 European Commission (2020a), Secure 5G Deployment in the EU: Implementing the EU Toolbox. Brussels: EC. Retrieved from https://eur-lex.europa.eu/legal-content/EN/TXT/?uri=COM:2020:50:FIN

70 European Council (2020a), EU-China Summit via Video Conference (June 22, 2020).

71 European Council (2020b), EU-China leaders' Meeting via Video Conference (September 14, 2020).

72 Grieger, G. (2020), *EU-China Relations: Taking Stock after the 2020 EU-China Summit*, European Parliament Think Tank. Strasbourg: EPTT.

73 Koty, A. (2021), European Parliament Votes to Freeze the EU-China Comprehensive Agreement on Investment, *China Briefing* (May 27, 2021).

74 Sarsenbayev, M. and Véron, N. (2020), European versus American Perspectives on the Belt and Road Initiative, *China & World Economy*, 28(2), pp. 84–112.

75 Smith, J. and Taussig, T. (2019), The Old World and the Middle Kingdom: Europe Wakes Up to China's Rise, *Foreign Affairs* (September/October).

76 Plummer, M. (2019), Ibid.

77 Baschuk, B. (2020), U.S Targets $3.1 Billion of EU and U.K. Imports for New Tariffs, *Bloomberg* (June 24, 2020).

78 Brunsden, J. (2020), Airbus to remove subsidies in attempt to end US dispute, *Financial Times* (July 24, 2020).

79 Garcia, H. (2019), Europe in the midst of China–US strategic economic competition: what are the European Union's options? *Journal of Chinese Economic and Business Studies*, 17(4), pp. 403–423.

80 Anderson, S. (2020), Biden Says He Will End Trump's Tariffs On Chinese-Made Goods, Aide Walks Back Statement, *Forbes* (August 6, 2020).

81 Garcia, H. (2019), Ibid.

82 Ibid.

83 Wolfe, R. and Mavroidis, P. (2020), WTO Dispute Settlement and the Appellate Body: Insider Perceptions and Members' Revealed Preferences, *Journal of World Trade*, 54(5), pp. 667–698.

84 Hoekman, B. and Mavroidis, P. (2020), To AB or Not to AB? Dispute Settlement in WTO Reform, *Journal of International Economic Law*, 23(3), pp. 1–20.

85 European Commission (2020b), The WTO Multi-Party Interim Appeal Arrangements Gets Operational. Retrieved from https://policy.trade.ec.europa.eu/news_en

86 Ullah, A., Aria, A. and Akhter, M. (2020), EU Trade Policy amid US-China Trade Confrontation. *Journal of Social and Political Sciences*, 3(1), pp. 90–102.

87 Smith, J. and Taussig, T. (2019), Ibid.

88 Plummer, M. (2019), Ibid.

89 Garcia, H. (2019), Ibid.

90 Ibid.

91 European Union Chamber of Commerce in China (2019), European Business in China – Position Paper 2019/2020.

92 Lin, L., Woo, S. and Wei, L. (2020), China May Retaliate against Nokia and Ericsson If EU Countries Move to Ban Huawei, *The Wall Street Journal* (July 20, 2020).

93 Westad, O. (2019), The Sources of Chinese Conduct: Are Washington and Beijing Fighting a New Cold War, *Foreign Affairs*, 98(5), pp. 86–95.

94　Lester, S. (2020), *What Would Trade Policy Look Like Under a President Joe Biden?* Washington, DC: CATO Institute.

95　Helleiner, E. (2002), Economic Nationalism as a Challenge to Economic Liberalism? Lessons from the 19th century, *International Studies Quarterly*, 46(3), pp. 307–329.

96　Koffman, J. and Szlajfer, H. (1990), How to Define Economic Nationalism? A Critical Review of Some Old and New Standpoints, in Szlajfer, H. and Droz, L. (eds), *Economic Nationalism in East-Central Europe and South America*, Geneva: Droz, pp. 17–54.

97　Harlen, C. (1999), A Reappraisal of Classical Economic Nationalism and Economic Liberalism, *International Studies Quarterly*, 43(4), pp. 733–744.

98　For a detailed policy prescriptions of neo-liberal economist group led by John Williamson, see Spence, M. (2011), *The Next Convergence: The Future of Economic Growth in a Multispeed World*, London: PICADOR, pp. 92–93.

99　Schoenbaum, T. and Chow, D. (2019), The Peril of Economic Nationalism and Proposed Pathway to Trade Harmony, *Stanford Law & Policy Review*, 30(1), pp. 115–196.

100　McCorriston, S. and Sheldon, I. (2020), Economic Nationalism: US Trade Policy vs. Brexit, *Ohio State Business Law Journal*, 14(1), pp. 64–99.

101　Brewster, R. (2018), The Trump Administration and the Future of the WTO. *The Yale Journal of International Law Online*, 44, Duke Law School Public Law & Legal Theory Series No. 2019-10.

102　Ibid.

103　Chow, D., Sheldon, I. and McGuire, W. (2019), The Revival of Economic Nationalism and the Global Trading System, *Cardozo Law Review*, 40(5), pp. 2133–2170.

104　Bown, C. and Irwin, D. (2019), Trump's assault on the global trading system and why decoupling from China will change everything? *Foreign Affairs*, 98(5), pp. 125–137.

105　Brewster, R. (2018), Ibid.

106　Bown, C. and Irwin, D. (2019), Ibid.

107　Chow, D., Sheldon, I. and McGuire, W. (2019), Ibid.

108　Bown, C., and Irwin, D. (2019), Ibid.

109　Chow, D., Sheldon, I. and McGuire, W. (2019), Ibid.

110　Hogan, B. (2017), Online Social Networks: Concepts for Data Collection and Analysis, in Fielding, N., Lee, R. and Blank, G. (eds), *The Sage Handbook of Online Research Methods*, 2nd ed., Thousand Oaks, CA: Sage Publications. pp. 241–258.

111　Schneider-Petsinger, M. (2020), *Reforming the World Trade Organization: Prospects for Transatlantic Cooperation and the Global Trade System*, Research Paper, US and the Americas Programme, London: Chatham House.

112　Van Grasstek, C. (2019), *The Trade Policy of the United States under the Trump Administration*, European University Institute, Robert Schuman Center for Advance Studies, Working Paper RSCAS 2019/11.

113　Bown, C. and Irwin, D. (2019), Ibid.

114　Noland, M. (2018), US Trade Policy in the Trump Administration, *Asian Economic Policy Review*, 13, pp. 262–278.

115　Chow, D., Sheldon, I. and McGuire, W. (2019), Ibid.

116　Lester, S., Manak, I. and Kim, K. H. (2019), Trump's First Trade Deal: The Slightly Revised Korea-U.S. Free Trade Agreement, CATO Institute, *Free Trade Bulletin*, No. 73.

117　Noland, M. (2018), Ibid.

118　Bown, C. and Irwin, D. (2019), Ibid.

119　For example, see Heo, Y. and Doanh, N. (2020), Is NAFTA Trade-Creating or Trade-Diverting, *Economic Papers*, 39(3), pp. 222–238. For the sub-period of

1989–2016, however, trade diversion effect was not strong enough to offset trade creation effect.

120 Vakulina, O. (2019), US tariffs: EU vows to retaliate, *Euro News* (October 4, 2019).

121 Kennedy, S. and Tan, S. (2020), Decoupling between Washington and Western Industry, *CSIS* (June 10, 2020).

122 Capie, D., Hamilton-Hart, N. and Young, J. (2020), The Economics-Security Nexus in the US-China Trade Conflict Decoupling Dilemmas, *Policy Quarterly*, 16(4), p. 28.

123 Ravenhill, J. (2013), Economics and Security in the Asia-Pacific Region, *Pacific Review*, 26(1), pp. 1–15.

124 Bown, C. (2019), *Phase One Trade Deal: Steep Tariffs Are the New Normal*, Washington, DC: PIIE.

125 Wyne, A. (2020), How to Think about Potentially Decoupling from China, *The Washington Quarterly*, 43(1), pp. 41–64.

126 Van Grasstek, C. (2019), Ibid.

127 Wyne, A. (2020), Ibid.

128 Lighthizer, R. (2020), The Era of Offshoring US Jobs Is Over, *The New York Times* (May 11, 2020).

129 Shalal, A., Alper, A. and Znegerle, P. (2020), U.S. Mulls Paying Companies, Tax Breaks to Pull Supply Chains from China, *Reuters* (May 18, 2020).

130 Lighthizer, R. (2020), Ibid.

131 Mitchell, T. (2020), US companies defy Trump's threats about 'decoupling' from China, *Financial Times* (September 9, 2020).

132 Lee, Y. (2020), Exclusive: Foxconn to Shift Some Apple Production to Vietnam to Minimize China Risk, *Reuters* (November 26, 2020).

133 Capie, D., Hamilton-Hart, N. and Young, J. (2020), Ibid., p. 31.

134 Pierce, S., Bolter, J. and Selee, A. (2018), *US Immigration Policy under Trump: Deep Changes and Lasting Impacts*, Washington, DC: Transatlantic Council on Migration.

135 Pierce, S., Bolter, J. and Selee, A. (2018), Ibid.

136 Yang, Y. (2020), US-China Tech Dispute: Suspicion in Silicon Valley, *Financial Times* (January 21, 2020).

137 Hickey, C., Merrill, C., Chang, R., Sullivan, K., Boschma, J. and O'Key, S. (2021), Here are the Executive Actions Biden Signed in His First 100 Days, *CNN Politics* (April 30, 2021 updated).

138 Brandt, L. and Rawski, T. (eds) (2008), *China's Great Economic Transformation*, Cambridge: Cambridge University Press.

139 Engardio, P. (2005), China Is a Private-Sector Economy, *Bloomberg Businessweek* (August 21, 2005).

140 Bolle, M. and Zettelmeyer, J. (2019), Measuring the Rise of Economic Nationalism, *PIIE, Working Paper*. Washington D.C.: PIIE.

141 Ching, F. (2018), China: Deng Xiaoping Era Ends with Start of Xi Era, *Ejinsight* (September 6, 2018).

142 Institute for Security and Development Policy (2018), Made in China 2025 Backgrounder (June 2018). Retrieved from https://isdp.eu/content/uploads/2018/06/Made-in-China-Backgrounder.pdf

143 Sutter, K. (2020), *'Made in China 2025' Industrial Policies: Issues for Congress*, In Focus, IF10964, Washington, DC: Congressional Research Service.

144 McBride, J. and Chatzky, A. (2019), *Is 'Made in China 2025' a Threat to Global Trade?* New York: Council on Foreign Relations.

145 The Economic Times (2020), China Won't Follow Others towards More Protectionism, *The Economic Times* (January 22, 2020).

146 Capie, D., Hamilton-Hart, N. and Young, J. (2020), Ibid., p. 31.

147 Link, J. (2019), How Huawei Could Survive Trump, *Washington Post* (June 10, 2019).
148 Berend, I. (2000), The Failure of Economic Nationalism: Central and Eastern Europe before World War II, *Revue économique*, 51(2), pp. 315–322.
149 Colantone, I. and Stanig, P. (2018), The Trade Origins of Economic Nationalism: Import Competition and Voting Behavior in Western Europe, *American Journal of Political Science*, 62(4), pp. 936–953.
150 Bolle, M. and Zettelmeyer, J. (2019), Ibid., p. 2.
151 Koeth, W. (2018), From "Global Europe" to Trade Defense: The EU Responds to Trump and China, European Institute of Public Administration (EIPA), *Working Paper*.
152 Kirkegaard, J. (2019), Chinese Investments in the US and EU Are Declining – for Similar Reasons. *PIIE Policy Brief*, PIIE-CF40, pp. 11–12. Washington D.C.: PIIE.
153 Koeth, W. (2018), Ibid.
154 Balsa-Barreiro, J., Vié, A., Morales, A. and Cebrián, M, (2020), Deglobalization in a Hyper-Connected World, *Palgrave Communications*, 6(1), pp. 1–4.
155 Biancotti, C., Borin, A. and Mancini, M. (2017), *Euroscepticism: Another Brick in the Wall*, Rome: Bank of Italy.
156 Czaika, M. and Di Lillo, A. (2018), The Geography of Anti-Immigrant Attitudes across Europe, 2002–2014, *Journal of Ethnic and Migration Studies*, 44(15), pp. 2453–2479.
157 Doshi, R., (2020), *The United States, China, and the Contest for the Fourth Industrial Revolution*, Prepared Statement before the U.S. Senate Committee on Commerce, Science, and Transportation, Subcommittee on Security.
158 Yang, Y. (2020), Ibid.
159 Hawksworth, J. and Fertig, Y. (2020), What Will Be the Net Impact of AI and Related Technologies on Jobs in China? *Report, PwC Economics*, London: PwC.
160 Nikkei Asia (2020), China Aims to Reach 'New Level' of Prosperity by 2035, *Nikkei Asian Review* (October 29, 2020).
161 Ibid.
162 The State Council of the People's Republic of China (2017), China to Invest Big in 'Made in China 2025' Strategy. Retrieved from http://english.www.gov.cn/state_council/ministries/2017/10/12/content_281475904600274.htm
163 Stern, N. (2010), *China's Growth, China's Cities, and the New Global Low-Carbon Industrial Revolution*, Leeds: Centre for Climate Change Economics and Policy, London: Grantham Research Institute on Climate Change and the Environment, pp. 8–9.
164 Feng, H. and Tang, D. (2017), China could peak carbon emissions in 2023, China Dialogue (November 2017). Retrieved from https://chinadialogue.net/en/energy/10232-china-could-peak-carbon-emissions-in-2-23/
165 Ito, A. (2020), Digital China: A Fourth Industrial Revolution with Chinese Characteristics? *Asia-Pacific Review*, online publication, pp. 50–51.
166 Ibid., pp. 52–57.
167 Ibid., p. 66.
168 Carsten, P. and Raman, R. (2016), Alibaba Buys Control of Lazada in $1 Billion Bet on SE Asia Ecommerce, *Reuters* (April 12, 2016).
169 Tourk, K. and Marsh, P. (2016), The New Industrial Revolution and Industrial Upgrading in China: Achievements and Challenges, *Economic and Political Studies*, 4, pp. 187–209, p. 194.
170 Nikkei Asia (2020), Huawei Enters a New World: How the US Ban Will Affect Global Tech, *Nikkei Asian Review* (September 14, 2020).
171 Xie, J. and Chen, Q. (2019), Huawei 'de-Americanizing' Its Phones, *Global Times* (December 5, 2019).
172 Giglio, M. (2019), China's Spies Are on the Offensive, *The Atlantic* (August 27, 2019).

173 Kuo, C., Shyu, J. and Ding, K. (2019), Industrial Revitalization via Industry 4.0 A Comparative Policy Analysis among China, Germany and the US, *Global Transitions*, 1, pp. 3–14.

174 Grewal, D. (2008), Ibid., pp. 202–203.

175 Freeman, O. (2020), *5G Smart Factories Slash China's Cement Production Costs*, Norwich: Manufacturing Digital Magazine.

176 Schwab, K. (2016), *The Fourth Industrial Revolution*, Geneva: World Economic Forum.

177 Lee, K., Malerba, F. and Primi, A. (2020), The Fourth Industrial Revolution, Changing Global Value Chains and Industrial Upgrading in Emerging Economies, *Journal of Economic Policy Reform*, 23(4), pp. 1–12.

178 Lemstra, W. (2018), Leadership with 5G in Europe: Two Contrasting Images of the Future, with Policy and Regulatory Implications, *Telecommunications Policy*, 42(8), pp. 587–611.

179 Santos, C., Mehrsai, A., Barros, A., Araujo, M. and Ares, E. (2020), Towards Industry 4.0: an Overview of European Strategic Roadmaps, *Procedia Manufacturing*, 13, pp. 972–979.

180 European Commission (2016), Identification and Quantification of Key Socio-Economic Data to Support Strategic Planning for the Introduction of 5G in Europe, Final Report, Luxembourg: Publications Office of the European Union.

181 Federal Register (2019), Exec. Order No. 13873, May 17, 2019, Vol. 84, No. 96, pp. 22689–22692.

182 Kaska, K., Beckvard, H. and Minárik, T. (2019), Huawei, 5G and China as a Security Threat, Tallinn: NATO Cooperative Cyber Defence Center for Excellence (CCDCOE), 28.

183 Buchholz, K. (2020), Which Countries Have Banned Huawei? Statista.com.

184 Parker, G., Fildes, N. and Warrell, H. (2020), UK Orders Ban of New Huawei Equipment from end of Year, *Financial Times* (July 15, 2020).

185 European Commission (2019c), Joint Communication to the European Parliament, the European Council and the Council, EU-China – A Strategic Outlook, JOIN(2019) 5 final, Strasbourg: European Commission.

186 European Commission (2019d), Recommendation on Cybersecurity of 5G Networks, Commission Recommendation (EU) 2019/534 of 26 March 2019, *Official Journal of the European Union*, pp. 42–47.

187 European Commission (2020c), Europe Boosts Investment with €70 Million in 5G with Strong Focus on Connected Transport by Launching 11 New Project, Publication 16 June 2020. Retrieved from https://digital-strategy.ec.europa.eu/en/news/europe-boosts-investment-eu70-million-5g-strong-focus-connected-transport-launching-11-new-projects

188 Ibid.

189 Rose, M. (2020), France Won't Ban Huawei, but Encouraging 5G Telcos to Avoid It: Report, *Reuters* (July 5, 2020).

190 Chazan, G. and Fildes, N. (2020), Germany Crackdown Set to Exclude Huawei from 5G Rollout, *Financial Times* (September 30, 2020).

191 Busvine, D. (2020), Huawei asks Germany Not to Shut It Out of Building 5G Networks, *Der Spiegel* (July 31, 2020).

192 Eurostat (2020), China-EU – International Trade in Goods Statistics. Retrieved from https://ec.europa.eu/eurostat/statistics-explained/index.php?title=China-EU-international_trade_in_goods_statistics

193 International Monetary Fund (2017), Germany: 2017 Article IV Consultation – Press Release; IMF Country Reports No. 17/192 (July 2017), p. 8, Washington DC: IMF.

194 Schafer, M. (2018), The Fourth Industrial Revolution: How the EU can lead it, *European View*, 17(1), pp. 7–11.

195 Ancarani et al. (2019), Backshoring Strategy and the Adoption of Industry 4.0: Evidence from Europe, *Journal of World Business*, 54, pp. 360–369.
196 Gramlich, J. (2020), Americans give the U.S. low marks for its handling of COVID-19, and so do people in other countries, Research on Coronavirus Disease (COVID-19) September 2020, Washington, DC: Pew Research Center.
197 Porterfield, C. (2020), China Bans Travel from the U.K., India and Other Countries with Higher Coronavirus Infection Rates, *Forbes* (November 5, 2020).
198 Petri, P. and Plummer, M. (2020), East Asia Decouples from the United States: Trade War, COVID-19, and East Asia's New Trade Blocs, PIIE, *Working Paper* 20-9, Washington D.C.: PIIE.
199 Dorussen, H. and Ward, H. (2010), Trade Networks and the Kantian Peace, *Journal of Peace Research*, 47(1), pp. 29–42.
200 Cohen, D. (2006), *Globalization and Its Enemies*, Cambridge: The MIT Press, p. 5.

> *The enemies of globalization are arrayed in two opposed camps … one camp, to simplify, is that of the Mullahs who denounce the "Westernization of the world" and the other camp is that of the enemies of capitalism, who fight the exploitation of workers by capital. The first fight the war between civilizations, the second the global class struggle. Despite their differences, these two opposing camps find themselves cling to the idea that globalization imposes a model that people do not want.*

7 Is Free Trade Passé?

In this book, I started by introducing the network theory and its usage in a framework of the global trading system, underlining how understanding the connections and linkages between nodes and the main participants of a system can lead us to know the world better both in a practical and schematized sense. I followed by defining inner and outer networks, digging deep into the usage of key terms like networking power, network power, networked power, and network-making power, which are the baselines for defining a leading node and the powers it holds toward the other components of the network. The difference between relational (more resembled by a friendship, for example) and affiliational (which we can find in a group or organization) networks was expanded upon, explaining how they are related to social studies and our research in general.

Due to the broad scope of social network analysis (SNA) and thanks to the studies that have been made in an array of disciplines, I was able to dig deeper, to analyze and understand additional tools that could be useful to unravel the dynamics behind many of the inter-connections of the global trading system. Specifically, I paid attention to the *positioning of the nodes*, which is defined by how nodes are disposed and how they interact with each other. Degree and direction would tell us how interconnected a node could be and toward which party its messages (or signals) will be sent. The phenomenon of *homophily* was also explored, and further attention was paid to different kind of networks (whole, partial, ego, and modal). The role of leading nodes and the importance of additional middle-man players inside a networking environment were explained through such terms and concepts as hub, switch, modem, and router. Considering the high degree of complexity of a global-based network, providing definitions for concepts like *network of networks* and *multilayered networks* in general, could not be disregarded. Indeed, an overview of academic work on interconnection, interdependence, and the role of international relations in issue linkage constituted the basic but essential work, for making assessments on regional agreements and global trade conflicts between hegemonic powers.

Taking advantage of all these notions, I then used network theory to examine some of the most influential mega free trade agreements (mega-FTAs) to assess their influence in a world in which multilateralism finds itself at the crossroads. The spotlight was given to the European Union (EU), the Comprehensive and

DOI: 10.4324/9781003305705-7

Progressive Agreement for Trans-Pacific Partnership (CPTPP), the US–Mexico–Canada Agreement (USMCA), and the Regional Comprehensive Economic Partnership (RCEP). These agreements (and institution, in the EU's case) all provide a solid base for the further increase of possibilities in the world of global trade and, consequently, in relations between multilateralism and each member. The EU appears to be led by its internal institutions (and, to an extent, by influence of Germany and France), which are following the so-called European Values shared by most of its members. The CPTPP led by Japan after the withdrawal of the US will surely be a hot topic considering the upcoming debate about an eventual return of its former leading node and the clash that could ensue between the US-led and the China-led networks. USMCA, while less influential relatively to the other regional trade agreements analyzed, is still relevant considering the state of polarization that the US keeps maintaining in its macro area.

The core of the debate about the competition of the US-based network versus the China-based one started to be unwrapped by underlining the objectives each respective network operates and pursues. Each country's stance, strategy, internal/external networks, and overall structure were depicted and analyzed using the tools we first introduced in the early chapters.

I then conducted a more in-depth analysis of this topic by extrapolating the main strategies utilized by each country to counter each other's attempts at gaining the upper hand. Not only are the 'anti-China' and the Belt and Road Initiative (BRI)-type networks included as examples, but further analysis of future characteristics and strategies revealed how the change of presidency in the US and the systemic problems brought on by events such as the COVID-19 pandemic managed to completely shift each country's strategy and foreign policy amid the multilateral crisis we have been witnessing for the last several years. For the US, we noticed a shift in policies based on different views of key values like Green Deals, clean energy, digital transformation, and alignment with the so-called European Values (which could be translated in Western Values if the US adopts them). China will instead have to deal with an increasingly difficult situation to maintain its BRI network.

Ultimately, each of the four waves that are challenging and strongly influencing the multilateral environment and the global trading system was presented. These would be the COVID-19 pandemic, the US–China trade war, economic nationalism, and the Fourth Industrial Revolution.

The coronavirus pandemic obviously shook the global economy and will directly impact how countries will operate both in the short and the medium term. Specifically, while the US struggles to contain the virus, China supposedly will try to leverage its recovering economy and get an early advantage compared to countries that are still struggling with containing the contagion. However, early talks for the allocation of the Stability Mechanism and the internal dispute regarding Eurobonds are events that both reminded the international community that European unity is far from completely achieved. I can say that the EU's bias toward multilateralism will probably be overshadowed as the US capitalizes its raw strength and sheer size to focus on bilateral deals. Many links of the sub-networks that deliver the global public goods are now being severed while most nodes are alienated in the process.

The US-China trade war has its own implications, but it does not represent the only set of problems causing deglobalization. We can clearly see how both China and the US want to polarize the attention of both their spheres of influence in order to prevent the rise of a singular hegemonic power. This strategy, moving along with the introduction of new FTAs and global projects like the BRI or the 'anti-China' network, will have to cope with other and recent challenges that will shape the global geopolitical balance in the next several decades.

Going more in depth into this topic, CPTPP and RCEP 15 will definitely replace some of the trade destroyed by the COVID-19 and the US-China trade war. A study shows that CPTPP and RCEP 15 together will more than offset global losses due to the US–China trade war. In that sense, the prospects of a trade war and recurrent pandemics raise incentives for an effective implementation of RCEP and the expansion of CPTPP in the future.[1]

As I mentioned, economic nationalism and the Fourth Industrial Revolution are also hot topics that will reshape how countries operate and trade. While the first will define a driving sentiment that future leading governors will have to take into consideration, the second will provide new tools that will supposedly change the landscape of the world as we know it.

The reasons for which I used network theory is that, after defining various types of network power, I was able to explain many of the connections between the leading node (in our specific case, US and China) and all the other surrounding nodes, both in inner and outer networks.

The analysis of the so-called mega-FTAs made it possible to better understand the past and future developments of the nodes involved. It also helps us to point out how the trade world shifted from a multilateral approach to one oriented toward bilateralism (or regionalism). We can make useful assessments for the future by considering FTA networks of the US and China, their partners' positions as nodes, and the networking strategies of the two and wrap up the analysis of the upcoming global trading system.

The ideology of liberal multilateralism in global trade represented by the World Trade Organization (WTO) cannot withstand the pressure of current circumstances.

First, a head-on collision within each node is inevitable between inner and outer networks. The attempt of the US and its allies to create and maintain a liberal multilateral trading system faces serious problems inside the countries. The inner networks have gravitated toward economic nationalism, support of isolationism, protectionism, and power-based bilateralism. The expanding liberal economic order has led to significant economic and political setbacks inside the liberal states themselves. The powers of the domestic nodes are therefore moving their states in the direction of a closed societies. Indeed, some leading nodes are aggressively seeking to sever multi-connected links in their outer networks.

Second, the WTO has failed not only to introduce new standard on demand but also to maintain its dispute-settlement mechanisms. Its power is weakening as alternatives have proliferated over the past three decades. Additionally, powerful states are contributing to the WTO's gradual demise by neglecting the various signs of the collapse of the multilateral trading system.

Third, because leading states widely use issue linkage as part of their negotiation strategy, global trading networks have become part of the multilayered network of foreign diplomacy. As we can observe from China–Russia or US–EU relations in the wake of the war in Ukraine, trading nodes are interconnected both horizontally and vertically. Because the policymaking procedures of states are intertwined, the strategic objectives, the configuration of the nodes, the contents of the standards in various networks, and the manner in which the nodes are linked all lead to important differences in decision making between states. Only when the intensity and extensity of the links between the nodes from all dimensions are fully measured can the final impact on the network from the action of nodes be adequately predicted.

Fourth, the US has begun to establish a hub-and-spoke system in which it is the only hub. Former US President Donald Trump initiated the construction of this bipartisan networks with its traditional allies. As a result, many states are now involved in relational trading networks, in which communication becomes unilateral and asymmetric. China is also building a network, in which a leading vertex (China) is bilaterally linked with many peripheral points. Hierarchical information flows from the state to non-state actors in many liberal states are also facing challenges from more interactive communication patterns.

The multilateral trading system in place for the present is built on three main ideas: first, countries are sovereign, but they place voluntary and mutual limits on the exercise of their sovereignty; second, countries can expect to extract mutual gain from free trade; and third, power should play a smaller role, and powerful countries should be constrained, either by law or by their own recognition of mutual self-interest (Van Grasstek, 2013).[2] However, it is a system that cannot be sustained in the face of leading states that wish to act contrarily, because such states are no longer constrained by the rule of law. The US and China have clearly failed to place voluntary limits on their own sovereignties.

Finally, many global firms that operate in China have begun to reconsider the adjustments made to their production-sharing network, i.e. the global value chain (GVC). Some multinational corporations have already scaled back their operations in China, which might eventually lead to their exodus from China especially when the Chinese Communist Party's (CCP) risks increase beyond acceptable levels. The two factors that emerge from this observation are the COVID-19 pandemic and the continued trade war between the Group of 2 (G2) countries. Both these factors have raised the level of China risk, more specifically, the CCP risk in the global community. Stability became more important than efficiency in the GVC. The direction of the GVC has changed, moving toward reshoring, onshoring, nearshoring, and diversification. The scope and the speed of changes in the GVC will ultimately depend upon the magnitude of risk and uncertainty perceived to exist in China. Due to US security concerns, some tech firms will have to redesign their geopolitical ecosystems. Obviously, the Chinese government will not stand for the exodus of foreign firms and investors from China and will respond with countermeasures, including incentives and disincentives to retain some investment sources and attract new ones. It is through the interactions of the two forces that the magnitude and intensity of the exodus from China will be determined.

If leading states want to rescue and restore a failing multilateral trading system, they will need to draft blueprints for the future. This new vision should set a balanced standard between developed countries and developing countries, as well as between inner networks and outer networks. The system can only be saved by the introduction of a new standard and the normalization of a mechanism for dispute settlement.

Within a network-based global trading system, I assert that states must balance their internal interests of the domestic nodes with the external interests of the globalists. If the two are not compatible, then conflict is inevitable. The multilateral trading system can only be maintained when external network interest and national interests are reconcilable. A possible solution would be for leading states to pursue inclusive globalization by providing effective compensation through an upgraded program for universal trade adjustment assistance. When groups that have been alienated by globalization are fully persuaded of the necessity of globalization, the expansion of economic nationalism triggered by populist governments can be stopped.

As the international liberal order is in decline,[3] it is not surprising to see how the nodes and links in the global trading system are slowly changing in terms of their interactions with each other. Trade agreements are also changing, from multilateral to mostly bilateral and plurilateral. Tekce and Acar (2008)[4] note that "the new FTAs tend to be far smaller in initial membership (i.e., largely though not solely bilateral) compared to the existing FTAs which had a preference for shallowness or narrowness in issue coverage but broadness in terms of membership." This trend is fueled by the fact that the Doha Round negotiations for the WTO remain unfinished, making the WTO less appealing for its members to utilize.

In future decades, there will likely be two competing trading networks, one being China-led and the other US-led. China will try to transform its economy from an export-oriented, investment-driven to the economy driven by domestic consumption. Dual circulation strategy of President Xi is a somewhat wishful attempt at shifting a major consumption source from foreign to domestic players. Only when China successfully emerges as the world's biggest consumer, bringing its population of 1.4 billion into the system to replace the US as the final destination of exports, and reducing risks and uncertainties caused by the Chinese government, China-led trading system and the red GVC network will survive.

The USA's engagement policy with China since 1978 has been a disaster and failure, in spite of years of patient waiting in the hopes that liberal democracy would take root in China. The alternative approach did not guarantee the democratic and liberal transformation of China either, as the US policies of threat, balance, sanction, boycott, and critique are more likely to reinforce the authoritarian milieu than to change it (Mueller, 2021).[5]

In the era of upcoming rivalry between the US and China, each node will seek to maximize its influence over geopolitically important networks. The US will attempt to contain China by not allowing it to grow into a regional hegemon and dominant power in East Asia. The US-proposed IPEF is a vital part of efforts to strengthen its ties with countries in the region. In the process, these two superpowers will fight strategically to draw Russia, Korea, Japan, Vietnam, and India into their respective orbits. The ongoing push and pull between different state actors, the agents of globalization, and supporters of nationalist movements can make or break the global trading system. From a network perspective, the viability for American and Chinese hegemony will ultimately depend on the structure and power factors of the networks that each creates for the world. The networks that can offer the world a better set of public goods will prevail in the end.

The outlooks do not have to be entirely negative, though. As we saw with many of the successfully developed mega-FTAs, plurilateral networks and sectoral agreements appear to be on the rise and drawing the attention of the leading protagonists of this second Cold War. China's outward investment bolstered its capacity to seek allies that, however, wanted to dip into the endless possibilities offered by the huge Chinese domestic market. This scenario prompted a strong response from the West, which kept looking for more opportunities and eventually was driven to seek its network of allies as well. Although with Trump much of the plurilateral efforts to strengthen the Atlantic alliance and to unify some of the most influential west-based nodes were halted, the outlook of a US-based networks that could lead different sets of parties to link up to a building bloc mechanism appears to be positive for the future of multilateralism as a whole.

The EU, shaken by the COVID-19 pandemic more than China and the US, managed to show great unity despite the drawn-out difficulties. After many discussions, the *New Generation EU* plan was approved, and each member started to make plans in order to make use of these new resources provided by the Union. Even while dealing with the UK, although for much of 2020 it looked like a *no deal* situation was the most probable outcome, supposedly the most troublesome talks and negotiations between the parties have been completed.[6]

The middle-power countries, with their collective influence, are also gaining more traction as they look at the bigger picture. Indeed, many of them want to refuse to accept a bipolar division of the networks. Instead of engaging in a network rivalry, they expect the US and China to cooperate and compete. Apparent is the fact that most of the US alliance partners are economically tied to China. The impact of each member of key FTAs like RCEP or CPTPP nurtures plurilateralism and makes it harder to define who is going to be a clear winner among the two biggest players. The Association of Southeast Asian Nations would be a fitting example of a powerful player that is getting more leverage while dealing with giants like Japan, China, and the US. Even considering the hegemonic competition, alliances and deals among countries with different economic sizes appear to be significant while evaluating the outlook of the whole analyzed area.[7]

Although the golden era of multilateralism and globalization might be long past, I just underlined some key signals that tell us how the international trading framework is indeed working toward an expanded alliance-based network system. The future development and unfolding of major events, such as the changes in the USA's strategy with the Biden administration, G2 hegemonic war, the formation of new sectoral or plurilateral agreements, the evolution of economic nationalism and technology, and finally the outbreak of a global pandemic, will reshape the future of global trading networks. All these problems can be summarized by the previously mentioned four waves of rising threats to free trade and open society, which will halt multilateralism and global trade development for at least one generation. The outcome is not yet certain, but I believe that in the long run, globalization will ultimately triumph, and indeed, there are reasons for hope.

Notes

1 Petri, P. and Plummer, M. (2020), East Asia Decouples from the United States: Trade War, COVID-19, and East Asia's New Trade Blocs, *PIIE Working Paper Series*, Washington D.C.: PIIE.
2 Van Grasstek, C. (2013), *The History and Future of the World Trade Organization*, Geneva: World Trade Organization, pp. 3–38.
3 James, H. (2021), Globalization's Coming Golden Age, *Foreign Affairs*, May/June, pp. 1–16. James argues that globalization process has a life cycle with the phases of globalization, slobalization (slow down+globalization), deglobalization, nobalization (no+globalization), and reglobalization. He examined the historical cases of 1840s famines and the 1970s oil shocks for the cycles. His optimistic view on globalization is well summarized in his conclusion: "The challenge of the new upswing in the cycle of globalization will be to find ways to learn and adapt – increasing the effectiveness of government and business – without compromising fundamental values (p. 15)."
4 Tekce, M. and Acar, S. (2008), *From Multilateralism to Bilateralism: The Impact of Free Trade Agreements on Global Trade Policies*, Marmara University Journal of Economic and Administrative Sciences, Istanbul: Marmara University, pp. 116–117.
5 Mueller, J. (2021), China: Rise or Demise? *Policy Analysis*, No. 917, pp. 1–33. Washington D.C.: CATO Institute.
6 Cameron-Chileshe, J. and Khan, M. (2020), EU Member States Begin Process to Approve Brexit Trade Deal, *Financial Times*, London: *Financial Times* (December 26, 2020).
7 Details on the *New Generation EU* plan can be found at: https://ec.europa.eu/info/strategy/recovery-plan-europe_en.

Index

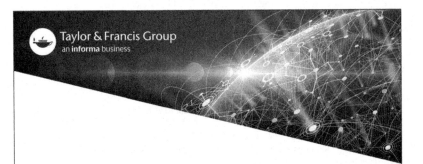

Printed in the United States
by Baker & Taylor Publisher Services